Mark Tully

NO FULL STOPS IN INDIA

VIKING
Penguin India

VIKING

Penguin Books India (P) Ltd, B4/246 Safdarjung Enclave, New Delhi- 110 029, India
Penguin Books Ltd, 27 Wrights Lane, London W8 5TZ, England
Penguin Books USA Inc., 375 Hudson Street, New York, New York 10014, USA
Penguin Books Australia Ltd, Ringwood, Victoria, Australia
Penguin Books Canada Ltd, 10 Alcorn Avenue, Toronto, Ontario, Canada M4V 3B2
Penguin Books (NZ) Ltd, 182–190 Wairau Road, Auckland 10, New Zealand

First published 1991
Reprinted 1991, 1992 (Twice)

Set in 12/14 pt Lasercomp Baskerville

ISBN 0-670-81919-0

CONTENTS

LIST OF ILLUSTRATIONS

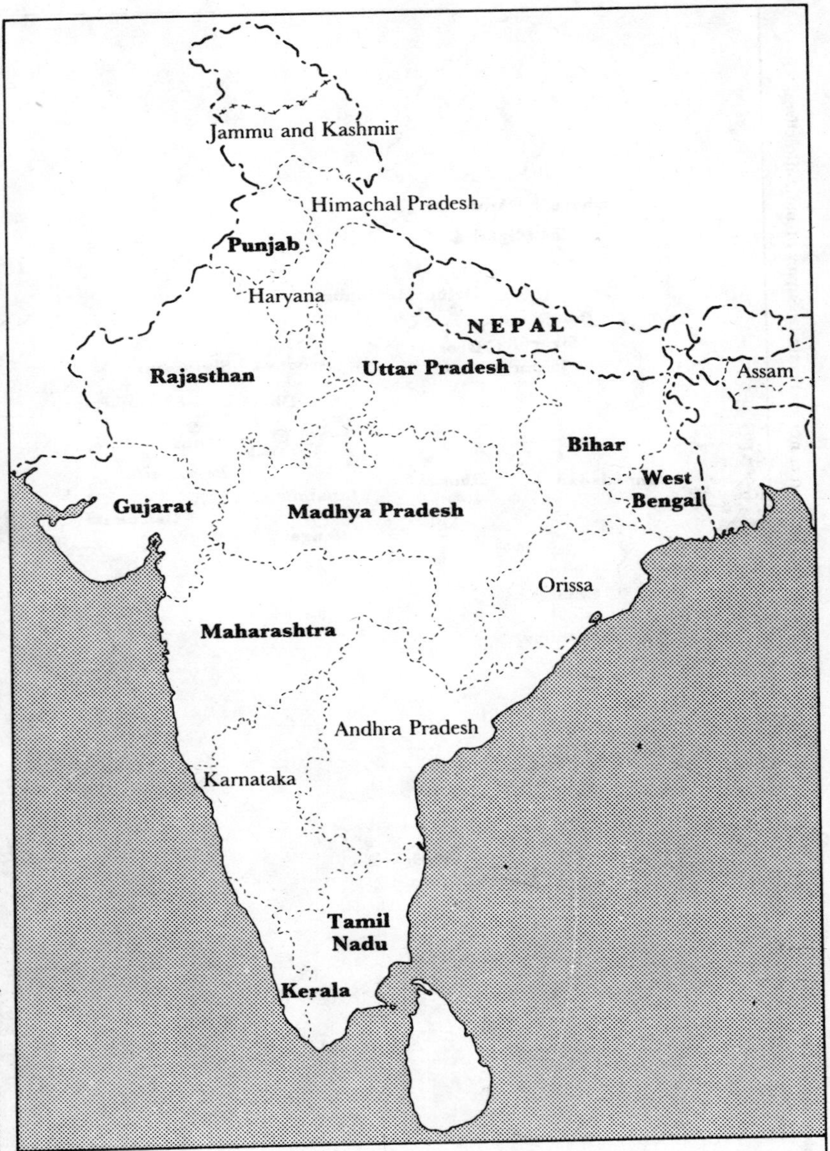

Indian States States in bold have important mentions in the book

The international boundary of the map on this page is neither purported to be correct not authentic by Survey of India directives.

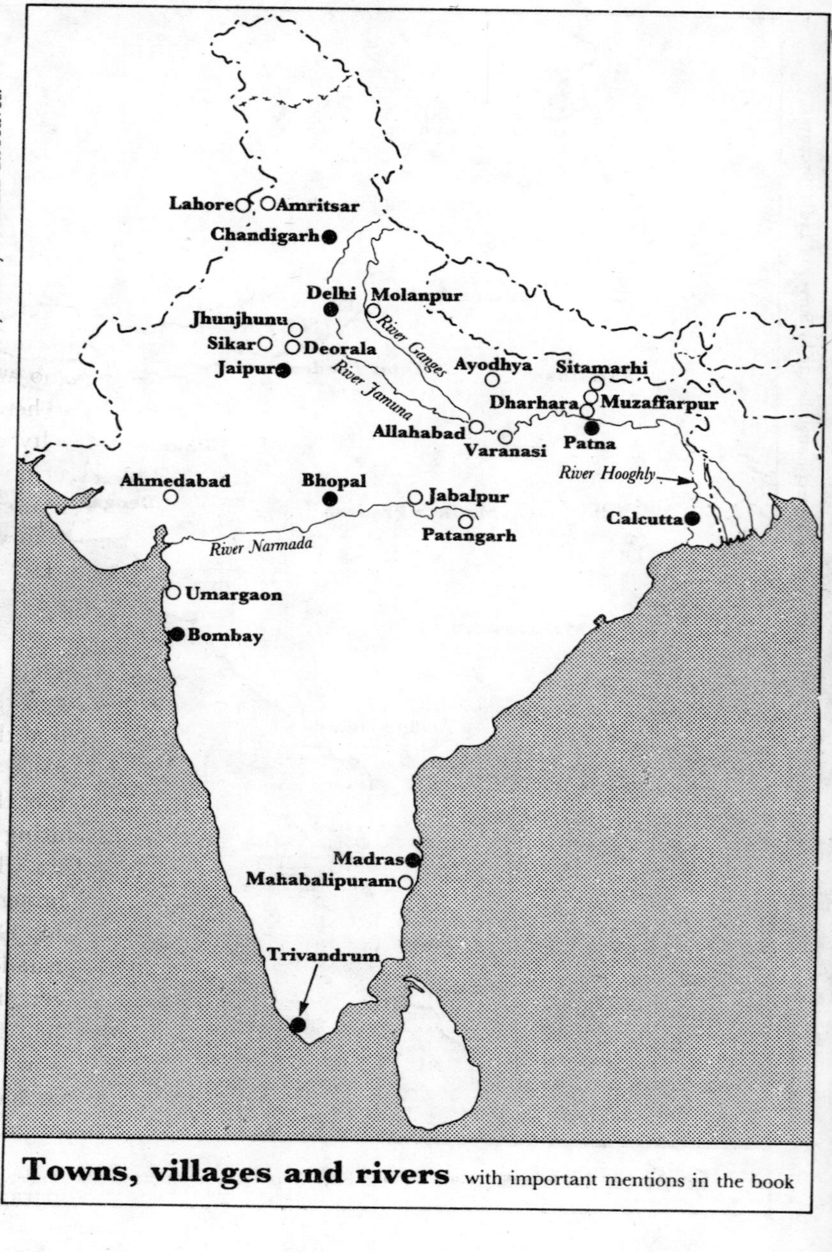

Towns, villages and rivers with important mentions in the book

The international boundary of the map on this page is neither purported to be correct not authentic by Survey of India directives.

ACKNOWLEDGEMENTS

The greatest temptation journalists face is to regard the stories they write as their own. They are not: they are the stories of those who are involved in the events reported. It's not the journalist who is the hero, it's those who suffer the famines or floods, those who fight cruelty or oppression, those who govern and those who oppose them. Never do I feel this more strongly than when I walk away from natural disasters with the material recorded for what I know will be 'a good story', leaving the victims to their suffering.

Let me say from the start, then, that this book is not mine – it belongs to all the people whose stories I have told, and of course to India. It also belongs to those who helped in the telling. It belongs to Gillian Wright, on whom I relied from the time when we planned the book together to the final corrections. She travelled with me, shared the insights she has gained from her deep reading and long experience of India, did much of the research and took responsibility for much of the drudgery which inevitably goes with the final stages of producing a book. The book also belongs to many patient people at Penguin who put up with my procrastination and, when the stories rambled, brought me back to the straight and narrow. It belongs to my agent, Gill Coleridge, who arranged for Penguin to publish me and persuaded them that I would eventually deliver as the delays grew longer and longer. It belongs to the BBC, and particularly to Alan Hart, for arranging six months' leave for me. It belongs to my colleagues in the Delhi office of the BBC, Satish Jacob and Avrille Turner, who have given me invaluable advice and help. And belongs to my wife, Margaret, and my family, who encouraged me to keep going.

The portrait of Ram Chander for Chapter 1 and photographs

ACKNOWLEDGEMENTS

for Chapter 3 are reproduced by permission of Rajesh Bedi, those for Chapter 5 by permission of Pramod Pushkarna and *India Today*, that for Chapter 6 by permission of Saibal Das and *India Today*, and that in Chapter 7 by permission of Raghu Rai. My thanks to them all.

Mark Tully, June 1991

INTRODUCTION

'How do you cope with the poverty?' That must be the question I have been asked most frequently by visitors to India. I often reply, 'I don't have to. The poor do.' It's certainly true. I live a very comfortable life in Delhi, while the taxi-drivers who have lived opposite me for fourteen years have to sleep in their cars in the cold winter and on a charpai or light bedstead in the open during the hot weather. I have a three-bedroomed flat. The taxi rank is their home. My foreign guests expect the taxi-drivers to take them back to their hotels whatever hour of the night it may be. Before leaving, they will check the fare with me to make sure the taxi-drivers don't get a few more rupees than they are due. That's the way my guests usually 'cope with the poverty'.

The crocodile tears that have been shed over India's poor would flood the Ganges, so there's no need for me to add my drop to them. No matter how much it may upset my guests, it's better to be honest and admit that I've learnt to live with India's poverty. The only excuse I can give is that I'm not alone in this: most prosperous Indians – and indeed the prosperous in all parts of the world – have learnt to live with the fact that millions of Indians live below what economists have defined as the poverty line. Millions more don't have adequate housing and sanitation. The fact that we, the fortunate of the world, still live with India's poverty is a scandal. India – which barely rates as a trading nation, which has no oil to export, which has no monopoly of any other essential commodity, which has not adopted a hostile ideology, which can threaten only its smaller neighbours – does not count in the capitals of the West. It ought to count if we really cared about coping with poverty.

The successful capitalist countries of the world are rejoicing in the downfall of communism, and in the West we are talking of the final triumph of our civilization as though it was now proved that there was no other way ahead but ours. But our civilization has still to show that it can provide for the poor of the world. A great deal of evidence indicates the opposite – that the West has harmed the poor and continues to harm them. After all, it was our civilization which left India a poor and backward country. A. Vaidyanathan writes in the *Cambridge Economic History of India* of the 'impoverished economy' which was the raj's legacy to India. He says, 'Altogether the pre-independence period was a period of near stagnation for the Indian economy. . . . There was hardly any change in the structure of production or in productivity levels. The growth of modern manufacturing was probably neutralized by the displacement of traditional crafts, and in any case was too small to make a difference to the overall picture.' It is also our civilization that India has tried to follow since independence, with results which certainly could not be described as a triumph.

There are many reasons why India in particular should make us in the West aware of how much remains to be done in the developing countries and of how many difficulties have still to be overcome before anyone speaks of triumph. One is obviously the size of the problem India faces. There are countries which are poorer than India, there are countries which have made far less economic progress, there are countries which don't have even the rudiments of a modern state, but there is none which has so many poor people. India's nearest rival in this respect is China, but the World Bank's *World Development Report* (1990) shows that there are more than twice as many poor people in India than in China, and more than four times as many extremely poor people.

China is a communist country but India is a parliamentary democracy – surely that's another reason why we should take the plight of India very seriously. China's achievements could mean that it is communism which will triumph in the war against poverty and democracy which will be defeated. I think that that is unlikely, but those who are now talking of the victory of freedom should perhaps ponder the strange fact that one of the freest countries in the world, which has made an all-out effort since independence to eradicate its legacy of poverty, has been much less successful in this than its communist neighbour. Of course India's achievements in some fields are more impressive than China's, but the fact remains that communism has provided better education, better health services and more food and clothes for its poor than democracy has.

In the *Indian Express* of 17 June 1990, the eminent Indian economist Amartya Sen wrote, 'It is important to understand the élite nature of India to make sense of India's policies.' He has, for example, compared India's success in providing higher education with what he has called 'the shocking neglect of elementary education'. Why has giving every man a vote not meant the transfer of power from the élite to the majority who in India are undoubtedly the poor? I believe one of the main reasons is that India's élite have never recovered from their colonial hangover, and so they have not developed the ideology, the attitudes and the institutions which would change the poor from subjects to partners in the government of India. Democracy has failed because the people the poor have elected have ruled – not represented – them. The ballot-box is only the first stage in democracy.

If all that were wrong with India were a particularly bad hangover from the raj, there might well be room for optimism. After all, even the worst hangover evaporates eventually, and in the twenty-five years I have known the country I have seen many of the more obvious relics of colonial rule disappear. India is no longer a land dominated by brown sahibs imitating the ways of the white sahibs who used to rule them. But India is still a land dominated by foreign thinking, and I would suggest that that thinking is just as alien as the brown sahibs'. Colonialism teaches the native élite it creates to admire – all too often to ape – the ways of their foreign rulers. That habit of mind has survived in independent India.

India's most successful students no longer knock at the doors of the colleges of Oxford or Cambridge: they now prefer Harvard or Yale. But what do they learn there which is relevant to their country? The scientists are versed in technologies aimed at reducing the role of human beings in production, although labour is India's greatest asset. The doctors want to practise medicine which provides the latest and most expensive techniques of healing individuals, whereas India's need is for public health, preventive medicine and simple cures which can be administered by paramedical staff trained inexpensively. The business-school graduates know how to administer complicated corporations with billion-dollar assets – the sort of corporations which will put out of business the small, labour-intensive and unsophisticated industries that India is officially committed to encouraging. All this is not surprising, because America is concerned about educating students to propagate the American way of life and keep its economy expanding.

What makes matters worse is the cultural imperialism of the West, an imperialism now strengthened by our success in the battle with communism. We don't need armies to hold down our modern colonies, we don't need viceroys to administer them on our behalf: our economic might holds them in captivity, and our apparent success ensures that they accept, if not enjoy, their slavery. Today most Indians see no alternative to our culture at the end of this century, just as their grandparents and great-grandparents saw no alternative to direct colonial rule at the start of the century.

The best way to destroy a people's culture and identity is to undermine its religion and its language. We, the British, did that as India's rulers and we continue to do that as part of the dominant culture of the world now. It is true that the British rulers of India were very cautious about Hinduism, especially after the Mutiny. Unlike some colonial powers, we did not attempt to convert India to Christianity. But we did create the impression that our religion was superior to Hinduism. As a child in Calcutta, I remember being told that Muslims were superior to Hindus because at least they did not worship idols.

At independence, India adopted the contemporary Western view that common sense dictates that religion be confined entirely to the personal domain and kept out of all public life – to put it at its kindest. What in fact the majority of people in the West have done is to consign religion to the rubbish bin. 'Modern' Indians inevitably follow our example, and anyone who does not believe in keeping religion out of all forms of public life is regarded as 'communal' – that is to say, totally biased in favour of his own religious community. The élite's so-called secularism inevitably degenerates into disrespect for religion. But the vast majority of Indians, who do not enjoy the benefits of modernity, still believe that religion is one of the most – if not *the* most – important factors in their lives. I have to admit to believing that the West is paying a very heavy price for its lack of religion, but it has made the economic progress to achieve other goals in life – ephemeral though they may be. What I think is manifestly wrong is to disturb the religious beliefs of those who have no hope of any other comfort, which is exactly what we have taught and are still teaching the Indian élite to do. Not surprisingly, this is producing a backlash in India – Hindu fundamentalism. The greatest Indian leader of the century, Mahatma Gandhi, vas a deeply religious man, but he campaigned tirelessly against the excesses of his own religion, Hinduism – particularly the humiliation of Harijans or untouchables. At the same time, he knew the danger of ridiculing rather than reforming religion. He believed that, in India at least, politics needed religion. In his autobiography he said, 'I can say without the slightest hesitation, and yet in all humility, that those who say religion has nothing to do with politics do not know what religion means.'

A central tenet of what passes for the post-religious ideal is the equality of all men. But, although all men may be equal in God's eyes, they can never be equal in the eyes of other men, and because of that basic flaw in the doctrine of egalitarianism we in the West now talk of 'equality of opportunity'. The pursuit of equal opportunities for all has many achievements to its credit, but this ideal too is going to be realized only if there is another life after this one. Our differences of opportunity start the moment we are conceived. The gap widens as we live in different families, go to different schools, are inspired or bored by different teachers, discover or fail to discover our individual talents and are given or not given the resources to develop those talents. So it goes on throughout our lives. There will always be winners and losers. The alienation of many young people in the West and the loneliness of the old show the suffering that egalitarianism inflicts on those who do not win, the superficiality of an egalitarianism which in effect means equal opportunities for all to win and then ignores the inevitable losers. Imagine how many losers there must be in a country like India where many children have their physical and mental growth stunted by malnutrition, where many parents are forced to regard their families as economic assets to be exploited in the child-labour market as soon as possible and where education is often seen as a waste of time because it does not lead to jobs or a better life. Imagine also what would happen if egalitarianism and its companion individualism destroyed the communities which support those who start life with no opportunities.

For all that, the élite of India have become so spellbound by egalitarianism that they are unable to see any good in the one institution which does provide a sense of identity and dignity to those who are robbed from birth of the opportunity to compete on an equal footing – caste. Caste is obnoxious to the egalitarian West, so it is obnoxious to the Indian élite too. The *Statesman*, one of the daily papers of the English-speaking élite, recently published an article by Bernard Levin in which he told Indians what to think of the caste system. He said,

> The roots of such evil [the caste system] go very deep; so deep that until very recent times those condemned through the accident of birth to occupy throughout their lives the lowest place (and in India the lowest place is low indeed) accepted their fate without any sign that they resented it or that they could and should have a different and better one. Many abominable cruelties have been practised on the low castes and tribes; at one time hardly a week went by without a Harijan being murdered because he had taken water from a well the use of which he was denied and thus polluted it.

This article was applauded by the English-speaking élite in India. One way to discredit any system is to highlight its excesses, and Levin is right to say that the caste system has many of these. But what the constant denigration of the caste system has done is to add to the sense of inferiority that many Indians feel about their own culture.

It would lead to greater respect for India's culture, and indeed a better understanding of it, if it were recognized that the caste system has never been totally static, that it is adapting itself to today's changing circumstances and that it has positive as well as negative aspects. The caste system provides security and a community for millions of Indians. It gives them an identity that neither Western science nor Western thought has yet provided, because caste is not just a matter of being a Brahmin or a Harijan: it is also a kinship system. The system provides a wider support group than the family: a group which has a social life in which all its members can participate. In the September 1989 issue of *Seminar* magazine, Madhu Kishwar, one of India's leading feminists, wrote, 'Even though the survival of strong kinship and community loyalties has some negative fallouts the existence of strong community ties provides for relatively greater stability and dignity to the individuals than they would have as atomised individuals. This in part explains why the Indian poor retain a strong sense of self-respect.' It's that self-respect which the thoughtless insistence on egalitarianism destroys. Madhu Kishwar also pointed out that the support system provided by kinship ties still provides greater social security than the combined effects of all the schemes that successive socialist governments have introduced to help the Indian poor. Every Indian government so far has thought it necessary to adopt socialism as its political creed, but none has tried to adapt that Western doctrine to the special needs of India.

The attack on Indian languages started in 1835 with what the *Oxford History of India* rightly describes as a 'fateful decision' by the governor-general, Lord Bentinck. He ruled that 'the great object of the British Government ought to be the promotion of European literature and science.' He therefore directed that all funds available for education should be 'henceforth employed in imparting to the native population knowledge of English literature and science through the medium of the English language'.

The spread of English as an international language has given a new impetus to this onslaught on the languages of India. The upper echelons of Indian society regard English as one of the greatest gifts of the British. They have made it the language of the exclusive club they belong to, and parents who see half a chance of getting their children admitted to the club will make any sacrifice to provide an English-medium education for them. The élite are not concerned that English has impoverished Indian languages and stood in the way of the growth of an indigenous national language. They insist that English must be preserved as the common language of multilingual India, even though less than 3 per cent of the population have even a basic understanding of it. Yet the irony is that we, the British, laugh at India's zeal for our language, and Indian accents and Indian English have long been a fruitful source of jokes. In my many years with the BBC in India, I have often had contributors rejected because of their 'thick accent'. 'It's too Peter Sellers', I am frequently told. I hear thick European accents on the World Service – accents which are certainly very difficult to understand on the crackly signal that reaches Delhi. I doubt that many BBC producers would tell a Frenchman that his accent was unacceptable: they are only too happy to find Frenchmen willing to speak our language. The French take an enormous pride in their own language: the still colonized élite of India do not.

India has followed Western economic thinking too. When socialism was in fashion, Nehru rejected Mahatma Gandhi's plea for development from the villages upward and concentrated on trying to create an industrialized nation through centralized planning. Now that the West has rejected socialism, the Indian élite talk of liberalizing the economy, making consumerism the engine of growth and allowing the wealth created to 'trickle down' to the poor. The irony is that, during the years when Rajiv Gandhi was liberalizing the economy, the growth in employment declined – and that's the growth rate that matters most in India.

An Indian friend of mine attended a conference at Oxford in the middle of the rejoicing over the downfall of communism in Eastern Europe. When asked what he thought about the triumph of democracy, he replied, 'I don't think it's democracy which has triumphed – it's consumerism. And that's a disaster for us.' You have only to watch the advertisements on Indian television to see how successful consumerism is in India too, even though most

Indians have no hope of buying the goods advertised. We, the advocates of consumerism, might not be too happy if the day ever came when they could buy the goods. The average Indian's annual consumption of commercial energy is the equivalent of 210 kilograms of oil. A Briton consumes the equivalent of 3,756 kilograms of oil. India's population is around 900 million. If each Indian were to start consuming the amount of commercial energy a Briton does, that would mean the world finding the equivalent of an extra 3,190 million tonnes of oil each year. Imagine what consuming that would do to the greenhouse effect, not to mention its effects on oil and other energy reserves.

Of course it's not just consumerism that has distorted the Indian economy: many of its ills can be blamed on socialist controls which have protected inefficient and often corrupt industrialists. But I don't think it's good enough to say that all would be well if India amended its policies, liberalized its economy and concentrated on competing in the world market rather than protecting its own market. That would mean massive investments going into products which few could afford. In spite of all the controls, investment is already slanted in favour of the élite. To take one example, private transport is beyond the wildest dreams of most Indians, but the streets of Delhi are nevertheless clogged up with Japanese-designed cars and scooters which can compete in the international market. For the less affluent there are only decrepit, outdated and fuel-inefficient buses quite incapable of providing an efficient service even if the roads were cleared for them. There has been no development of suburban railways worth the name, and not even any attempt to relieve the burden of the poor man's taxi-driver – the cycle-rickshaw puller. He does not enjoy the fruits of modern aerodynamics, metallurgy or engineering. His vehicle hasn't changed in the twenty-five years I have known Delhi – it's still inordinately heavy, and doesn't even have such modern aids as gears.

In its 1990 report on poverty, the World Bank suggested that those developing countries will be most successful which 'promote the productive use of their most productive asset – labour' and provide 'basic social services to the poor'. Officially, India has spent the last forty or more years trying to do that. On paper, or in theory, it has not failed: laws have been passed and funds have been voted to provide social services. The failure has been in the implementation of the laws and the disbursement of the funds. To implement and supervise the laws and policies, the élite who dominate the administration would have to go into the countryside and become involved in the lives of the villagers, but they resist even being moved from the state capitals, where they enjoy the comforts of modern conveniences, to the district headquarters. There's an entertaining Hindi novel, *Rag Darbari*, about the futility of the government's efforts in the countryside. Its author, Shrilal Shukla, writes:

In the old days when the white men ruled India, the Rest Houses where they stayed while touring villages were built on river banks or in valleys, forests and mango groves – that is, wherever the poetry of Wordsworth, Rabindranath Tagore or Sumitranandan Pant came to mind. Such things as dust and bustle, cholera, smallpox and plague, starvation and poverty, ugliness, bad manners and unpleasantness found it very difficult to reach them. . . . Now there have been hundreds of experiments in which brown sahibs have gone from the town to the country, stayed in a village for a few days, drunk the local water and returned alive and kicking without any contagion or disease. By means of jeeps which stir up typhoons of dust day and night, one thing has been settled – India, which until now had been located in the towns, is spreading into the villages.

The cynical Shrilal Shukla was himself a member of the élite cadre of government servants – the Indian Administrative Service. He knows how experimental the stays in the villages have been, and how administrators leap into their jeeps at the earliest possible moment to rush back to their comfortable quarters in some government compound and clear the dust from their lungs with purified water, aerated soft drinks or stronger medicines.

If an industrialist does take advantage of the various tax and other concessions available to those who venture into the countryside, he will import all his key employees from the cities and provide them with houses, schools and health centres so that they do not have to interact with the locals or take any interest in improving their facilities. Very often all the locals get is jobs as cleaners and a little trade. Until administrators, doctors and teachers spread out from the cities and settle in the countryside, no end of investment in school buildings or health centres will provide the effective social services which the World Bank rightly says are so essential for balanced development.

The failure to deliver has brought democracy into disrepute. During the 1989 general election, I asked a labourer who he was going to vote for. He replied, 'What does it matter? Whoever I vote for will put my vote in his own stomach.' Disillusionment with politicians has spawned its own vocabulary. One phrase which has gone straight into Hindi without translation is 'vote-bank'. It means the politician's practice of trying to build up the support of a caste or religious community by making promises specific to its members – promises that are not fulfilled. Another telling usage is the word 'kursi' or 'seat'. In political terms, this is the seat on which an office holder sits, and has come to signify the unscrupulousness with which a politician fights for that seat and the tenacity with which he sticks to it if successful. Then there is '*Aya ram gaya ram*', or 'He's just come and he's gone.' That describes the many politicians who change their parties with each fluctuation in their political fortunes. A '*note chapne ka machine*', or a currency-note printer, refers to a scheme involving large sums of money from which the politician will take his cut. Most political pundits credit the Indian voter with great wisdom because he has consistently thrown out politicians who fail to perform, but the system does not seem to allow anyone to make radical changes, so the time will surely come when the Indian voter will lose faith in the system too.

India has shown that democracy alone is not enough – nor, incidentally, is economic growth. What are required are politics and a political system which are relevant to India's past traditions and present circumstances. In *Rationalism in Politics and Other Essays*, the political scientist Michael Oakeshott wrote, 'Those societies which retain, in changing circumstances, a lively sense of their own identity and continuity (which are without hatred of their own experience which makes them desire to efface it) are to be counted fortunate, not because they possess what others lack, but because they have already mobilized what none is without and all, in fact rely on.' The élite who dominate modern India believe that all that's good comes from outside and are certainly not without 'hatred of their own experience' but do 'desire to efface it'. We in the West do not hate India's experience: we despise it and believe that what we have to offer is far superior. As satellite television spreads, it will be even harder for the many courageous but uninfluential Indians who realize the rightness of Oakeshott's words to fight the pressure from outside. They will become more and more marginalized. It's my belief that if we are really serious about coping with India's poverty we too have to show far greater respect for India's past and perhaps even learn from it ourselves, for we have still not shown that we have the answers to poverty. We must be aware that our way of life is encouraging thinking and policies which increase poverty and instability in the less prosperous parts of the world. Development is more than mere economics.

I am well aware that I will be accused of advocating a return to some golden age of India which never existed. Many will say I am trying to drag India backwards – to deny it the fruits of modern science and technology and to rob it of the freedom of democracy. Such critics are, I believe, in effect accepting the claim that there is now only one way: that Western liberal democracy has really triumphed. Of course India must live in today's world, and its citizens must feel that they are progressing and prospering. India must keep abreast of all the latest knowledge, but it must adapt that knowledge to its own problems, it must build on its own traditions and beliefs. In *The Mind of Mahatma Gandhi*, Gandhi is quoted as saying, 'My *Swaraj* [self-rule, or independence] is to keep intact the genius of our civilization. I want to write many new things but they must all be written on the Indian slate. I would gladly borrow from the West when I can return the amount with decent interest.'

It should be possible for India to preserve its own genius and to build a nation according to its lights, for, as Sarvepalli Radhakrishnan, the philosopher who became India's second president, said in his edition of the Upanisads, 'The characteristic genius of the Indian mind is not to shake the beliefs of the common man but to lead them by stages to the understanding of the deeper philosophical meaning behind their beliefs.' But the Western world and the Indian élite who emulate it ignore the genius of the Indian mind. They want to write a full stop in a land where there are no full stops.

The stories I tell in this book will, I hope, serve to illustrate the way in which Western thinking has distorted and still distorts Indian life – I might almost say they are parables. They provide no answers to India's poverty, but I believe they do suggest where we should begin to look for those answers – in India itself.

— 1 —

RAM CHANDER'S STORY

Bed tea or chota hazari (small breakfast), as we used to know it when I was a child in Calcutta during the last days of the raj, is one of the luxuries of my life in India. It's one I would be able to appreciate more if I had the self-discipline not to drink until eleven o'clock or so at night, eat a vast dinner and then go straight to bed, even though I know my digestion will only just be starting to cope with such excesses when the time comes for me to get up. Waking up would be easier if I had a more old-fashioned servant: some of those who lived here during the raj have admitted that they knew it was time to get up when they felt their cheek and realized they had been shaved. My Ram Chander's banging on the door is not much more kindly than the hammering of the corporal's baton at the end of my bed when I was in the army.

Ram Chander, or 'Chandre' as I have come to know him, is not one of those smooth, smart, silent, servants of the raj. He would stand, if he ever stood straight, about five foot four. He doesn't stoop, but he always seems to lean – perhaps because anything akin to a straight line is abhorrent to him. No amount of encouragement will make him eat three meals a day, so he is thin almost to the point of emaciation. He caught smallpox as a child, and so his face is pockmarked and one eye is covered by a glaucous film. Whatever clothes he wears become instantly crumpled, and his hair, although thinning, has a will of its own. Chandre speaks no English, for which I am to blame since I have never made any effort to teach him – in this city of snobs, I don't want to lose one of the few opportunities I get to practise my Hindi.

It would be surprising if Chandre were a Jeeves, because he

comes from a caste which is not normally promoted beyond the lowest ranks of the servants' quarters – he is from the bhangi or sweeper caste, at the bottom of even the Harijan caste hierarchy. But Chandre is no upstart; the success he has made of his life has not gone to his head. I can imagine that in these egalitarian days many will regard it as the height of condescension for me to describe his becoming my servant as a success, but that is the way Chandre looks on it because he is a lot better off than most people from his village.

Condescension is a trap which anyone who writes about his servant can easily fall into. The word 'servant' itself shocks liberal consciences, but that is what Chandre is. So why do I want to write about him? One reason, of course, is because I think that I have a good story to tell. I also hope that his story will show those who have a horror of the caste system that a Harijan is a human being. Ever since Mahatma Gandhi awoke India and the world to the suffering of Harijans, they have been much pitied. But all too often those whom we pity become pitiable. Our concern, our anger about their plight, denies them humanity. Above all, I hope that I am paying a tribute to the affection that Chandre and I have for each other.

Chandre does not know the year of his birth. That's not uncommon in an Indian village, where life is still not measured exactly in ages – the ages for joining and leaving school, the legal age for marriage, or even the legal age to vote. These all exist in law, of course, but rural India has never been a great respecter of that. All that Chandre does know is that he was still a child when the jhagra or troubles took place.

The troubles – the partition riots of 1947 – found Chandre and his mother in Lahore. His mother was working as a sweeper in a lunatic asylum. Chandre told me, 'My father was not alive by then. He was a big strong man, like you, but he died about a year after I was born. He died in one minute, at night.' Chandre did not know what had happened in that minute.

I asked Chandre what he remembered of the bloodshed in Lahore. He replied with his usual brevity, 'Much rioting.'

Lahore, the magnificent capital of Punjab, became part of Pakistan after partition, and Hindus like Chandre's mother fled to

Delhi. No one knows exactly how many fled or how many Muslims tried to make their way to Pakistan in what must surely have been one of the greatest upheavals of history. About half a million people were killed, many of them butchered in trains. Chandre and his mother were lucky. He remembers that the train journey from Lahore to Delhi, a distance of about 300 miles, took several days. He also remembers a mob stopping the train.

'On the way, near the start of the journey, someone attacked the train. I don't know who. The carriage was crowded, great big men were weeping, we were all scared. We shut all the windows and doors, and I hid under a seat. Then the military came and we reached Delhi safely.'

After that adventurous beginning to his life, Chandre could well have just settled down to being one of millions of Harijans working on the land in Uttar Pradesh, India's most populous state. His village is Molanpur, post office Gavvan – a villager always describes his home by his local post office – district Badayun. It is about four hours' drive from Delhi. Chandre's family was better off than most Harijans because they did own some land. According to Chandre, his grandfather had at least ninety bighas (fifteen acres) but he lost a lot of that to the Ganges, which meanders where it likes through the soft soil. His uncle was still farming about fifty bighas when Chandre was a boy, grazing the buffaloes and goats. His mother used to make ghi, or clarified butter, from the buffaloes' milk and sell it in the bazaar at Gavvan, only a mile away by foot. As soon as he was strong enough, Chandre was taught to plough with bullocks. Then he worked the year round in the fields – sometimes his family's and sometimes other people's which his family had taken as share-croppers, sharing the produce with the owners on a fifty–fifty basis.

Chandre was perfectly happy. 'Farm work goes on twelve months of the year. We lived well and I was never hungry.'

'What about school?' I asked Chandre when I was trying to piece together the story of his childhood.

'There was no school in my village. I learnt to read from my own children.'

There was actually a school, I discovered later, but it didn't teach much which seemed relevant to working on the land, and Chandre had no other ambitions at that time.

'If life was satisfactory for you, how did you come to Delhi?' I asked.

'Oh, that was because of the big row.'

I imagined there had been some massive dispute over land which had driven Chandre out of his village. But not at all – it was a sudden storm, although it must have been brewing for some time.

'I left home because I argued with my mother. She told me to go, otherwise why should I go?'

'But why did your mother tell you to go?'

'Because she got angry with me.'

'There must have been some reason for her getting angry with you.'

'I suppose there was. I did have a bad temper.'

'So you lost your temper.'

'No, not me – my mother.'

Extracting information from Chandre was trying my patience, so I said rather irritably, 'Chandre, I don't understand. What was the row about? Surely your mother didn't just get angry for no reason at all.'

That at last got Chandre going. 'Well no. One evening I returned home to find the buffaloes and bullocks lowing because they hadn't been fed. I said that my cousin should give the buffaloes green fodder. I said that I spent the whole day working in the fields and what I brought home everyone ate, so why couldn't my cousin at least look after the animals and give the fodder. My mother said, "If you leave the house there'll be no fighting." That night I was sleeping in the fields while the maize was growing, to keep away the wild animals. In the field I thought, "My mother has never spoken to me like this in the whole of my life and so I should go." I left the next morning from the fields and no one knew that I had gone. No one knew where I had gone. I had eighty rupees with me and the clothes I was wearing.'

It is quite possible that Chandre would have cooled down and returned to his village to make peace with his mother had he not met a member of his biradari or subcaste on the road – described by Chandre as one of his relatives. Chandre has an army of so-called relatives, who are always demanding his attendance at weddings, funerals or other family occasions. He asked Chandre where he was going, and Chandre replied without thinking, 'To find work.'

His relative said, 'But you have work in your village and you have land, so why do you want to go outside.'

Then Chandre told him the story about his mother. His relative replied, 'Your mother should not have spoken like that. You have done right. You can come with me – I have work in Delhi.'

So Chandre arrived in the capital of India with just the clothes he was standing up in and his eighty rupees. His relative was living in what is known as a jhuggi-jhonpri, that is a cluster of one-roomed shacks normally consisting of mud walls and rusty corrugated-iron roofs. Even someone as short as Chandre could not stand up inside the jhuggi. The jhuggi-jhonpri had sprung up on the edge of a construction site because, as usual, the contractors had made no attempt to house the migrant labourers building in this case a hospital. Chandre's relative was working as a labourer, carrying sand and bricks on his head.

The next day, Chandre's relative sent him off to buy atta or flour for making chapattis, but Chandre was never to return. It wasn't that he didn't want to return – he had nowhere else to go and was very grateful to his relative – but he just got lost. When I asked Chandre how he could have got lost when there must have been plenty of atta shops nearby and plenty of people to ask the way back to the construction site, Chandre replied, 'I crossed the road to the shop, bought the atta and then forgot the way.'

'But it must have been a big construction site. Some people must have known the way back to it,' I said.

'Yes, it was a big site, but I didn't know what to ask for. I had only arrived the night before, so I didn't know. I wandered around all day and in the evening I found myself in Akbar Road.' Akbar Road is one of the tree-lined avenues of the original New Delhi. Its colonial bungalows set in large gardens are occupied by ministers, senior civil servants and service officers. Chandre must have walked a long way from north Delhi to get to this, the most sought-after part of the capital. The burra sahibs of independent India live like their colonial predecessors in an artificially sanitized zone, removed from all the discomforts suffered by the people they are governing or administering. Chandre was overcome by the alien orderliness of it all.

'There were no people on the streets, no shops. So I finally realized that I was completely lost and there was no one to ask. It was getting dark, I had nowhere to go, so I just sat down by a rubbish heap and started to cry. I couldn't think of anything else to do.'

'Did you spend the night on the streets?' I asked.

'No. You remember our dhobi [washerman], Sohan Lal? A friend of his came by and asked me why I was crying. He said, "Don't worry. Come with me," and that night he gave me food and a place to sleep. He asked me my caste and I said I was a bhangi. But he didn't mind. He was a dhobi.'

'Did you feel uneasy because you were a sweeper, not from their caste?'

'No, there was nothing like that. I didn't feel like that. I spoke to Sohan Lal and his family and they didn't let me feel anything.'

I was a little surprised by this, so I said, 'Sohan Lal's family had absolutely no reason for taking you in. You were not related. They didn't know your family. They didn't come from the same area.'

'No, they just felt sorry for me when I told them that I had arrived in Delhi the night before, had been told to go and buy atta and had got lost. They said, "You stay here until you find your relative, otherwise you will die."'

Chandre could well have died or got lost in the underworld of Delhi if Sohan Lal's family had not taken pity on him. To this day, Chandre remains a very nervous traveller. Recently he was sent by train to Allahabad to meet me. Before I left, I assured him that the Prayagraj Express terminated at Allahabad, but a tired Chandre told me he had sat up all night in case he missed the station.

Sohan Lal's family lived in the servants' quarters at the back of a large compound in Akbar Road. A senior naval officer called Nayar was living in the bungalow – he must have been an admiral to qualify for such spacious accommodation. Chandre was taken to see Nayar Sahib the next morning. Nayar telephoned a friend who was looking for a sweeper and suggested that he took on Chandre. But Chandre once again failed to reach his destination.

'Nayar Sahib's sweeper told me to go behind the Ashoka Hotel where I would find a house and to ask there about the job. There was no house – just a big hotel – so I wandered round all day and then luckily found my way back to Nayar Sahib's house in the evening.'

'What did Nayar Sahib say?'

'He called the dhobi and asked him whether I got the job. The dhobi told him that there was no house where the sweeper had sent me. So the sahib called in the sweeper and asked him why he had told me to go to the wrong place. The sweeper said he had gone for the job himself – I suppose it was better paid. Anyhow, Nayar Sahib got very angry with the sweeper and said, "This man will work here now." '

Chandre worked for Nayar Sahib for five years – or at least that is as he remembers it: I am a little doubtful whether a senior naval officer would have remained in one posting for so long. Anyhow, it was during Nayar Sahib's time that Chandre met and married his wife. Under normal circumstances Chandre's marriage would have been arranged for him by his family and the biradari or subcaste, but he had not had any contact with his village since he had arrived in Delhi. So it was that Nayar Sahib acted as the head of Chandre's biradari – or perhaps it would be more accurate to say his marriage-broker. It all happened very suddenly, as Chandre explained in his laconic way.

'A man was running off with a girl in Nayar Sahib's time. He came to the compound where I lived. We were all on duty, so the women asked him who he was, where he had come from, what caste he was. He got frightened and ran away. Perhaps the police were after him. He left the girl behind and didn't come back. Then, after some days, all the compound people – the dudh-wallah [milkman], the mali [gardener], the dhobi and all the rest of them – went to the sahib. He called the girl. She told him she had no relatives in Delhi and was not married. The compound-wallahs suggested the marriage. The sahib asked if she wanted to stay with me. So it was fixed.'

'Did the sahib ask you whether you wanted to marry the girl?'

'I can't remember. The sahib took us to a navy place in his car where we had an official marriage and put our thumbprints on the papers.'

Chandre did not bother to find out about the man who had brought his wife to the compound.

'I never asked my wife. She didn't tell me either. Later her mother did say that a man used to come to their house, but they didn't know who he was. It appeared to be something about love. My wife was very beautiful.'

'What about her caste?'

'She told Nayar Sahib she was a sweeper, so I took her to belong to the same caste as I did.'

Neither Chandre nor his new wife made any attempt to contact her family. That, like most things in Chandre's life, happened by accident. One day the newly-weds were together in a market near Akbar Road when they were spotted by his wife's sister-in-law, who worked there. She ran up to Parvati, Chandre's wife, and asked her what she was doing with a man. Parvati explained that she was now married, and so the sister-in-law took the couple to the hospital where Parvati's parents were working. They were, according to Chandre, 'happy at the marriage'. But Chandre still did not tell his own family and biradari.

Eventually the inevitable happened and Nayar Sahib was posted. A new Anglo-Indian naval officer took over the bungalow in Akbar Road. He was, according to Chandre, a little more inquisitive.

'I never used to go back to my village like the other servants do. One day the new sahib asked me why I didn't. He then asked me about my village, its name, the name of the post office, the name of the tehsil [revenue area] and district. Then he sent a letter to my mother. She came to Delhi and we met again. For five years I had not seen anyone from my village.'

I asked Chandre what he had felt when he first saw his mother after so many years. He shook his head slowly and said, '*Kuch nahin*' – 'Nothing.'

'After all those years, nothing?'

'Nothing, I suppose,' he said.

Nevertheless, Chandre was apparently glad to re-establish his connections with his village because he started going home again. There inevitably he came under pressure from his relatives to find jobs in the big city for them too. To demonstrate his status as a man of the world, he gave the job in Akbar Road to his sister's husband and moved on to a guest-house where he was the sweeper for three or four sahibs. When they left, all the staff lost their jobs and the cook and Chandre set off to find work as a team. They worked together for three years and then the cook introduced Chandre to one of his relatives – Garib Prasad, a long-serving BBC cook. It was through Garib Prasad that Chandre first came to work for me. Neither of us can remember the year exactly, but it must have been about 1972.

At that stage in my family's life the household was dominated by Garib and his wife, who somehow managed to look after my children as well as her own seven. The Garibs were part of our family, and Chandre did not, I am ashamed to say, impinge on our lives very much. Garib belonged to the old school of servants who believed that the cook was the boss. What is more, he did not really approve of Chandre's frequent absences in his village – absences which were always extended well beyond the day he had promised to return. Eventually Garib decided that we must have a sweeper who could be relied on, and Chandre returned to his village for good – or at least that was what he thought. He was quite happy about that, because there was no one to look after the land. There was another reason for Chandre's return to the village. It was in his words the '*aurat ka chakkar*' or 'trouble with the woman'.

Chandre was not shocked when I asked whether that meant that his wife was involved with another man or that he was involved with another woman. He smiled and said, 'It does happen sometimes in the village – you can't do anything about it – but it wasn't that trouble. I told you that my wife was very fair. But she also suffered very badly from fits. She had them very often.'

'So you went back to look after her.'

'Yes. That was why I kept on taking a holiday from you, and in the end Garib said I would have to go, so I did.'

By this time Chandre had a daughter, Rani, and a son, Mahesh. After Chandre's return, his wife bore him another son. He died soon after birth, and Chandre's wife died two or three days later.

Chandre stayed in the village until his son, Mahesh, fell ill. He then returned to Delhi to stay with his sister and get treatment for Mahesh. He managed to get a job cleaning some offices and re-established his contacts with the domestic servants' circle. That, he explained, was how he came back to my house.

'Garib was ill in the Mool Chand Hospital near where you were living then. He called for me and said that I should join him again, because he had not found a sweeper he could work with. So I came back.'

Neither my wife – Margaret – nor I knew about all those machinations, but we were very happy to have Chandre back again. In so far as he ever showed any emotion at that stage in our relationship, Chandre seemed to be reasonably pleased too.

Two years later Garib died. We were all heartbroken – especially my children. Garib had been with us since we first came to India, fifteen years earlier. None of us could imagine an outsider in Garib's kitchen, so we hit on the idea of Chandre – who was by now very much an insider. When Margaret put this to Chandre, he turned it down flat. He said, 'I can't do it, because I am not a good enough cook.'

Margaret tried to persuade him. 'You have been working with Garib and other cooks for so long you must have learnt something about cooking.'

'No. I am a sweeper, and I am very happy. I would not like to let you down or to make you angry with me because the food was not good.'

Margaret refused to give up. 'Come on, Chandre,' she said. 'I have seen you cooking sometimes. When Garib was tired he used to sit on the chair and tell you what to do.'

'Yes, but Garib isn't here to tell me what to do now,' said Chandre with flawless logic.

'I will teach you,' offered Margaret.

But Chandre had an answer to that one: 'It would not be proper for you to spend your time in the kitchen.'

Margaret knew how stubborn Chandre could be, so she decided to leave it for the moment, saying, 'Well, Chandre, I don't know what we can do, because all the children say they won't have anyone else.'

The matter was left for a few days, during which Margaret and our daughters did the cooking – much to Chandre's horror: he had never seen a memsahib working in the kitchen except when there was something really special to be cooked.

Garib's death left us with the problem of his family too. His eldest son was now in a good job with an advertising agency, but the rest of the family still had to be looked after. What was worse, if we took on another cook he would have demanded Garib's quarters and there would have been nowhere for the family to go. We discussed this problem with Garib's eldest son, and he came up with an answer which has worked to everyone's total satisfaction ever since. He suggested that Mamaji, as we all knew Garib's wife, should work in the kitchen with Chandre. That would give her an income, and something to take her mind off the loss of her husband. Sham Lal, Garib's son, didn't see any problem in his mother working with a sweeper as cook, and promised to put the idea to her when he felt she was sufficiently recovered. He soon managed to persuade her, on condition that Chandre handled the cookbook – that accounting horror left over from the raj. Chandre had an apparently irrefutable answer to that one: 'I can't read and write well enough to do the cookbook. I never went to school.'

Margaret agreed that she would do the cookbook, and Chandre, seeing that we were all utterly determined to get him in the kitchen, agreed to serve an apprenticeship under Mamaji. It soon became apparent that Chandre knew much more about cooking than he had admitted. It also emerged that Chandre was not totally illiterate, and after a few months he took charge of the cookbook too.

It is now ten years since Garib died and Chandre took over. Margaret and I are separated – a matter of great sadness to Chandre and Mamaji, but they get on very well with Gilly who lives with me. Chandre's style is very unorthodox, but I wouldn't change him for the best-trained servant in India, and his cooking is superb.

Chandre, like all good servants, is the real ruler of the house. If I go to sleep again after his early-morning knock, he'll say, 'I thought you had a lot to drink last night.' In the evening, he gives me an old-fashioned look if I move on from beer to whisky. Chandre won't allow me to serve drinks to my guests: he says, 'Sahib, I am the servant in this house and this is my job.' Towards the end of the evening he sometimes comes and joins in the conversation, leaning on a bookcase which divides the room. He doesn't say much unless the conversation turns to religion, as it does from time to time. Then he will often express his certainty that there is a god up there. Chandre controls my eating as well as my drinking. As soon as breakfast is over he'll insist on knowing what's wanted for lunch, and as soon as that's over I have to turn my attention to dinner. He is in charge of the cookbook, and nothing comes before keeping that up to date and in funds. Chandre doesn't have it all his own way – Mrs Garib gives as good as she gets in the kitchen – but basically Chandre is the boss.

He's at his most imperious when keeping unwanted guests away. In India, a man's home is very much not his castle: everyone feels free to call at all times. I much prefer this to the nuclear family and the formality of Britain, but there are times when I have seen enough of someone – or indeed of everyone. Then Chandre comes into his own, lying with the utmost conviction to keep unwanted intruders out. There was, for instance, the occasion when the car was parked around the corner and all the lights were off in the flat downstairs, to give the impression we were out. We were actually sitting watching television upstairs in the office. Even upstairs we heard the impatient hammering on the front door, but we weren't worried because we were sure Chandre would deal with the intruders. A few minutes later Chandre came upstairs, looking slightly unsure of himself.

'Sahib, when I went to the door I found a lot of people in khaki with guns. I thought the police had come, so I was very worried and I thought of shutting the door. Then I thought, supposing they get annoyed? We don't want to get taken to the police station. So I came to ask you what to do.'

I couldn't think of any reason for the police to come to get me, but in India it's always best to stay on the right side of the law so I told Chandre to go down and ask them whether their business couldn't wait until tomorrow because I was very busy broadcasting to London. I find that this is usually quite an effective excuse. Chandre was soon back again for more advice.

'Sahib, I can't tell them to go away,' he said. 'They are the security guards for Chaudhuri Devi Lal – he has come to see you.'

I agreed with Chandre that we could not turn the redoubtable chaudhuri, or headman, away, and so I went down to welcome him and apologize for the delay.

Chaudhuri Devi Lal was then the chief minister of Haryana and was soon to become the deputy prime minister. At seventy-five, he is the patriarch of the Jats, the Indian farming caste which dominates the villages surrounding Delhi. Some six feet two inches tall, broadly built, with a good head of white hair and a deep gravelly voice, he is every inch a leader. The chaudhuri is hated by the élite because he is proud of his rural background and makes no pretence to the sort of sophistication they admire.

Chandre always remembers another occasion when Chaudhuri Sahib came to call. This time it was breakfast. Chandre had laid on what we all thought would please the chaudhuri's rustic tastes – egg brujia (a sort of spiced scrambled egg), a vegetable curry, lassi (liquefied curd) and crisply fried parathas. All seemed to go well until Chaudhuri Sahib said to Gilly, 'These are very good parathas. What oil do you use?'

'Groundnut oil,' replied Gilly.

The chaudhuri hurriedly dropped his half-eaten paratha. In a shocked tone he said, 'You don't use ghi.' Then, realizing that he had to provide some excuse for not finishing his meal, he said, 'You know, my doctor has told me to restrict my diet.' In towns ghi is considered a luxury, but to a self-respecting farmer it's the only acceptable cooking medium.

Devi Lal never came to breakfast again, but this hasn't spoilt our friendship, though Chandre is disappointed that the chaudhuri didn't find time to come to the house after becoming deputy prime minister.

Chandre really comes into his own when there is a big party and we have to call in outside caterers. Then he regards it as his job to see that the bearers don't get drunk or remove too many bottles for themselves. Chandre can also produce a meal under the most adverse circumstances. Corbett Park, the national park just below the foothills of the Himalayas, is better known for its tigers than for its cuisine. We take Chandre with us whenever we go, because even without a kitchen his performance far outstrips that of the cooks working for the contractor who runs the café there. One evening, after he had reluctantly been for an elephant ride and seen a tiger, Chandre was crouched over a kerosene stove outside our quarters. Suddenly the pots behind him clattered. Chandre turned, saw two green eyes staring at him in the semi-darkness and ran inside. When we came back we found the cooking pots all higgledy-piggledy, our dinner spilt on the floor and no sign of Chandre. We shouted for him and he came out looking shaken. 'Sahib, a tiger came,' he said. 'I saw his eyes. So I ran.'

My son Pat was not convinced, and said, 'Chandre, if a tiger came into this compound there would have been a hell of a hangama [uproar]. There are so many people here. They would have seen it.'

But Chandre insisted that it was a tiger. Pat, who was tired after a day in the jungle, went into his room and threw himself on to his bed. There was a sharp hiss and Chandre's tiger shot out of the door. Chandre had got the family right, but not the species – it was a scruffy domestic, but not domesticated, cat.

We Europeans always like to impose our ideas on our servants: we feel we are doing them good and, of course, at the same time storing up merit for ourselves. It was inevitable, therefore, that we should all concern ourselves with the education of Chandre's son, Mahesh. Arrangements were made to get him enrolled in the best government school in the locality, and off he went. No one thought much more about this until one day I saw Mahesh pedalling one of the cycle-rickshaws which ply between the main road outside our house and the railway station. This was now not a question of some vague merit we hoped to earn, it was much more serious than that – the izzat or honour of the household was at stake. I rushed inside and called Chandre.

'What the hell is Mahesh doing pulling that rickshaw?'

Chandre looked rather sheepish and said, 'I can't get him to stay at school and so he has decided to earn his living. He says that he can't hear and then the master beats him.'

'What do you mean can't hear?'

'He says that he has some trouble with his ears. I have been to see the master and he refuses to have Mahesh back. He said, "I don't want a boy like that in my school."'

'Well, for God's sake get him off that damn rickshaw!'

Mahesh didn't seem too unhappy to be forbidden to pull a rickshaw, which is very hard work indeed. The next step was to get him to a doctor. This we did without too much difficulty, but when an operation for his ears was suggested Mahesh once again flatly refused to cooperate. He said he would rather die than go into hospital. So that seemed to rule out education. The next best thing was some sort of training. Fortunately Babu Lal, one of the mechanics who run an open-air car-repair business on the taxi rank opposite us, agreed to take on Mahesh. I have to say that his attendance there is not much more regular than his attendance at school, but Babu Lal is more tolerant than the master. Obviously you can take Mahesh to water but you can't make him drink. My only consolation is that he did learn to read and write before getting himself expelled from school.

It does not redound to my credit that it was many years before I visited Chandre's village, although it's only about four hours' drive from Delhi. Chandre is very proud of his village and of its temple, but somehow I had never found time to go there. Then one day Chandre came into my office and said, 'Sahib, can I have a loan of 20,000 rupees?' I was somewhat taken aback, because Chandre's personal and family problems had usually been solved with smaller sums. When I asked why he wanted this large loan,

Chandre looked sheepish and said, '*Rani ki shadi*' – 'For Rani's wedding.'

I knew that Chandre's daughter, Rani, was only about sixteen, and that we were all meant to be encouraging late marriages to help with family planning and the emancipation of women. But I also knew that once Chandre had made up his mind there was no point in arguing. So I said to him, 'I hope you have found a good boy for Rani. She is a very good girl.'

'Yes,' replied Chandre. 'When I was in my village, the chaudhuri of our biradari came to see me. He is an old friend. He asked whether I would like him to fix a boy for my daughter. I said yes, but I didn't hear anything for six or seven months. Then the chaudhuri came to me and suggested that I should agree to give Rani to one of his relatives.' He explained the relationship by saying that the chaudhuri's son would be Rani's '*nand ka devar*' when she married. After drawing several family trees, I came to the conclusion that Rani's fiancé was the chaudhuri's son's wife's younger brother. Relationships in northern India are very complicated to unravel, because there is a separate word for each relative. It's not, for example, good enough to say 'cousin': you have to know the word which means 'my elder maternal uncle's son'.

After we had sorted out that little problem, Chandre went on to tell me that the rishta, or proposal, had already been formally accepted. 'In our biradari,' he said, 'we from the girl's side have to go to the boy's village. There we take the rishta and it is formally accepted. I went with fourteen people including Mahesh. Twelve came from Delhi, two from the village. I had to take with me sweets, fruit and 150 rupees in cash to give to the boy's family. They gave us a feast and so the rishta was pukka.'

'Was that all you gave?' I asked.

'Oh no. I had to take the suit length for the boy of terry cotton, shoes, a shirt and a gold ring. I had to take five kurta pajamas [loose-fitting tunics and trousers] for the boy's father and uncles, and five saris for the ladies of the family. It cost about 4,000 rupees.'

'But you didn't want a loan at that stage?'

'No, I have some money saved up in a drawer in the house.'

'In this house!' I said angrily. 'You know we have had three burglaries.'

'It's locked in a drawer downstairs. The burglar only steals from the office upstairs,' replied Chandre with perfect logic.

'Why on earth don't you use a bank? It'll be much safer, and you may get interest.'

'No, I don't trust banks. You may have to pay a bribe to get the money out. Many people have told me that.'

Bribes are usually only paid to get loans, but I gave up and asked Chandre whether Rani's fiancé was literate. Gilly and Avrille, who works in our office, had told Chandre a hundred times to make sure he married Rani to a well-educated boy who could get a good job. But Chandre hadn't bothered to find out what his future son-in-law's educational achievements were. They turned out to be minimal. Chandre insisted it would all be all right, because he knew the family well, but it wasn't until after the marriage that he learnt that the boy's father had two wives and innumerable children.

Chandre's biradari has not yet been corrupted by the middle-class practice of giving dowries, and so he was not presented with a long list of goods which he would have to provide in order to get his daughter married. Nevertheless, Chandre himself drew up a fairly formidable list of gifts to give to the couple. It was, quite naturally, a question of izzat or self-respect for Chandre to show that he was able to provide for his daughter properly. This was Chandre's list:

one television set,
one scooter,
thirty-one degchis (handleless saucepans) and other cooking pots and pans,
thirty-one saris for the women and
seven kurta pajamas for men of the boy's family,
five saris and five silver ornaments for Rani,
one tin trunk,
one wall clock,
one wristwatch for the boy,

two chairs,
one table,
one sofa,
one bed with bedding,
2,500 rupees cash.

Total value: 80,000 rupees.

When Chandre asked for the loan, I had no idea that he would be incurring so much expenditure – I grandiosely thought that I would be financing most of the wedding. It never, for instance, occurred to me that Chandre would provide a scooter for his son-in-law, because I had never seen any of Chandre's relatives riding one. But, as the day of the wedding drew near, the extent of Chandre's commitments became clear as the back room of our house started to fill up with all the gifts. I thought that I should step up my contribution, but Chandre said, 'No. All I want you to do is to come to the wedding, even though it is in my village and it will not be very comfortable for you.' That was how I came to pay my first visit to village Molanpur in Uttar Pradesh.

Gilly, Avrille and I set off for Molanpur on the day of the wedding – a day that had been selected as auspicious by Nirottam, a Brahmin living on the embankment at the back of the village. We met up with Satish Jacob, my long-standing colleague in the office, at a dhaba or roadside eating-house owned by a pehlvan, or wrestler, in Gajraula, a small town on the main road from Delhi to Lucknow. There is a whole host of dhabas there because long-distance buses from Delhi stop to allow their passengers to eat. The competition is stiff so the food is good, but the pleasure of eating it is somewhat reduced by the highly offensive odour from a chemical factory on the edge of the town. The leaves on the trees were shrivelled – presumably due to pollution from the factory – and I did wonder what chemicals had penetrated the wrestler's food, but we were all hungry and so I didn't raise that question.

Rattan Singh, the retired wrestler, was sitting cross-legged on a charpai, his face unshaven, his eyes hidden behind dark glasses. He said very little – his presence was enough to ensure the smooth flow of food in his dhaba. He was once the champion of northern India, but he had retired several years ago. The surrogates he now employed to fight for him were strutting around wire cages outside the dhaba. They had swollen red combs instead of cauliflower ears, and battered beaks instead of broken noses. They were better-fed than the guests at his dhaba, getting regular meals of raisins and almonds. Rattan Singh assured me that his fighting cocks were just as formidable as he'd once been.

After we had joined up with Satish and eaten our lunch, we turned off the national highway to Lucknow and drove along the road to Gavvan, the town near Chandre's village. It was April – one of the hottest months of the year. The brain-fever bird's cry rose higher and higher up the scale as it screeched, 'It's getting hotter, it's getting hotter, and I can't *stand* it, can't *stand* it, can't *stand* it.' I thought I would get brain-fever too if I didn't stop our little red van and take a break in one of the cool, green mango groves which flanked the road, but we were late – as always – and couldn't disappoint Chandre.

We passed through the town of Hasanpur, where white-capped Muslims lounged in the shade of mosque courtyards waiting for the evening prayers and the break in the fast of Ramzan, the Muslim month of fasting. In the centre of the town a fine old family house built around a cool courtyard still survived. Much of its plasterwork was intact, but the finely carved wooden balconies were collapsing and the whole place had an ill-kempt air about it. Clearly it was soon to fall victim to the greed of the contractors, who were just waiting to complete the transformation of Hasanpur into yet another hot and ugly concrete cauldron.

Leaving the town, we passed two immaculate white bullocks shaking their heads in unison as they laboured under the yoke of a cart carrying vegetables to market. In the countryside, horse-drawn traps or tongas and bullock carts have still not totally surrendered to three-wheeled phut-phuts of all shapes and sizes emitting all forms of pollution. At first the land was quite fertile. Shisham trees lined the roads, and young sugar cane sprouted in the fields. On the bank of one field we saw a black redstart, his tail quivering energetically. He too was apparently suffering from brain fever, because by now he should have been on his way up to the Himalayas. As we went on, the land became more barren –

wild charas or cannabis grew in the scrub, the bushes were stunted, the date-palms had been mutilated by villagers always short of fodder for their goats and cattle. The earth was dusty and white – the sort of soil that makes me feel hot just to look at it. What agriculture there was seemed comparatively primitive. We passed two more bullocks, this time plodding round and round in circles turning a Persian wheel – a form of irrigation which has been replaced by electric and diesel pumps in the more prosperous areas of northern India.

Eventually we reached Gavvan, where Rani's wedding had been arranged. As we drove into the town, we were flagged down by an anxious Chandre who had been here since the morning. He had apparently forgotten that I'd told him we'd be lunching in Gajraula. Knowing Chandre's deficient sense of direction, I was relieved to be told that he'd brought one of his young relatives to ride ahead of the van on a scooter and lead us to the village.

We drove through the town, paid a two-rupee toll to cross a bridge and then turned right down an even narrower road. The area around the village was more productive than the scrubland we had just passed through. This was the season for sunflower as well as arabi, a root crop with leaves like elephant ears. One field was guarded by a scrawny scarecrow. The tarmac soon gave out and we bucked and reared along a mud track leading to Molanpur, the scooter-rider performing miraculous feats of balance to remain wheelborne. Eventually we came to the village, but we didn't stop. We passed the village pond, with the inevitable black buffaloes wallowing peacefully in it, and drove on until we came to a cluster of mud houses – Chandre's basti. Harijan bastis, or settlements, are always on the outskirts of villages.

There were six thatched houses with mud walls built around an open space of about eighty by seventy feet. More houses were built off the courtyard facing the track, which led in one direction to the main part of the village and in the other direction to the embankment protecting Molanpur and its lands from the Ganges. I had expected that we would be surrounded by curious villagers as soon as we stopped, but everyone was far too busy with preparations for the wedding to bother about us. Chandre got out and led us into the courtyard, where he showed us his house with a certain amount of diffidence. It had a low doorway without a door and one room in which I could just about stand up. Chandre said, 'I have had the thatch done again for the wedding, but it's not really all right for you to sleep in so I've made another arrangement.' I assured Chandre that we would be quite comfortable, but he was not convinced, as he was used to seeing me in much more luxurious circumstances.

The whole basti was decorated with strings of paper flags. Banana trees had been placed on each side of the doorway of the hut where the marriage ceremony was to take place. New mango leaves – symbols of prosperity – were strung above the doorway. The walls of all the huts and the ground of the courtyard had been covered with a fresh paste of mud and cow dung. On the walls, the paste had been worked into intricate patterns – peacocks and elephants had been moulded on to it and the women of the basti had painted animals and men fighting each other inside and outside the houses. The style was very similar to many of the tribal paintings I have seen in central India. Those are now much admired as 'folk art', but I have never heard or read of 'the art' of the Harijans of western Uttar Pradesh – I suppose because they lack the glamour of tribals.

The last-minute preparations for the arrival of the barat, the bridegroom's party, were being made. A tractor trailer carrying chairs and a generator was being unloaded outside the basti. A canvas awning was being erected on wooden poles – one of the elderly women said scornfully, 'It's not very big.' Mahipal, one of Chandre's relatives who works in our office, was washing himself under a pump. He and our dhobi had arrived by the overnight bus from Delhi.

Chandre took no part in the preparations. He seemed to assume that all would be all right in the end. His only concern was that we should live life as we were used to living it. He said, 'It's five o'clock and you haven't had any tea.' Then he insisted on sitting us down at a table complete with tablecloth and went off to brew up. An old lady with a face lined like a prune, no teeth and small, round Mahatma-Gandhi-style spectacles squatted in front of Gilly and started to massage her feet, whimpering, sighing and muttering to encourage herself. Chandre came back to ask where we had put the beer. It had been hidden in the back of the van, because I wasn't quite sure about the proprieties. Chandre doesn't drink himself, and I thought that it might be inappropriate for me to drink at the wedding. I asked tentatively, 'Will it really be all right for us to drink beer. Won't someone object?'

Chandre said with some annoyance, 'I have arranged everything. The whole village wants to welcome you, and I have told them that you will drink beer.'

I could have wished for a somewhat different image to precede me, but there was nothing I could do about it now. If I didn't drink beer, Chandre would, I supposed, lose face. Anyway, there was the ritual of tea to get through first.

After tea, Avrille and Gilly were taken off to see the bride. Rani was being groomed for the coming wedding. Her hair had been oiled and her limbs smeared with turmeric paste, which is said to make skin smooth and fair. She was wearing an old sari borrowed from a relative, which made her look grown-up. In Delhi, like other young girls, she always wore a shalwar-qamiz – baggy trousers and a long shirt. The sari was an indication of her new status – of a married woman. She was an unconventionally pretty girl, with a dark complexion, prominent cheekbones and very large, bright, brown eyes. Ever since her engagement, she had glowed with confidence. Although she coyly refused to comment when asked what she thought of her fiancé, her smiles showed that she certainly had no objection to the match. Now that her wedding day had come she was still enjoying being the centre of attention, but she was tense because the great changes which lay ahead had at last dawned on her. 'Today we had a puja [act of worship],' she told Gilly and Avrille. 'The kumhar [potter] came, and we made offerings to Boorhe Babu. If you do that, then he stops you getting seep – light-brown patches on your skin. I shan't see you today, unless you come here to see me. I have to stay in this house now, because the barat may come any time.'

While I was waiting for Gilly and Avrille to come back, the cows appeared over the top of the embankment in a haze of dust.

They were being driven home for the night by young boys. Then two buses drew up on the embankment and the barat emerged. I had expected Chandre to go out to greet it, but he was nowhere to be seen. The young men came first – dressed in gaudy, tight-fitting trousers, with open-necked shirts which clung to their narrow chests. They gaped and giggled at me and then walked on, some of them holding hands. The older men followed, dressed for the most part in traditional cotton kurtas. They politely ignored the strange foreigner seated at a neatly draped table solemnly sipping tea. The women had been left behind – in Chandre's biradari they don't travel with the barat. The bridegroom's party regrouped on the open ground on the other side of the courtyard, where they were served with soft drinks. Twenty-four hours of feasting had started.

I was not sure what to do next. Should I join in the festivities or should I not? I am easily embarrassed and hate sticking out like a sore thumb. Fortunately Gilly and Avrille returned quite soon, and, with my customary cowardice, I sent them off to find Chandre so that he could tell us what to do.

Chandre decided that it would be premature for us to join the other guests. 'You sit here,' he said. 'You will be more comfortable and I'll call some people to talk to you.' Chandre went off and came back with about ten members of his biradari. It was getting dark, so hurricane lights were produced and Chandre brought the beer. I certainly felt like a drink, but I also wanted someone to drink with. Unfortunately Satish had left sometime earlier, since he had to get back to Delhi, and Gilly and Avrille both thought it would be most unladylike to join me. So there I was, left alone with my drink. However my embarrassment soon wore off under the influence of the lukewarm beer and the conversation.

One of the elders who came was Tau, a man of dismal countenance with a great moustache through which he filtered smoke from his hookah. 'Tau' means 'elder uncle', but he was in fact only Chandre's elder uncle's son – he'd gained the title of 'Tau' because he behaved and looked like an elder uncle. Tau offered the hookah stem to me, but I politely declined. I enjoy many Indian tastes, but the hookah has always defeated me. I nearly choked to death on one in Raja Bazaar in Rawalpindi.

Inevitably the conversation soon got round to weddings. Tau said, 'Ram Chander is lucky. In my younger days the barat stayed until there was no food left in the basti. Nowadays they usually go after one day.'

Gilly asked, 'Do your boys and girls ever get married on their own, for love?' The women laughed, and one said, '"Love" – we don't understand the meaning of the word. These men just think we are there to do the work for them – from morning right through until we go to sleep at night they keep us at it.'

Another woman said, 'That's true, but if you have a good man you become fond of him.' It was harder to understand the women than the men, because they rarely went out of the village and so their dialect was not affected by the Hindustani spoken in towns.

Kamal, a very intelligent younger relative of Chandre's, said, 'Only the educated people get married like that. They perhaps get to know each other in school. For us, an elopement is a great disgrace. I think that's right.'

Gilly quoted an old saying: '*Jab mian bibi razi, to kya karega kazi*' – 'When a boy and a girl agree, not even a qazi [a judge, one of whose duties is the registration of marriages] can do anything about it.'

The villagers laughed, and Kamal said, 'Han, you have said absolutely right. But then we don't encourage that sort of thing. We prefer to arrange it through our customs, because a young girl and a young boy – what do they know?'

I was reminded of the headman of a village just outside Delhi with whom I'd once discussed marriage. He'd said, 'In England you marry the women you love. In India we love the women we marry. You fall out of love after marriage. We fall in love after marriage.'

When I related the headman's views, Tau grunted: 'All this love talk! It has nothing to do with life in villages. Only those who don't know anything about how we live would talk of it.' That ended that conversation.

After a lengthy silence, during which Tau bubbled gloomily on his hookah, I attempted to get things going again by asking about changes in the life of the village. An elderly man with thick glasses, and wearing a rather grubby Gandhi cap, said, 'In my view the worst thing that has happened is that the police have started coming into the village. In the old days the police never came – we used to sort out our quarrels ourselves or with the panchayat [village council]. But nowadays people keep running to the court or the police station. They waste a lot of money, and achieve nothing. The police are not just. They always side with the richer person, so no matter how much you offer them you can't beat someone with more money.'

'But surely,' I asked, 'under the panchayat system you also suffered, because you were the poorest community and you were the sweepers.'

'Han, of course that was there,' the elderly villager replied. 'But, you see, many of our quarrels were among ourselves and we have our own panchayat in our biradari so they sort out the quarrels. Even when we had quarrels with the other castes, the leaders of the panchayat knew that the village could not do without us and that if too much injustice was done to us we would not do the necessary work. So it wasn't that injustice was always done to us. In a village in those days everyone knew their place, but so did everyone have a place.'

'Why do people go to the police now?'

'I'm not certain. I think maybe it's to do with the government. The government and the politicians are always saying they will do everything for us, and people believe this – even though they are always going to the government and getting nothing. Nowadays, you see, everyone thinks that only the government can do anything. Even if a person gets a good job, he doesn't think it's a suitable job unless he is an employee of the government. That's why everyone goes to the government for justice too, because they think only government justice is proper justice.'

Chandre walked into the courtyard, looking rather solemn. He came up to Tau and said, 'Now we must do the accounts. It'll be too late if we don't start now.' Tau, who was still sitting cross-legged on the ground, looked up at Chandre and said, 'Call them all, and I'll come.'

Now the real business of the wedding was to be done. Members of Chandre's biradari are expected to contribute to each other's daughters' weddings. Each person notes down the contribution he has made and then hopes to be reimbursed when his daughter gets married. The proceedings this time were supervised by a diminutive old man drowned by a giant yellow turban. He was the chaudhuri of the biradari. The chota chaudhuri, or small chaudhuri, who was actually very much larger than his superior, was there too. The negotiations took nearly three hours, but Chandre told me they went off without any serious argument. This seemed to be largely because of Chandre's good nature. I asked him whether everyone had paid his dues. 'No,' he said – 'but then they never do. My closest friends did, and others paid something, but I don't like to fight about money. You know how much money I have given to Hari Ram – my real brother, who works near Delhi – and you know he has never given anything back to me.'

Tau apparently never contributed to weddings but always took part in the negotiations. He had told me he earned only a pittance, and so I suggested to Chandre that he lacked the wherewithal to contribute to weddings.

Chandre replied, 'He's got money, but if he doesn't want to give back what I have given for his weddings I am not going to cause any trouble.'

When the business session was over, Chandre came back to us and said, 'You'd better come out now, because the barat procession will be arriving soon.' Gilly asked Chandre, 'But aren't you going to change to receive the barat?' He was wearing a distinctly dirty white shirt and a pair of trousers which had formed part of his uniform several years ago. Chandre ignored that question and went off to see what the caterers preparing the wedding dinner were up to.

We went out to the open space in front of the basti to join the villagers waiting for the barat. For some two hours we were continuously reassured, 'It's coming soon'; 'It's on the point of coming'; 'Now it's coming'; 'It'll be here any moment.' But the barat procession didn't appear. Chandre sent off a series of spies to find out what was happening, and each one returned with an assurance that the barat was on its way. The procession was obviously delayed because the bridegroom's party were still tanking up. It's the privilege of the bridegroom's relatives to arrive drunk, but they take it amiss if the bride's relatives have been drinking. By ten o'clock in the evening, even the laconic Chandre was becoming a little worried. He said to Kamal, 'I hope they won't arrive too much in drink, because then there could be trouble with some of the young men.' Kamal replied, 'There's nothing you can do about it. It's their occasion to make merry.'

Eventually we saw a bright light in the distance moving towards us. It seemed to move very slowly and to stop frequently. As the light got nearer, we picked up the sound of a deep baritone voice amplified by vast loudspeakers singing a hit from an old Bombay film – '*Mere sapnon ki rani, chale ao*' – 'Come, queen of my dreams.' Actually it was the raja who was coming to Chandre's Rani. The procession halted again just before rounding the last corner. Some children ran towards it, but they were called back – tradition demands that the bride's party must wait for the arrival of the procession. The music faltered, and I wondered whether everyone, including the bandsmen, was having a last pull on the bottle before entering the no-drinking area. If so, it must have been a quickie, because the music soon picked up again and the head of the procession, brightly lit by Petromax lights, rounded the corner. Chandre's generator chose this moment to give up and so we – the receiving party – were plunged into darkness.

The first thing I saw was a zoo jigging up and down vigorously. There were white storks, gaudily striped tigers, black bears, and monkeys – all made of papier mâché and cotton wool, and all held aloft by young men dancing the bhangra. The bhangra is a Punjabi dance which has now become standard at all north-Indian weddings and has deteriorated into a hybrid pop form heavily influenced by Western jiving and Indian film choreography. The Hindu gods mingled with the menagerie. There were pictures of Krishna, famed as a lover; the ever-popular monkey-god Hanuman; and Ram with his wife Sita, the hero and heroine of the epic the *Ramayan*, which was top of the television charts at the time. Even the then prime minister, Rajiv Gandhi, was numbered among the Hindu pantheon for this wedding.

Next came the singer. Miraculously, no one tripped over the wires which connected his microphone to the generator bringing up the rear of the procession. He was accompanied by bandsmen in red uniforms with flat hats and white plimsolls. There were trumpeters, clarinettists and even a sousaphone-player blowing their hearts out. Behind them came the hero of the night, Manoj, sitting on a peacock throne wearing a golden turban and garlands of currency notes round his neck. The throne was set on a converted jeep covered with bright-coloured bulbs flashing in circles, diamonds and arcs like rainbows. It looked like a gigantic jukebox. Behind the jeep came the generator, spewing out black smoke. I said to Gilly, 'Manoj looks like a Hindu god seated on a throne.'

Gilly replied, 'He's either a very bad-tempered or a petrified god.'

Manoj certainly didn't look as though he was enjoying the barat. Everyone else was. Perhaps that was the problem – maybe he was like the bridegroom who would have preferred to have stayed back for the party rather than gone off on his honeymoon. It was certainly going to be a very dull night for Manoj. When the procession came to a halt in the space in front of the basti, Manoj meekly descended from his chariot and went into the house where he was to be married. There he was tended to by his sisters. He could hear the beat of the drums and the cries of the dancers – by then we had all got swept up in the bhangra. He had to sit and think about his future with a young bride whom he didn't know at all.

Such thoughts didn't trouble Chandre – by now the proud proprietor of a show which was clearly going very well. He came up to me and said with satisfaction, 'It's a big barat, isn't it?' I replied, 'It certainly is.'

The next stage in the wedding was the evening feast. In most Indian communities the bride's party has to feed the barat before they themselves can start eating. In Chandre's biradari it was a free-for-all. Outside caterers had cooked chana (chick-peas) and potatoes, the sabzi or vegetable was loki – a kind of marrow. For a dessert there were laddoos – sweets made from gram-flour and sugar. Food was served on paper plates instead of the traditional dried leaves. Chandre did not change for dinner.

After dinner, the party started again. Fireworks added to the excitement. The air was thick with the acrid smell of biris or cheap cigarettes, the smoke from the fireworks and the fumes of the barat's generator. The members of the barat breathed the sour smell of cheap country liquor, but I saw only one young man who was obviously drunk. He was led away by his friends, presumably to rest and sober up. There was no disorderliness, no fighting.

I saw Mahipal and two other young men making their way through the chaos with charpais on their head. Sensing that they were meant for us, I went over and asked where they were going. Mahipal said he was taking the charpais to the temple on the embankment, about a quarter of a mile away, where arrangements had been made for us to sleep. I persuaded Mahipal that we would be quite happy sleeping in the courtyard, and so he took the charpais back. We went to bed under the night sky outside Chandre's house. That was a decision I was to regret.

It wasn't until the fireworks, music and dancing ended at five o'clock in the morning that I managed to get any sleep. The respite didn't last long – I was soon awakened by loud snoring. At first I thought I had been woken by my own snoring – that has happened. But then I came to my senses and realized that the offender must be someone else, because the snoring had not stopped. I looked across to the charpais where Gilly and Avrille were sleeping peacefully, with their mouths shut. Neither of them was the culprit. The snoring was unusually loud but very regular and seemed to be coming from almost under my charpai, but when I leant over the edge of the bed I could see nothing. I gave up, covered my head with my sheet and somehow managed to get to sleep again. At first light I was woken up by a young girl removing a large log of wood from a hole in the mud wall just by my charpai. There was a great deal of grunting and snuffling and a huge black sow crawled through the hole on bended knees. A long, thin snout, fangs and a comb of bristles along her back showed that the blood of a wild boar ran in her veins, so it would probably not have been a good thing if I had tried to stop her snoring. Wild or not, however, the sow had a very good relationship with the young girl, who drove her past my charpai and out towards the fields, crying 'Harrrrr, Harrrrr, Harrrrr!'

A few minutes later we were brought steel mugs full of steaming sweet tea, and Chandre's relatives enquired solicitously about the next of the day's problems – what they called 'lavatory'. I lacked the dexterity to perform my morning offices squatting in the fields and so gladly accepted the offer of the facilities in the hostel of the nearby temple. Gilly and Avrille disappeared with Chandre's sister-in-law for their ablutions, which were more thorough than mine. They had full-scale bucket-baths, dousing themselves with water from a huge brass pot while hidden from the other guests by a mud wall built as a screen to one side of the courtyard in Chandre's sister-in-law's house. My ablutions did little for my appearance, which was by now beginning to resemble Chandre's on the night before, but after their baths Avrille and Gilly looked as though they had spent the night in a luxury hotel. I waited for breakfast, while they went off to see Rani.

We had been told that the auspicious time for the wedding ceremony had been set for the early morning, but Rani had still not bathed or put on her wedding finery. She was sitting in the room beside the courtyard where the wedding was to take place, attended by her female relatives. She stared at the floor and wouldn't speak – wedding nerves had got the better of her. Eventually she admitted that she hadn't slept all night. For most of the time she had stayed inside the room, but occasionally she had gone out into the courtyard to serve water to her guests. 'Poor child,' said Chandre's sister-in-law. 'At times like this a girl should have her mother near her. We are doing what we can, but a mother is something special for a girl.' As Gilly and Avrille left, they heard the sister-in-law offering motherly advice to the young bride. 'Respect your mother and father-in-law. Live with them in peace and listen to what they tell you. Look after your husband. Above all, don't fight with anyone in your new home.'

While the girls were away, Chandre came to keep me company. I asked him what he had done all night. 'Nothing,' he said with surprise. 'Come on, Chandre,' I said. 'Did you talk to people?'

'Yes,' he replied.

'What about?'

'I asked them, "Is everything all right?" They said, "Yes, it's fine." But everyone wanted to know about you. They said the best thing about the wedding was that you, my sahib, had come.'

Seeing my embarrassment and disbelief, Chandre said, 'Honestly. It's true.'

I hurriedly changed the subject to Chandre's still unkempt appearance. 'You really can't go to Rani's wedding ceremony in those clothes,' I said.

'No,' he agreed. 'I have got some new clothes. You'll be surprised when you see them, but I have still got a lot of work to do.'

'What work?' I asked. 'Surely it's nearly time for the marriage to take place. You said it would be early in the morning because that was the auspicious time.'

'Well, if we aren't ready, it can't be,' said Chandre with his customary logic.

'But what is this work?' I insisted.

'Well, I've got to cook your breakfast, haven't I?'

'No,' I said firmly. 'We can go without that if necessary. Why don't you go and get changed so that the marriage can start?'

But Chandre could not be budged. All I could achieve was to persuade him that he should start cooking breakfast at once.

After breakfast we hung around watching cooks kneading a mound of atta into dough for chapattis, to be baked in a tandoor or oven they had dug in the ground. This was the start of the preparations for the main feast. The members of the barat were waking up and straggling bleary-eyed into the fields for their lavatory.

We wandered around aimlessly until a miraculously transformed Chandre reappeared to take us to the ceremony. His hair was neatly brushed, he was closely shaved and he was wearing an immaculately pressed, cream silk kurta with matching trousers. I had never seen him look so smart.

The wedding took place in the small courtyard of the house where Rani was staying. We were very touched to see that she was wearing the pink sari we had given her. The edge of her sari was drawn over her face. Manoj was sitting next to her, wearing a smart suit buttoned up to the collar and a pink turban topped with a crown made of silver and gold paper covered with flowers. The couple were sitting on the ground under a conical thatch supported by three upturned ploughs. A stick stood in the middle of this mandap or platform with mango leaves and earthen pots tied to it. Women sat in one corner of the courtyard singing songs of rejoicing. Relatives filed past Manoj and Rani, touching her feet and smearing tilaks on his forehead, and putting money into a steel tray by the fire. No Brahmin priest was involved in the ceremony, but the elderly chaudhuri who had supervised the business transactions the night before squatted by the fire reciting mantras and dropping herbs into the flames.

Eventually the chaudhuri told the couple to stand up. He tied Manoj's scarf to a white cotton shawl which Rani was wearing and gave them a gentle shove towards the fire. Manoj led his bride around the flames seven times – a marriage is said to be a bond which lasts seven lifetimes. Some of the bridegroom's party let off fireworks, but this was soon stopped by the elders from Chandre's side. The couple then went inside the house to be 'worshipped' by the guests. Rani, according to tradition, should not have lifted her veil until she reached her in-laws' house, but happily for all of us she did show her pretty face, now smiling shyly. She wore a heavy gold ring through her nose, and a pendant on her forehead hung from a gold chain pinned to her parting.

Chandre had slipped out before the ceremony ended – he had received a message that the cooks were refusing to start baking the chapattis until they were given a bottle of liquor, and he had gone to find them one. He was back and waiting for us when we came out of the house after paying our respects to the couple. 'Come quickly,' he said – 'I want you to see the pigs.' There they were in the open space in front of the basti – two monsters, trussed up in the back of a three-wheeled minitruck. As they were being lowered to the ground, Chandre said to me with pride, 'One weighs more than a quintal [a hundredweight].' I was relieved that the pigs had come from outside and that my friend of the previous night was not to be sacrificed.

None of us wanted to watch the slaughter, but Chandre insisted. Mahipal came forward with a long iron spike, knelt beside the larger of the two pigs and stabbed it through the heart. Then we knew what to squeal like a pig means. After the pigs' bristles had been singed off with burning straw, Mahipal washed off the black, charred hair under the pump and started to cut the carcasses up into small pieces for the curry. The meat was cooked in huge, black metal pans, stirred with bamboo sticks.

While the guests were waiting for their feast, they were kept amused by a magic-wallah and three young men who specialized in dances appropriate for a day when fertility was very much on people's minds. Two of them were young and slim; they were dressed in saris with false breasts filling out their blouses. The third was slightly older, his teeth were stained by pan, or betel-leaf, and he looked thoroughly dissipated. He was dressed like a monkey with a large tail and a larger penis, which he used to good effect to entertain the guests and arouse the young dancers. They wiggled their hips and wobbled their false breasts seductively to the music of bagpipes – not instruments I would have associated with this sort of entertainment. Eventually one of the young 'women' fell to the ground in ecstasy and the 'monkey' leapt on top of her to shouts of approval from the audience.

We were never to know what other entertainments lay in store for the guests, because Chandre came to call us for our lunch – chicken curry, which had been specially prepared for us because pork is one thing I won't eat in India.

As we had to get back to Delhi that night, Chandre excused us from waiting for the barat to move off and take Rani to her new home. The whole wedding party seemed to surround our little red van to see us off, but we eventually completed our goodbyes and were allowed to leave accompanied by our dhobi and his wife.

As we drove away, I thought how removed I had been from the wedding itself. I had been treated like royalty: the guests were honoured by my presence, but they kept their distance. I wondered whether I had been at fault – whether I should have made more effort to talk to members of the barat. Perhaps I should have stayed up all night. On many occasions I still have difficulty in knowing how to be a foreigner in India, but at the wedding I don't think it was entirely a problem of being a foreigner – I was Chandre's sahib, and the members of Chandre's biradari don't expect to be on intimate terms with their employer. Then again, the wedding was also very much an affair of Chandre's biradari, and I think that anyone from outside that tight-knit community would have felt a stranger. I have talked to Chandre about this since the wedding, and he has assured me that I did exactly what was right. I am still not sure: I would feel more comfortable if I had taken more part in the wedding, but that would have meant forcing myself on the guests, which can be just as condescending as standing slightly aloof – and incidentally a lot more embarrassing for everyone.

Within a year of the wedding in Molanpur, Rani had given birth to a son in hospital in Delhi. When Chandre first saw him he burst into tears, because the baby's left foot was twisted at a right angle to his leg. Rani, more sensibly, accepted the doctor's assurance that this could be put right by six months in plaster.

When Rani returned from hospital, Gilly and Avrille took her aside and explained how putting off her next child would help her to look after herself and her baby's health, and would mean that the family would be better off. Her husband, Manoj, was unemployed. They suggested an IUD and told her it would not harm her or her baby, or prevent her having children later on. It transpired that Rani already knew all about family planning from friends and television – all she needed was some help in going about it. So the next day she went off happily with Gilly to the local Marie Stopes clinic. Manoj put up some opposition, but Rani handled him efficiently and he was won over. Unfortunately, the women of his village were not amenable to persuasion. When the baby's foot had been straightened and Rani returned to her in-laws' home, the women there insisted she have the IUD removed – they thought she had been immoral to interfere with herself.

Chandre was much exercised about getting a job for his son-in-law. Avrille sent Manoj and Rani for an interview as domestic servants for an executive of a Middle East airline. When they came back, Chandre came to me with a long face and said, 'I don't know whether I should let Rani live in the house of a habshi.' 'Habshi' means 'Negro'.

I told Chandre rather pompously that there was nothing wrong with Africans, and anyhow this man was an Arab. Chandre replied, 'That's all right, but Rani says that the habshi wants her to cook beef.'

'Well, you sometimes cook buffalo here.'

'That's true. But these people, they eat too much meat.' I couldn't budge Chandre, but Rani herself overruled his objections and the couple went off to work for the airline executive. Unfortunately Manoj didn't take to domestic service – it was nothing to do with the beef, it was just that he didn't like the work – so he's now back in his village waiting for me to find him a more congenial job.

Shortly after Manoj gave up domestic service, Gilly and I returned to Molanpur. When I started to write Chandre's story, I realized that I needed to know more about his village. With Chandre as guide, we managed to get lost within a mile of the village – which didn't seem to surprise any of his biradari. It was a cool winter afternoon. There was a cloudless, bright-blue sky – the sort of sky that welcomed me when I first came to Delhi in 1965, though a foul, throat-rasping smog now characterizes winter in the Indian capital. Without a wedding to motivate it, Molanpur was looking a little shabby. The thatched roof of one of the houses had collapsed, and the paintings on the walls had faded. There were piles of dried cow-dung where we had stood to welcome the barat.

The first thing I wanted to do was to see the field from which Chandre had run away to Delhi. Chandre said he would send some chokras – young boys – with us. He never bothers to visit his own fields, which are cultivated for him by a member of the

Yadav farming caste. On the outskirts of Molanpur, some Yadav farmers were crushing sugar cane to make gur or jaggery – coarse brown sugar. A pair of bullocks yoked to a shaft walked round and round in a circle. The shaft turned two drums, between which the cane was crushed. A young boy walked behind the bullocks, clicking his tongue, flicking their tails and occasionally thwacking them with a stick of sugar cane to make sure their monotonous task didn't send them to sleep. Nearby, the glutinous green juice squeezed out of the cane simmered in an open black pan at least five feet in diameter. The pan was heated by an oven dug into the ground and fuelled by crushed cane and eucalyptus leaves. Even the water used to wash out the pan after each boiling was not wasted – it was given to the cattle to drink. The farmers told me that this was the only industry in the area, and it was very much a seasonal affair. Molanpur had done quite good business in hand-sewn shoes, but the cobblers had lost out to nasty, cheap plastic products.

We crossed the bandh or embankment which protects Molanpur from the Ganges and walked towards the sacred river. The mud path was baked hard by the sun. A sea of yellow stretched away into the distance on both sides – the bright yellow of mustard and the lighter yellow of ripening wheat. The boys didn't know exactly which of the small fields belonged to Chandre, but they assured us that some of them did. Clumps of sainta grass fifteen-feet tall hid the Ganges from us. We asked the boys how far the river was, and when they said a mile or so we decided to walk on.

Indian villagers are notoriously bad measurers of distance, but fortunately these boys were not too far out. When we reached the sacred river, the sun was going down behind broken clouds. It was what is known in the villages of northern India as a 'partridge-feather' sky. The setting sun cast a glittering golden band across the waters of the Ganges. The ragged banks and islands of sand testified to the river's wanderlust – the Ganges knows no boundaries. A man stood waist-deep in the water, praying with his face turned towards the fast-setting sun. It was one of those many moments when I think, 'I can never leave this country.'

As we walked back to Molanpur, villagers were returning

home – on their heads, bundles of the long grass which is used for thatching and making furniture. Fires were glowing beside the tube-wells where farmers were settling down to keep watch on the pumps which would irrigate their fields throughout the night. The boys asked me to get them jobs in Delhi. I tried to persuade them that I didn't have any influence with the government, but I don't think they were convinced.

That night we again sat down inside the basti where we had waited for the wedding to start. Chandre's relatives gathered around us. Tau, who had never contributed to Rani's wedding expenses, brought out his hookah. Chandre's nephew Kamal said, 'Most of us smoke biris or cigarettes now.'

Hari Singh, the Yadav farmer who worked Chandre's land, sat on the edge of a charpai. If most of what I'd read about caste in Indian newspapers had been true, he should never have allowed himself to be seen in a Harijan basti. I had once asked Chandre how he could trust a man outside his biradari to farm his land for him – especially when that man came from a higher caste, and a caste which was notorious for brutalities against Harijans. Chandre replied, 'We went to the embankment and he swore by the baba [Hindu holy man] of the temple that he would not cheat me. I don't think he has. In fact he is a friend. When his wife was ill, he brought her to Delhi and he stayed with me while his wife was in hospital.'

I asked the Yadav what his biradari thought of this friendship with a Harijan. He said, 'In this village there are not those sort of problems. We mostly keep ourselves to ourselves, but if some work has to be done with another caste we do it. That's why I look after Ram Chander's farming.'

It was the biradari that I really wanted to talk about. I thought that, as a younger man, Kamal might have had doubts about the system, but he said, 'It's still very important. We help each other in the biradari from birth until death. When anyone dies, one or two hundred people will collect for the funeral and will take the ashes to the Ganges. Men and women come. Only biradari people help you in times of trouble.'

Gilly asked, 'Do you ever make someone hookah pani bandh

these days?' Everyone except Tau laughed, and Kamal said, 'He's the only one we could make that, because he's the only one who smokes a hookah.' 'Hookah pani bandh' means being barred from smoking the communal hookah or drinking water with members of the biradari – social ostracism. Chandre thought for some time and then said, 'Actually there was a case, although it's very rare now. It was because of my cousin Ramu. Someone spoke badly about his daughter, saying she was living a dirty life. He reported it to the panchayat and they found the man had done wrong.'

'How long did the bandh last?' Gilly asked.

'I think it was about a year,' Chandre replied. 'Then he asked for forgiveness and he was made to pay a fine.'

'Can we meet the chaudhuri of the biradari?' I asked.

Kamal replied, 'Yes. That's not difficult. We'll take you to Gavvan tomorrow to see him. But I want to ask your help, Sahib. You must do something about Tau. He has had his pay cut by the government from sixty rupees to thirty each month.'

'Thirty rupees a month,' I said with surprise. 'I thought you could earn thirty rupees in two days working in the fields nowadays.'

'Yes, thirty rupees,' Kamal replied firmly. 'It's a disgrace.'

'What work do you do, Tau?' I asked.

The old man said, 'I am a sweeper.'

'Yes I know that,' I replied – 'but where?'

'In the government school on the embankment.'

Eventually I extracted the whole story from the taciturn Tau. He had been cleaning the school next to the temple for many years. He had been paid sixty rupees a month for his labours. Recently the headmaster had called him in and said that the government inspectors had instructed that he should be paid only thirty rupees. The headmaster couldn't explain this. I suggested that maybe the headmaster was pocketing the other thirty rupees himself. Tau grunted, 'It's possible.'

'How much do you sign for?' I asked.

'I don't know. I make a thumbmark.'

I turned to Kamal and said, 'Why don't you ask to see the

register, so that you can see what Tau is signing for? My guess is that the headmaster is taking the money. I can't believe that, with all the money government employees get nowadays, Tau should only be paid thirty rupees a month.'

'It's very difficult for us to interfere,' Kamal said. 'If we make too much trouble, Tau will lose his job altogether. I can't go to see the master sahib. He will just say it's not my business.'

After finding out that the headmaster lived in the nearby town of Gavvan, I suggested that we might go and see him the next day. Kamal thought that was a good idea, but I wasn't entirely certain.

'Supposing the master sahib is annoyed by my visit,' I said. 'He may not say so to my face, but he may take it out on Tau when I have left.'

'That's possible,' Tau grunted again. 'Then you will have to come back.' Everyone laughed except for Tau, who did not see what was funny about such a common-sense remark.

'All right,' I agreed – 'I'll go to see the master sahib. But first of all you must show me the school you clean tomorrow.'

'I won't be cleaning it,' Tau replied – 'it's Sunday.'

'I know, but you can still show it to me.'

'I suppose so.'

On that somewhat unpromising note we left the problem of Tau until the next day and started to clear up some of the questions I had about Chandre's wedding.

That night, because it was quite cold, it was decided that we should sleep inside Chandre's one-room house. Two charpais and thick razais or quilts were provided for us. A small oil-lamp was set in a niche in the wall. Just as we were going to sleep, Kamal walked through the open doorway with a cricket bat. 'What on earth is that for?' I asked.

He replied, 'To hit dogs with. They come in during the night.'

Fortunately they didn't. Nor was I woken this time by the sow.

The next morning Tau had lost interest in the whole venture, so Chandre took us to the temple on the embankment with one of his nephews. The village had woken up by the time we set off. My friend the sow had been let out. The goats had been tethered and were nibbling greedily at branches of jamun trees. Brown and white puppies were sucking at the sagging breasts of their emaciated mother. The chickens had flown down from their roosts on the thatched roofs and were scratching furiously for their breakfast. Grey babblers – known in India as 'sat-bhai' or 'seven brothers', because they are said to go around in groups of seven – were rummaging noisily in the piles of dried cow dung. The residents of the basti were returning from their ablutions. A family party was disembarking from a bullock cart outside the next-door basti, which belonged to the dhobis. They were going to the Ganges for the naming ceremony of their son.

The temple had been built in honour of a Hindu saint called Hare Baba, who had died as recently as 1971 with the words 'Hare Bol', or 'Speak the name of God', on his lips. Chandre told me with pride that the baba was credited with building the thirty-mile-long embankment to protect Molanpur and 6,999 other villages from the Ganges when it flooded. An old pilgrim told me that the baba had miraculously built the embankment in six months, because he was so moved by the plight of the villagers in a great flood in 1922. The pilgrim said, 'I remember we all had to climb into trees. We even had to defecate from the branches.' A retired official of the Uttar Pradesh Roadways who spent his time visiting the holy places of India gave us a guided tour.

The main temple was built around a courtyard. Its centrepiece was a shrine with a life-size alabaster statue of the baba sitting upright, complete with beard and black spectacles. He was wrapped in a saffron robe, had a red tilak on his forehead and was sitting upright as that was the position in which he had been buried immediately beneath the spot where his statue now stood. Hindu saints are sometimes buried, sometimes thrown uncremated into rivers. Under the shade of the tall trees outside the main temple there were smaller shrines. Monkeys climbed over the roof covering the image of the monkey-god Hanuman. A small group of women were pouring Ganges water over a lingam – a phallus, the symbol of Shiva – which a dog was licking happily. The non-stop chanting of 'Hare Bol, Hare Bol' could be heard. Chandre said, 'The chanting hasn't stopped since the baba died.'

Tau's school was about fifty yards away. It was a large building with several classrooms. Pious platitudes were painted on its walls. One said, 'It is our duty to work, the fruit is in the hands of God.' If Tau could have read it, he might well have thought, 'You can say that again.' There was no way, as far as I could see, that anyone should be paid just thirty rupees a month for keeping that school clean.

Back in the village, Chandre made breakfast for us and we discussed plans for the visit to Gavvan to see the headmaster and the chaudhuri. Tau agreed to come with us, but insisted that someone else would have to do the talking. We found Maulvi Ayub Khan, the headmaster, in a small brick-built house. The master explained to me that the rates of pay were set by the basic-education official. Apparently the sweepers didn't have a union, unlike the peons or messengers, and that was why they got paid so badly. I found it hard to believe that this pious elderly man would be stealing half of Tau's meagre pay-packet, and I retreated hurriedly before any other member of our party suggested that. It would have been highly embarrassing if the villagers had said that I had made such a suggestion.

As we were walking away, Chandre proposed that we ask the chaudhuri for his help in the matter. He was sitting in the sun outside his house, surrounded by members of the biradari. When he saw me, he leapt up with remarkable agility for a man who claimed to be eighty-one and gave me a smart salute. 'I was in the army as a sweeper,' he explained. He was still wearing khaki, topped by a yellow turban whose tail almost touched the ground. He was a very small man, barely five feet tall. When Chandre introduced me, he said, 'I know you. You came to Ram Chander's wedding. You did very well for him by paying for it.'

I protested that I had made only a very small contribution, but he wouldn't hear anything of it. 'No, no. I know what you did. I said the mantras at the wedding, so I know.'

I asked him how he had learnt the mantras. He replied, 'I was taught them. You don't have to know how to read and write to learn them. Now I'm teaching my son. You see, people in our biradari like to be married by an important man, otherwise there will be no evidence that they are married.'

I didn't quite understand this, so I asked Kamal to explain. He said, 'There is no book or register it's written in, so if there's a fight later about the wedding then you have to have an important witness to say they were married.'

'Yes,' the chaudhuri said. 'There are often fights within the biradari, and it's one of my main jobs to sort them out.'

I asked the chaudhuri about the case of hookah pani bandh, and he replied, 'I can't remember a case like that for many, many years. There can't have been, because I would have given the sentence.'

I turned to Chandre, who said, 'No, there was one years ago – when I was ploughing the fields.'

'You haven't done that for years, but last night you said it happened recently,' I replied.

'Maybe I did,' said Chandre. 'But now I know it was when I was still ploughing.'

The chaudhuri generously admitted that he might have forgotten the incident. With that misunderstanding cleared up, we got down to talking about Tau's problem. All agreed that his wage was shameful, and most felt that there must be some brashtachar or corruption somewhere. A smart young man who spoke a little English said that he earned a thousand rupees a month as a sweeper in the municipal offices. The chaudhuri said, 'This boy is like my prime minister, because he is a reading and writing man. I am like the president, and I also have a vice-president. We are all elected, so that gives us a status. But I don't know what we can do in this case.'

'But surely you have this status so you can do sifarish [make a recommendation] to some big officer.'

'We do sometimes do sifarish to the government officers,' the chaudhuri agreed, 'but that's to get people jobs. It doesn't work always – in fact not very often. Anyhow, this seems to me like the work of a sweepers' union, and you know there are no unions in the villages.'

So we left, no further forward with Tau's case. I assured him I would take it up with the Uttar Pradesh government myself, but I was not very optimistic.

When I got back to Delhi I did write to the commissioner for Uttar Pradesh, and to my surprise I got a reply: the government of Uttar Pradesh did not think the work Tau did merited more than thirty rupees a month. So much for my influence! I should never have interfered. I had done no good to Tau, and perhaps had harmed Chandre's standing in the village. He had given me such a build-up, and here I had failed on my one and only sifarish. But then probably it's only my pride which has been hurt. Chandre has, as usual, taken it all in his stride. When I next meet Tau he will, I suspect, be secretly rather pleased that his own dismal expectations were fulfilled.

— 2 —

THE NEW COLONIALISM

The celebrated Indian writer Nirad C. Chaudhuri, who now lives in Oxford, dedicated his *Autobiography of an Unknown Indian* to the memory of the British Empire, saying, 'all that was good and living within us was made, shaped, and quickened by the same British rule.' I admire Nirad Chaudhuri's scholarship, I envy him his felicity of style, I enjoy his humour, but I profoundly disagree with his views. Emperors don't quicken their subjects' cultures: they kill them. So, if Nirad Chaudhuri is right, there was nothing worthwhile in India before the raj, which would have been truly remarkable for a culture that had survived so long. That wasn't even the view of the British who ruled India. They studied Sanskrit and the Hindu scriptures, they wrote grammars of modern Indian languages and they preserved India's ancient monuments. But the raj could not have survived if we British had not been convinced of our own superiority, and so few Britons could not have ruled so vast a country if they had not also created an Indian elite who shared their conviction that British culture was inherently superior to their own. We were clever, not crude, rulers, and we realized the dangers of going too fast and too far – of the sort of resentment which caused the Indian Mutiny or the First War of Independence, whichever way you look at it. That was why we concentrated our efforts on creating that small élite and left the rest of India to itself. That élite – the India which applauds Nirad Chaudhuri – took over the reins from us and we continue to exercise our cultural hegemony over them – a hegemony preserved by the conviction that we are superior.

Cultural exchanges are one of the more subtle ways of imposing cultural imperialism. They create the impression that we respect Indian culture, while at the same time giving us the opportunity to exhibit our own superiority, or what we believe is our superiority. Over the last ten years or so, India has been persuaded to hold a number of impressive festivals in foreign countries – significantly, Britain led the field. These were matched by festivals of Britain and the other countries in India. The festivals of India undoubtedly increased interest in things Indian but they had no radical effect on life in our countries. The exhibitions in India were a hard and effective sell to the Indian élite who dominate Indian life.

In the small seaside town of Mahabalipuram, about thirty miles south of Madras, I came across a remarkable example of cultural imperialism through cultural exchange. It was the catalogue of the sculpture by the English artist Stephen Cox exhibited at the Delhi Triennial in 1986. Cox had spent some months in Mahabalipuram working with Indian temple sculptors. An official of the British Council told me that Cox had been given a scholarship 'to learn and to teach'. The catalogue of his works started, 'Art is unimaginable without a matrix of culture, even a parochial culture; it is inconceivable without a history; it cannot be separated from the properties of the materials of which it is made and these are themselves provided by that culture, history and by the physical world its peoples inhabit. All of these are elements of the web of language in which an art is expressed.' Further on, the author of the catalogue wrote, 'So Cox's art of sculpture is continually developing. He does not bring with him to India an inflexibly alien instrument, but one capable of growing by response to the rocks and to the human achievement that he finds.'

If I understand that aright, it means that Cox had gone to Mahabalipuram to learn about the culture of its sculptors and had then allowed that culture to influence his work. In Mahabalipuram, however, that was not the accepted view of what had actually happened. Ganapathi Stapati was the principal of the College of Architecture and Sculpture, and it was to him that Cox had turned for guidance. Stapati comes from a long line of shilpis, who are both architects and sculptors. His father was the first principal of the college in Mahabalipuram, and Stapati succeeded him. He had recently retired and was living in a small house on the main street of Mahabalipuram.

Stapati has written a detailed account of what he calls the 'grammar' of the ancient Vaastu tradition of art and architecture, the tradition he is keeping alive. I asked him how much Stephen Cox had learnt of this ancient culture, and was somewhat taken aback when the mild-mannered sculptor replied, 'He never learnt anything from me. I used to talk to him about spiritual things and sculpture, but he would say to me, "When I am with you I experience what you mean; as soon as I leave the room I lose it. What can I do? That is my culture." It is my opinion that he did zero here.'

'What do you think of the work he did while he was in Mahabalipuram?'

'He still has people working for him here. He is very commercial. He hasn't understood my craftsmen, my people. We are real creative artists. He is doing mechanical work; he is not moved; he is not aroused. In fact I said as much. On the last day that he was here, there was a reception for him where I spoke and I told the audience, "Stephen Cox has been here for months. He is carrying nothing from Mahabalipuram except a few pieces of stone." '

I thought that perhaps the two sculptors had got across each other – that there had been a personality clash – but Stapati said, 'I liked Stephen. He was honest and kind. I deliberately did not interfere in his work. I never went to the place he was working until the last day. Then I took the minister of education, and Stephen showed him the work.'

Contrary to the claim of the catalogue, there had not, in Stapati's view, been any meeting of cultures. He believed that Cox had learnt nothing from Mahabalipuram, and Stapati had certainly not been inspired by the Western sculptor's art. When I asked him for his views on modern art, he looked across at Sasikala, the wiry and energetic architect who had introduced us, as if to ask whether she felt he was going too far. She smiled and Stapati, encouraged, let rip.

'In the name of modern art you have dispensed with the

spiritual element of art. The whole world is carried away by these trends. We don't vibrate to modern art. The old masters like Michelangelo, they do affect us – they had imagination. Those who look at modern works and say "How beautiful!" are hypocrites.'

'Why do you talk so much of vibrations? Could you explain what you mean by that?'

'It is all part of the scientific and spiritual tradition we have been brought up in. It is complex and difficult to explain in English, but I will try. We believe there is a spirit in all things, and through sculpture we express in form the beauty of that spirit. The smallest unit is the atom. Ultimately they are united in form – in physical objects – but they also exist in space. Within us there is an inner space in which atoms vibrate, and these vibrátions are our feelings. When we see fine art, we vibrate to it – we are moved. When we create art through the discipline of our tradition, we create forms which mirror the vibrations within us. The poet becomes the poem; the sculptor becomes the sculpture. We are making images of the best within ourselves. Ours is not a realistic art, but in our sculptures we can give expression to the eternal spirit and, through symbols, to even the most subtle aspects of Hindu philosophy. Of course it takes years to master the grammar, the discipline, of our tradition.'

'How', I asked, 'would Stephen Cox be able to understand your tradition in a few months?'

'Stephen Cox never made the attempt to learn,' Stapati replied. 'He never questioned or asked my people. There are people who have learnt Carnatic music – they study for years. In that way sculptors could learn too. The British Council should send me one boy of fifteen or sixteen and leave him with me for six years. I will make him a master sculptor. Stephen Cox could not even work in our granite. He needed two or three years' continuous work to master it. He couldn't do that, so we gave him people to work for him. He could only put some finishing touches to the work. Come into my yard and I will show you what I mean.'

In the yard there were statues of different sizes, in different stages of completion. A seven-foot-high statue representing Tamil, the language of Stapati's culture, still needed some detailed work. The statue weighed three tons. Stapati took a piece of charcoal and drew some lines on her legs. He then coloured the lines with red ochre to make them indelible. 'These lines', he told me, 'will show the sculptor the shape and the depth he has to carve. I always carve the finishing touches myself. I have to put the eyes and the lips in.'

'Doesn't that make you like Stephen Cox?' I asked.

Stapati laughed, 'Oh no. Students often play tricks on their teachers, because they think that we know the theory but we can't actually carve. We always catch them out. You can't be a master unless you are first a craftsman. I started carving as a boy, like all traditional shilpis.'

Stapati went over to a five-headed statue of the elephant-god Ganesh, took up a pointed steel chisel and a hammer and started work. Sparks flew off the granite as he tapped at it. 'It's not cutting,' he said – 'it's pecking. One of these chisels will be blunt after five minutes. We have to have our own forge and blacksmith to sharpen the chisels.' He brushed away the dust with a piece of coconut fibre.

Britain itself is not very appreciative of the work of a traditional Indian mastercraftsman and artist like Stapati. Much of his work is commissioned by Indian communities abroad. He showed me a six-foot statue of the god Vishnu, destined for Kentucky. It was almost finished. The black granite had been oiled and was as smooth as skin. Stapati said, 'I could do much more work in Britain, but you make problems. It's very difficult to get permission to build temples. I have designed two, but we had to hide them in existing buildings. The one I have built in Manor Park in east London is inside an old church for which you no longer have any use. Your churches are all empty, but you won't let us put up our temples in their place. You have lost the spiritual basis of your culture and so perhaps you are now afraid of ours, because you realize that it does have a very strong basis.'

Stapati speaks English very clearly but sometimes has difficulty understanding the non-Indian version of that language, and Sasikala acts as his unofficial interpreter. Sasikala is passionately dedicated to the preservation of the Vaastu tradition. She and her husband, who is an engineer, have set up a society in Mahabalipuram to widen interest in the tradition and to make it relevant to the present times. In a statement the couple have issued about the society's aims, they have written:

> To many Indians, the turn that the country [India] has taken after the fifties has been of great concern. This era is described as the era of the second colonization. A colonialism that colonizes the mind in addition to bodies. The West is now everywhere, outside in structures, and in minds. The colonized Indian mind believes that all answers are from the West and acts accordingly. The priorities of the Indian society have been altered beyond recognition.

Sasikala and Stephen Cox did not see eye to eye. She felt that the English artist condescended to her hero, Stapati. She told me angrily, 'He used to make sneering remarks to me while Stapati was talking – remarks like "He doesn't understand", and "They have been doing the same thing for hundreds of years. It has lost its meaning for today." He seemed to think that I would agree with him, although I don't know why. He talked down to Stapati, but I don't think he could help it. With his learning and his success, he thinks he has to be superior. I think that this is inbred in the British, that they think they are superior.'

I showed Sasikala the British Council catalogue. After reading a few pages she threw it back at me, saying, 'It's bullshit. These people are very clever with words, but what does it actually mean? Read it time and time again and you will only get more confused.' She was equally dismissive of Stephen Cox's work. There were pictures in the catalogue of five sculptures representing the Indian concept of tanmantras, or the five senses. They were oval plaques of granite: one had nothing but a nose carved on it, another just had two eyes, a third a mouth, two ears protruded from a fourth, and a fifth plaque had just three lines – the marking of a devotee of the god Shiva. The ovals symbolize one of the Hindu creation legends.

Sasikala said to me, 'The tanmantras are the subtle elements which underlie the senses. You can't depict them by the physical organs which perceive the senses – that is just crude. We believe in subtle forms of symbolism.'

I realized that there must be more to Stephen Cox's art than using Indian ideas without fully understanding them. I also realized that I was not qualified to appreciate what that was, so I went to see V. Arunachalam, the young Indian sculptor who had worked with Stephen Cox and was indeed still working for him. I thought he would provide a counterbalance to the views of the traditionalists. He had a small yard opposite the drive of the hotel in which I was staying, about a mile out of Mahabalipuram. Arunachalam also came from a family of sculptors and had been taught by Stapati at the college in Mahabalipuram, but, unlike his guru, he wore Western clothes – a shirt and tight trousers. He said Cox had picked him because he was one of the few students of the college who spoke English reasonably well, and the two had struck up a good relationship.

Unlike his teacher Stapati, Arunachalam had grown to like abstract art, but he could not sell it in Mahabalipuram. He showed me with considerable pride photos of the statues he had carved for Stephen Cox. There were also several larger sculptures lying outside the palm-thatched hut which was the studio. He pointed to one and said, 'You see that one like a large peanut – that is the son of Shiva. It will go in a set of the holy family – Shiva, his wife and family. You may not understand it, but I have come to like it.'

Another flat piece of granite had one breast carved on it. Arunachalam went on, 'This will be Ardhanareshvara – that is, the traditional Hindu figure which is half Shiva and half Parvati, his wife.'

'But do you understand the way Stephen Cox handles these Indian themes?'

'As I see it, he is doing mixed Indian and European art. He uses the titles from Indian themes. I once asked him what a sculpture he was working on meant. He said, "I don't know. I just do it." In traditional art you have to know what you are doing. That doesn't mean that modern art is bad, but it is easy to sculpt.'

Arunachalam had shipped three containers full of sculptures to Stephen Cox in the previous year. 'Stephen sends me the drawings and I carve them. He puts the finishing touches to them,' he explained.

Unfortunately Stephen Cox was not in Mahabalipuram at that time, but I sent him a draft of this story. I was not surprised to get a very angry reply. Eventually we did meet.

Cox was hurt that Stapati, a man whom he liked and admired, had apparently so misunderstood him. Nevertheless he admitted that he regarded Stapati's work not as art but as craft. He also did not feel the spiritual element in the traditional carving at Mahabalipuram which Stapati was so proud of. Cox said to me, 'The obsessiveness in the craft of Stapati's work sterilizes it. I find the deification of simple objects – sometimes just a pile of bricks in a wayside shrine – more spiritual. They have been worshipped for years and are the by-products of devotion.'

I was puzzled. Stephen Cox was clearly a very sensitive and gentle person, so I couldn't understand why he wanted to work in Mahabalipuram if he didn't regard the town's carving as art. He explained to me, 'I was drawn to the place. I had never been anywhere like it before. The sound of hammers tapping everywhere from morning to night. The chance to put two feet into an environment that could trace its sculpture links with devotion in an unbroken skein reaching back to antiquity. You mustn't get me wrong – I admire Stapati as a great craftsman and a great temple architect, but I never went to Mahabalipuram to sit at his feet or to learn temple carving.'

I asked him about Stapati's allegation that Cox couldn't carve granite: that he would need two or three years' continuous work to master it. He replied, 'I can get anything I want out of a block of stone. I don't think it's necessary to do rough work, although I am capable of doing anything that is necessary. Stapati insists that a carver must learn his craft. This is a fundamental difference between an artist and a craftsman. Anyone can learn a craft.'

I admitted to Cox that I found it easier to understand Stapati's work than his. He smiled and said, 'You have only talked to Stapati and his disciples. There are Indian artists who admire my work.'

Stephen Cox was on his way back from Mahabalipuram after spending some time working with Arunachalam. I said to him, 'You object to my describing your studio in Mahabalipuram as an example of modern colonialism, but it seems to me you are doing exactly what the colonialists did: you are using cheap labour and raw material, finishing it yourself and selling it at a large profit.'

'I wouldn't say it was colonialism,' Cox replied; 'I'd say it's sound economics. I came here with a brief to carve for three months, but having been able to set up a system of working it seemed a terrible waste to let it go.' Then he laughed and said, 'Actually it's not that sound economics. It costs me a lot to come here and a lot to ship the work, and I also pay my workers more and look after them better than others do in Mahabalipuram. The rewards are not that great either, because Europeans don't seem to have taken off on the work I do here.'

Stephen Cox is undoubtedly a humane neocolonialist when it comes to business. That, presumably, is why his studio isn't doing all that well. Nevertheless, anyone who exalts his 'art' above someone else's 'craft' is implying superiority, and that's what cultural imperialism is all about.

Mahabalipuram has some of the finest examples of stonecarving in India. The 100-feet-high rock escarpment which runs along the back of the town, about half a mile from the sea, is a museum of mythology more than 1,000 years old. Lord Shiva watches an emaciated ascetic standing on one leg in a huge frieze carved on the face of the rock. The animals of the forest have gathered to see the miracle which is about to occur – so have mankind, the demigods and the snake people of the underworld. I love the cat at the bottom of the frieze, standing on his hind legs in imitation of the ascetic. So great is the cat's asceticism that he ignores the fat, tasty rats playing at his feet. The only difficulty is that we are not sure what the miracle is. The frieze, which one of the guidebooks claims to be the biggest bas-relief in the world, is known as the Penance of Arjun, one of the heroes of the great Hindu epic the *Mahabharat*. He performed a penance to persuade Shiva to give him a miraculous weapon to destroy his enemies. There are, however, some scholars who believe that the ascetic is not Arjun but Bhagiratha, who persuaded the gods to send the river Ganges to the earth.

Further along the escarpment, Krishna holds a mountain over the village of Gokula to protect the villagers and their cattle from the wrath of the rain god Indra. That frieze has been protected by a stone canopy. Then there is a cave with carvings showing Vishnu in his incarnation as a boar rescuing the goddess earth from the bottom of the ocean. Among the many other monuments there are five raths or chariots of the gods, also carved out of the rock. They are named after four of the five brothers who are the heroes of the *Mahabharat* and after the woman who was wife to all the brothers.

The beach at Mahabalipuram is dominated by the two pointed towers of the Shore Temple. It is believed there were once three. Spray, sand and wind have eroded but not entirely erased the carvings on the outer walls. Inside the three shrines of the temple, the deities have survived unharmed, except for one lingam whose top is damaged.

In spite of its magnificent art and the careful preservation of its traditions, most of the young carvers of Mahabalipuram are reduced to doing debased work. Walking up from the Shore Temple, I passed a shop selling small, stone images of the Hindu gods. The owner of the shop had advertised that he was an unemployed graduate from the College of Architecture and Sculpture. He claimed he couldn't find work because most temples in India were now being built out of concrete, not stone. When I picked up a small, black granite Ganesh, he said with engaging honesty, 'I am afraid it's not very good. There is no detail on it, but then he is popular with tourists – particularly foreigners.'

Tourism is another post-independence colonizer. At the top end of the market it has produced the five-star culture. That means the élite of India keeping up with the Kapoors by dining, staying, holding conferences and even marrying off their daughters in expensive hotels notable for insipid food which won't inflame fragile foreign intestines and for an excess of marble. Mahabalipuram caters mainly to the bottom end of the tourist market – the young people doing India on ten pounds a day. As most of them sell their hard currency to the young men who pester every foreigner on the beach, Mahabalipuram can't be doing much to replenish India's foreign exchange reserves – one of the justifications for tourism. Groups from the Soviet Union and eastern Europe trade in champagne and vodka, because their currency is not exactly hard.

There are several small restaurants offering fresh seafood European-style. In one I heard a young French girl complaining to her boyfriend, 'It's so simple to make salad oil – I don't know why they can't do it.' At another table, a young Englishman complained, 'I thought you should be able to get a good cup of tea in India of all places. When I asked for tea out of a pot, it came out all funny – mixed with milk.'

I did, I must admit, also see many young foreigners eating lunch in the Mamalla Bhavan, where for eight rupees – that's less than the price of a cup of tea back home – they were served a thali. A thali is a round tray with small bowls of vegetable curries, dals, pickle and curd. These are to be mixed with rice dolloped on to the centre of the thali. Second helpings come automatically, and third helpings are there for the asking. Rasam or pepper-water is provided to wash the meal down.

The proprietor of this excellent restaurant, Narayanswamy Janahardham, started thirty years ago selling ten meals a day. Now on a busy day he sells more than 1,000 lunches alone. Tourism in Mahabalipuram is so successful that it's threatening to take over the whole town. The restaurant proprietor told me that the government wanted to ban all further construction in the town, so that it could be developed for tourism. He was not amused: 'They want the people of Mahabalipuram to move out so that the tourists can move in. I am in favour of some development, but I don't see why it should be controlled by planners who don't live here but have houses in nice suburbs of big cities like Madras. Why should they tell us to get out of our own town?'

Walking along the beach at Mahabalipuram I had seen foreign girls tanning their bare breasts. I asked whether the citizens of Mahabalipuram objected to that too. 'I wouldn't say "object",' Narayanswamy Janahardham replied, 'but it is definitely bad. It doesn't fit in with Indian customs. Naked on the beach is not advisable. Our people will turn their heads away in shame. It is bad for the reputation of the West. What's worse is drugs,' he went on. 'It has not got bad here yet, but we will have to be careful not to go like Goa. There I am told that there is a big business in selling drugs to foreign tourists. In Mahabalipuram I know some boys who are selling ganja. I have told the police, but they have done nothing. But I must not complain too much – after all, tourism is good for business.'

Business is what modern imperialism is all about, and, in the developing world, promoting it is the main task of the British Council and the other arms of Her Majesty's diplomatic services: the Foreign Office and the Ministry of Overseas Development. In Tamil Nadu and its capital, Madras, I saw the slogan 'Be Indian, buy Indian' painted on the side of many lorries, but unfortunately the Indian élite still prefers to buy 'foreign'. Things have improved since the days when I first came to India, when departing diplomats found a good market for partly used lipsticks. But improvements in the quality, quantity and variety of Indian consumer goods have not conquered the market, because the old colonial mentality still survives – the servile mentality that believes that anything Indian must be inferior. Nothing has done more to keep that feeling alive than the English language.

It has often been said that if you want to destroy a people, first destroy its language. The British were too subtle to try that: they degraded Indian languages by installing a new language of the élite – English. Just as the British were quite happy to keep the caste system intact provided they were acknowledged as a superior caste, so they were quite happy to promote the study of Indian languages provided English was acknowledged as the link language of the élite. As English reinforced their superior status, the élite, not surprisingly, made no serious attempt to provide an Indian link language when the British left.

Nowhere is this failure more obvious than in Tamil Nadu. It is the one state in India where the television service, which is controlled by the central government, cannot transmit its Hindi news bulletins – even though Hindi is meant to be the national link language. Hindi, not English, is seen as a colonial language in Tamil Nadu – part of an attempt by the Aryan north to dominate the Dravidian south.

The battle against Hindi has been fought by the Dravidian parties, who have used the Tamil language and regional chauvinism to establish a hold over Tamil Nadu politics. They have ruled the state since 1967. The Dravidian message was spread through the Tamil cinema. The founder of the original party – which, like all Indian parties, has split into factions – was a film scriptwriter. The most famous Dravidian chief minister – M. G. Ramachandran, or 'MGR' – was a superstar actor. He had always played the role of a hero, a protector of the poor and oppressed, and so came to be seen as the incarnation of righteousness in the minds of millions of Tamils – particularly women. Although no one could argue that MGR provided an effective or honest administration, his faithful fans never blamed him. During the last three years of his life he was so ill that he could barely speak, but they did not lose faith in his leadership. When he died, in 1987, the state shut down. Millions of people flocked to his funeral in Madras, and those MGR fans who couldn't get there held funerals of his images. Grief even drove some of them to suicide.

I arrived in Tamil Nadu just after the election to the state assembly held a year after MGR's death. His wife and the film heroine who was close to him in his later years had quarrelled, both claiming to be his true successor, and so the Dravidian movement was divided yet again. MGR's arch-enemy, the Tamil film scriptwriter Karunanidhi, was returned to power – the beneficiary of MGR's failure to leave a political last will and testament.

One of Karunanidhi's early acts was to announce that children in Tamil Nadu government schools would start learning English only in the third year; earlier they had been taught English from the day they started school. Karunanidhi thought this a necessary gesture to show that he was a better Tamil patriot than MGR, but he did not intend it to be a serious attack on English. He needed English in his state, and indeed throughout the rest of India, otherwise Hindi would be the only possible link language.

The trouble with English is that it links only the élite. Because the teaching of English is so bad in most schools, less than 3 per cent of Indians are reasonably competent in the language. The British Council feels that Tamil Nadu is probably above the average and reckons that there is no 'zero level of English' in the state, which apparently means that everyone has at least some acquaintance with the language. If that is true, I can only say there is plenty of 0.001 level English in Tamil Nadu.

In Madras I found that, in spite of the Dravidian movement, the English-speaking élite had an effect on Tamil Nadu which had been and still was out of all proportion to its size. I was told of a small and courageous publishing firm which was doing something to redress the balance. I travelled to its office in a brand-new scooter-rickshaw whose driver, judging by his reaction to my attempts to urge caution, was certainly pretty near the zero level of English. The office was above a paint shop in one of the not-so-smart parts of central Madras. There I met S. Ramakrishnan, one of the partners of Cre-A Publications. He spoke excellent English but had chosen to publish in Tamil.

'It was an ideological, not a commercial, decision,' he told me. 'We want to do in Tamil what has not been done before. We have to extend the language, so that people can express themselves.'

Ramakrishnan believed that the use of English by the élite had stunted the development of Tamil. He said, 'As a publisher, I find that English is not a healthy thing. It limits the possibilities of the expression of experience. If I want to write a critical essay on film or theatre in Tamil it will be very difficult. Unless we do most of our communication in Tamil, a large section of the people will not be able to understand wide areas of experience. There will just not be enough Tamil works for them.'

Cre-A Publications is attempting to fill the gap by publishing Tamil books in new fields, but it is meeting with customer resistance. It found, for example, that a health-care manual had sold well because everyone was concerned about their health, but a book on environmental issues flopped. It flopped, according to Ramakrishnan, because 'it was outside Tamil-speaking people's consciousness'. The élite, however, are very environment-conscious – the environment is debated ad nauseam in the English-language press – but the English-speakers are not interested in reading Tamil.

'A well-educated Tamil household', Ramakrishnan said, 'will happily spend fifty rupees on an English paperback but will not think of buying a Tamil book. As they are the ones with the money, this severely limits our markets. Then we face competition from other Tamil publishers – particularly from what are known as monthly novels. They are printed on the cheapest possible paper and sell for only two rupees. It's difficult to wean people away from them, and from the same sort of romantic and sensational stories brought out in serial form in Tamil magazines.'

Nevertheless, Cre-A was making a valiant effort. One of its latest ventures was a Tamil translation of Kafka's *The Trial*. I couldn't imagine that that would bite deeply into the monthly novels' circulation.

Before I left Delhi I had been to see one of India's leading educationalists, Father Kunnankal, who had infuriated the old boys and parents of St Xavier's, one of the capital's leading day-schools, by changing the medium of instruction from English to Hindi. He came too from the south – from the state of Kerala, and so his mother tongue was the Dravidian language of Malayalam – but he also spoke fluent Hindi and, of course, English. As a result of his pre-Vatican-II Jesuit training, he could converse in Latin as well, although he told me that he did not find many people to talk to in Latin nowadays.

Father Kunnankal pioneered the change to Hindi at St Xavier's because he believed very strongly that the influence of English as the language of the élite was harming his country. Sitting in a small, spartan room in the residential quarters of St Xavier's, he said, 'I take the problem of English very seriously. It is the main cause of the dividing of India, and we are a deeply divided society. I often wonder whether we really want an equitable and egalitarian society. If we do, education should be a major measure for achieving it.'

'How', I asked, 'does English language as a medium divide society?'

Father Kunnankal was not wearing his habit – not even a clerical collar – but that did not make him any less austere and distant. When I asked that question he looked at me in astonishment, and I was reminded of the occasions at my public school when a form master had discovered that I hadn't done my prep.

'Of course it makes all the difference,' the priest said. 'It is very clear that education should be in the vernacular. If English continues, then all the best jobs go to those educated in that language. The pressure for English-language schools is also maintained. The educational entrepreneurs – including, I am afraid, all too often the Church – say, "If you want English, we will provide it." Meanwhile the government will go on teaching in the vernacular. That means you will get all the relatives of bureaucrats and ministers studying in private English-medium schools and they will have no personal interest in improving the government education.'

'How did you manage to persuade the parents and old boys of St Xavier's to accept Hindi?'

'The basic argument I used was that teaching in Hindi would not lower academic standards. I found many of the parents who spoke English had been educated in a vernacular language and I pointed out to them that I had too. With great reluctance they agreed to the change, but by now we have proved that you can have quality education in Hindi.'

'But what would you do about a link language? You are never going to persuade southern Indians to accept Hindi.'

'Well, I don't know about persuading. It could have been done if we had taken a courageous decision at independence. There has been at least one other occasion since then when I feel the nation would have been prepared to accept any decision the government took, but I had better not say when because I don't want to be accused of meddling in politics. The point is that English cannot be our national language. Apart from being foreign, it is only spoken by perhaps just 50 million people. Hindi can be understood by three-fifths of the population. The over-zealous propagandists of Hindi have created this opposition to it. The English-speaking élite have been only too happy to do what they can to foster this attitude. They despise Hindi and want it to be despised.'

In Madras I found that the Church, as one of the 'educational entrepreneurs', had moved into the Tamil market, but it was still under strong pressure from its customers to provide English-medium schools. Presentation Convent is situated in large grounds known as Church Park, on Mount Road – potentially one of the best commercial sites in Madras. The Presentation nuns were an Irish order, but there had been a ban on new foreign missionaries for many years and the Madras convent was almost entirely Indian. The nuns originally provided education just for the élite, but now they look after nearly 4,000 girls in three schools and one teacher-training college. Church Park was no longer its old spacious self. Sister Pamela – one of the senior nuns – told me, 'If we put up another five-storeyed building, we could fill it three times over.'

She was taking a class of trainee teachers. Two wore the habit of a Roman Catholic congregation. Only one wore a sari and the rest were in green skirts and white blouses. They had all just left school. Sister Pamela was sitting in front of a blackboard – the only educational aid I could see in the classroom. She was fair-skinned by the standards of the south, because she was an Anglo-Indian. When Sister Pamela invited me to ask the class why they had chosen to be educated in English, they all gave the well-tutored reply: 'Because it's an international language.'

'What about your national language?' I asked. That stumped the girls. Eventually one said, 'I don't mind Hindi.' The future teachers had given no thought to India's language problem – to them it was natural and right that English should be 'the medium of instruction'. Sister Pamela then dismissed the class, and the girls trooped obediently out on to the verandah. We went to the sister's office, where she explained the different educational institutions on the campus.

The newest was the Sacred Heart Tamil-medium school, started just seven years ago. The sister said, 'We find there is a demand for that school from drivers and people like that. The politicians and the bureaucrats who are always going on about Tamil, they send their daughters to our English-medium schools. They put a lot of pressure on us, because there is a great shortage of places in good English-medium schools.'

I told Sister Pamela of a college principal I had recently met in northern India who carried a revolver to protect himself from angry parents whose children he couldn't take because demand so far exceeded the supply of places. Sister Pamela said, 'It's not that bad here, but sometimes they do try to put pressure on us.'

'Do you succumb?'

'We try not to – let's leave it at that,' she replied firmly.

I then asked why there was such a demand for education in English.

'It has a snob value. Nowadays also, I am afraid, most parents want to send their children abroad for further education. They are only keen on them becoming doctors or engineers, and a foreign training puts you in a much better position whether you want to get a job or set up on your own.'

Very few Indian children go to foreign universities before getting an Indian degree. The shortage of places at good Indian universities – especially engineering and medical colleges – has created a narrow, highly competitive, exam-oriented education system which puts frightening pressures on schoolchildren. The best engineering students disappear down the brain drain; the doctors all want to practise high-tech medicine which has little or no relevance to the health of the vast majority of Indians. I asked Sister Pamela why the Church was helping to provide this élitist education.

'Things are changing now. I have already told you that we have started a Tamil school here. We have also closed down our élite boarding-school in the hill-station of Kodaikanal. The religious orders used to specialize in these English schools, although there were some exceptions – for instance, one of our schools here was founded as part of an orphanage for Anglo-Indians. At the same time, our parishes do run schools for ordinary Tamils.'

Those who argue in favour of Western culture and values for India claim that they have provided the only egalitarian challenge to the 'iniquities' of the caste system. This argument falls down on many counts – not the least being that down the centuries

Hinduism has thrown up several reformist movements without the help of Western values. The changes in the inequable class system in Britain were brought about by the industrial revolution and the wealth it produced. If India had been allowed to have its own industrial revolution instead of being forced to contribute to Britain's, who can say what influence that would have had on the caste system? What is more, the Church – which was supposed to be in the vanguard of the drive to 'civilize' India – itself fell victim to the caste system.

Christianity in southern India is very old. Tradition has it that St Thomas the Apostle was martyred in Madras. When the Portuguese Jesuits came in the sixteenth century, they found Syrian Christianity firmly established in Kerala. Obviously they could not let well alone, and a battle ensued – which is undecided to this day – between the proponents of the Syrian and the Latin rites. Kerala still has the only Roman Catholic cardinal loyal to the Syrian tradition.

The British brought with them further divisions to trouble Indian Christianity. St Mary's church in the fort in Madras claims to be the oldest Anglican church east of Suez. Consecrated in 1680, it still stands, with its spire and rectangular nave a remarkable tribute to the style of Nicholas Hawksmoor. The guidebook in St Mary's records an early Anglican chaplain's concern about the influence of the Roman Church on his flock.

We are told that 'Master Patrick Warner, the Chaplain of Fort St George, was much exercised in his mind because the English soldiers took unto them as wives the native Portuguese women and allowed the marriages to be conducted by Roman Catholic priests.' In 1676, therefore he wrote a long letter to the Directors [of the East India Company] complaining of the backsliding of soldiers, the drinking and dicing of Writers and Factors, and the sinful toleration of Sir William Langhorne, who had actually fired a salute in honour of the foundation of a Roman Catholic church within the walls of 'White Town'.

There was also rivalry between the Anglicans and the Catholics for Hindu souls. In numerical terms the Catholics won, but neither of the Churches made any great headway with orthodox

Hindus: the bulk of their converts came from the untouchable community and the tribes. One Roman Catholic friend of mine still refers to Harijan converts as 'powder-milk Christians', and there is no doubt that these people – the poorest of the poor – were attracted by the missionaries' promises to feed their bodies, rather than the prospect of spiritual nourishment. Nevertheless, the Harijans also expected Christianity to give them the dignity that they were denied by Hinduism, but here they were to be bitterly disappointed – especially by the Roman Catholic Church.

In many churches in Tamil Nadu, Harijans were separated from the rest of the congregation by a screen. They were not even united with the rest of the Church in death – special parts of cemeteries were set aside for them, and in at least one place, Trichinopoly, they had a separate burial-ground. The Church did little to educate Harijan Christians, concentrating its efforts on schools for the élite. As for ordination, that was almost unthinkable. A Catholic schoolmaster told me recently that, in the Krishna diocese, upper-caste Catholics still objected to taking Communion from a Harijan priest because they believed that the host would be defiled.

The Roman Catholic Church no longer insults its Harijan Christians so openly, but they are still very much a deprived majority. In the diocese of Madras, Harijans make up about 80 per cent of the membership of the Church yet they are represented by just five of the 200 diocesan clergy. There is only one Harijan bishop in Tamil Nadu – some say he is the only Harijan bishop in India – and he was not the man his community wanted.

In 1972, the see of Vellore fell vacant. The vicar-general was a Harijan, and his community felt that he should become their bishop. The Church thought otherwise, so the Harijan Christians went on the rampage, burning churches and threatening their clergy. The Church eventually compromised by appointing a Harijan to the diocese of Ootacamund, an ecclesiastical backwater in the Nilgiri Hills. Now the Church faces a new challenge from militant Harijans who are no longer prepared to accept casteism in the Church. They call themselves 'Dalit Christians'. Dr B. R.

Ambedkar, the Harijan lawyer who wrote the Indian constitution, first gave his community the name 'Dalit', which in Sanskrit means 'oppressed'.

In Madras there is a very active Dalit movement among the Christians. I met one of its young leaders – Paul Panneereselvan of the Dalit Liberation Educational Trust. He had recently organized a rally of Christian Dalits in Madras to demand that the government give them the same educational and job opportunities – 'reservations', as they are known – which had been given to Hindu dalits since independence. He had apparently faced stiff resistance from the Roman Catholic archbishop, resistance he overcame only by threatening to start a movement for a separate Dalit Church. Paul took me to meet two priests who had been helpful to him.

One of these was Father Manuel Alphonse, a Tamil Jesuit in his late thirties working in the All India Catholic University Federation. He told me that Harijan girls found it so difficult to become nuns that a special congregation had been founded for them. This did not achieve much, however, because the priests and the other congregations despised the Dalit order and so refused to give the nuns opportunities to serve the Church. The congregation was now apparently trying to get girls from other castes to join it, to improve its status. Father Manuel said that Harijan men faced difficulties in getting ordained. Most of the Harijan candidates for holy orders were not well educated, which gave the heads of seminaries an excuse for refusing them admission. Those who did manage to pass their exams were, according to the Jesuit, regarded by their teachers as 'irredeemably immoral'. Father Manuel went on to explain, 'One slip by a Dalit seminarian and he will be tipped out. In the case of a high-caste young man, the head of the seminary will say, "It was just a peccadillo. We will look after him and he will reform."'

The Jesuits are more enlightened than the bishops and the diocesan authorities. India has the second-largest Jesuit congregation in the world, and in Tamil Nadu there are about 600, of whom some fifty are Dalits. But Father Manuel said even the Jesuits had not been able to do much for Dalit Christians as a whole. 'The diocesan bishops don't like us interfering,' he explained. 'In fact, most of them regard us with deep suspicion and there are some dioceses where the bishops won't allow us to work. We also have difficulties with our own Dalits in the Society. They are ashamed of being Dalits, so, when they join the Jesuits, they change their names and disguise their backgrounds. They refuse to support Dalit causes, and even avoid making friends with other Dalits. The fact is that they are afraid of being looked down on if they are identified as Harijans.'

Father Manuel believed that the conservative leadership of the Indian Church was to blame for the attitude towards Dalit Christians. He described the Indian bishops as 'more Roman than Rome', and went on to say, 'Our Church has not even accepted the limited role that the Vatican now allows the laity to play. The trouble is that we have always been heavily dependent on foreign funds – especially funds from the Vatican. You can't build an indigenous movement on foreign funds – they lead to a sense of dependence, and you don't get leadership like that. In the case of America the boot is on the other foot. The Vatican relies on the American Church for funds and so it can afford to challenge even the Pope's authority.'

The Jesuits do appreciate the need for Christianity to be Indian in India and have been experimenting with Hindu symbols in their worship for many years. Much work has been done on the relationship between Hindu and Christian theology and traditions. Father Manuel believed that an Indian theology was emerging, a theology which would challenge the foundation stone of Christianity – the claim that Christ's incarnation was unique, the one and only incarnation of God on earth.

Father Manuel had already gone a long way down that road. He told me, 'Indian theology is based on the problems of living with Hinduism. We Christians are living with a very ancient civilization, which in many ways has better answers than we do. My family has been Christian for generations, but I feel closer to being a Hindu than a Christian. A man like Krishna makes more sense to me than Christ. Our modern élite have been influenced by Christianity. That's why they can't understand this country, where Hinduism is far more important than any concept of India.' It's not surprising that India's conservative bishops are wary of the Jesuits.

Paul's second friend was a Harijan parish priest in Ennore, an industrial area on the northern outskirts of Madras. St Joseph's Church stood in its own compound, set apart from the bazaar by a high yellow wall. The priest's house was at the far end of the compound. There was a small garden whose bright flowers were the first colour I had seen in the drab industrial suburb. A cage of budgerigars hung outside the door. An elderly barefooted servant told me that Father Paul Raj was out but said I could wait in his office.

Father Paul Raj got back just before the Mass was due to start. He came into his office buttoning up his white cassock and apologized that he would have to keep me waiting again while he said Mass. He offered me a cup of coffee and seemed surprised when I said I would prefer to go to the service.

'Functional' would be the only way to describe St Joseph's Church. It was an L-shaped, flat-roofed, yellow concrete hall. There were no pews or chairs, just red coir matting on the floor in front of the altar. There were some low benches in the extension built to the right of the altar, but they seemed to be reserved for nuns. Although it was a weekday – and a weekday which did not commemorate any red-letter saint or festival – there was a congregation of about fifty, as many men as women. An old woman hobbled past me to the front of the congregation, leaning heavily on a thick bamboo stick which served as a crutch. I noticed that another woman's ankle was swollen and disfigured by elephantiasis, which is now rare except among the very poor, but most of the congregation seemed relatively prosperous. A few mothers had brought their children. Most of the 350 families Father Paul ministered to worked in the factories of Ennore. The priest's house was built on to the back of the church and so he entered through a door behind the altar. He was wearing violet vestments, the liturgical colour for Lent, and was accompanied by two young servers wearing scarlet cassocks. The Mass was said in

Tamil. I discovered how uncomfortable that red coir carpet was when I knelt for the consecration.

After Mass, Father Paul sorted out a few problems with his parishioners and then took me back to his office. He was a young man, in his early thirties but already a little on the stout side. He had black wavy hair and a dark complexion. His mother was a Harijan, but his father was a caste Christian. He told me that he had almost always 'stood first' during the eleven years he had studied to become a priest, and that was why the priests in the seminary had not been able to prevent his ordination.

We spoke for nearly two hours about the problems of Harijan Catholics and the difficulties he faced as a Harijan priest. When he was first ordained, he had believed in fighting for the Dalit cause. He had called the Dalit Liberation Educational Trust into the country parish to which he had been appointed, and they had explained to his Dalit parishioners the ways in which the Church was exploiting them and had, as he put it, 'Fired them up with zeal to do something about it.' Regrettably for Father Paul. the zeal backfired.

His parishioners were very angry about the previous priest, who was not a Harijan. They believed that he had been a dishonest steward and were particularly upset that he had left the collection of rents from Church lands in the hands of local nuns, not to Father Paul, who had promised to use the rent to help them. The former priest wanted to return to collect the rent from the nuns, but news of the parishioners' new-found militancy had reached him, and so he kept away until there was a visit by the archbishop. Surely, he thought, the Harijans would not dare to make trouble in the presence of such an august dignitary. But he was wrong. Angry parishioners gathered outside the house where the archbishop was staying and shouted, 'Down with corrupt priests' and other slogans in a similar vein. The priest and a burly colleague he had brought in case there was any trouble were waiting there to see the archbishop. Fearing that he might hear the slogans, they tried to push their way through the crowd and escape. One of them was knocked over and badly bruised. The parishioners, who had never intended to lay hands on a priest, fell back in fear and the two men rushed into the house to complain to the archbishop. They told him that Father Paul had made false allegations about corruption and had incited his parishioners to attack them. Although Father Paul was not present when the priests were surrounded, the archbishop found in favour of the caste clergy and transferred the Harijan to Ennore, which was not a Dalit Christian parish. There, the archbishop reckoned, Father Paul would not find many takers for his Dalit liberation theology.

Father Paul had clearly learnt his lesson and was now resigned to preaching the gospel according to high-caste catholics. He said to me, 'I have learnt the hard way. There is nothing I can do by entering the struggle for the Dalit Christians because the caste clergy have captured all the important posts in the Church – the bishops, the provincials and all the rest of them. They will just say I'm doing it because I'm a Dalit and that I'm bringing caste into the Church – as if it wasn't there already.'

When I told Paul Panneereselvan that his friend was no longer fighting the fight with all his might, he said, 'I know. You really can't blame him. There is no point in our waiting for the Church to come to our rescue. We will have to fight our own battles.' He suggested that I should go with him to see how he was training the troops.

We went to a village where Paul was holding a meeting. It was near the town of Kanchipuram, famous for its temples and its silk. Paul was accompanied by a young woman called Maria Francina, who was a singer. As we entered the village of Arasankuppam, children ran up to our car chanting 'Dalit girl, Dalit girl, you will wipe away the tears of our community' – the words of a song she had sung when they had last been there.

The meeting was held in the village school, a one-roomed building furnished with two blackboards, one table and a few chairs – most of which were broken. It was a concrete box, with no trees to provide shade – a typical product of the public works department. The Indian government spends millions of rupees urging all and sundry to 'plant more trees', but it can't persuade its own public works department to set an example. Inside the school there were about a dozen young Dalits sitting on the floor.

The meeting started with songs by Maria Francina, whose peach-coloured chiffon sari embroidered with flowers – the dress of a smart town girl – contrasted with the simple checked cotton lungis and well-washed shirts of the village Dalits. The villagers were given songbooks and joined in enthusiastically. Other young Dalit men came in as the singing continued, and by the time Paul started the hard sell there were about forty sitting in front of him.

He first asked the young Dalits whether they were being oppressed by the caste Hindus. One reported that he had been forced to wash up his own teacup when a tea-stall owner had found he was a Harijan; another said there was a nearby village where Dalits were not served tea at the tea stall. There were complaints that caste Hindus refused to employ Harijans on their land, and one young Dalit said priests in a local temple were still not allowing Dalits to worship there. There were several complaints about caste Hindus not paying proper respect to Dalits. One young man said that, in his village, even a Harijan who had achieved the lofty status of a bank official was not shown respect. Another complained that his community always went to offer condolences to the mudaliar caste when a leader of that caste died, but that they did not reciprocate by commiserating with the Harijans on the death of one of their leaders.

Periodic attempts were made to keep the village children out of the schoolroom, but they proved futile. I wasn't quite sure why the attempts were made at all, because the children listened just as attentively as the young men, until their midday meal was ready. When he was chief minister, the film star M. G. Ramachandran had introduced free midday meals for all children. I was impressed that even on a Sunday a meal had been prepared in a remote village like Arasankuppam. I was less impressed with the meal itself – rice and a ladleful of spicy water with three or four very thin slices of carrot.

While the children were eating their lunch, Paul started the direct motivation of the Dalits. He asked the young men to stand up one by one and say who they were. One said, 'a Harijan'; another, 'a scheduled caste – that is, I come from a depressed community'; and one even said, 'I am an untouchable.' Paul told them, 'All those are labels. You must not accept them. They have been given to you by Brahmins and they mean "You are my servant, you are not my equal." ' He then mimicked a conversation between a Dalit and a high-caste Hindu. Folding his hands and wagging his bowed head from side to side, he said, 'Yes sir, yes sir, yes sir, I will do any work you ask me to. Please sir, yes sir, of course I will sir.' The audience laughed. Paul then went on to tell the Dalits, 'You are Dravidians – the original Indians who were here long before the Aryan Brahmins came along. You should be proud of your ancestry, not call yourself by names you are ashamed of. We Dalits have allowed ourselves to be oppressed because we did not use our brains.' He then went on to tell a story to illustrate his point. 'There was an exhibition in Madras of brains. A Brahmin's brain cost five rupees, the brain of a mudaliar ten rupees and the brain of a Dalit fifty. When a customer asked, "How come a Dalit brain costs so much?" he was told, "Because it's fresh – it hasn't been used." Scientists have shown that all people have the same brains and the same blood. If you are blood group A you can donate for a Brahmin of group A.'

Paul then changed gear. After writing three words on the blackboard – self-recognition, self-respect and self-reliance – he said, 'Come on. Some of you must have been standing up for yourself and your community – tell me what you have done.' The only graduate from Arasankuppam stood up and said he was running a night school for Dalits. The audience clapped enthusiastically. Another had helped widows to get the certificates they needed for government loans. There was more applause. The only other graduate in the audience said he had arranged for a candidate to stand in elections for the village council, but the upper castes had bribed the Dalits so they didn't vote for him. The graduate went on to say, 'The trouble in my village is that the young people say they prefer their own life of slavery and labour rather than change.' Another Dalit stood up and said, 'We will go from this village to your village and we will work among your young people so that they change their attitude.' Paul and the whole audience applauded loudly.

More young Dalits spoke of their efforts to inspire self-respect in their community, and then Paul again asked them individually, 'Who are you?' Some said, 'I am a Dravidian – one of the original community.' Others said, 'I am a son of the soil,' or simply, 'I am a man.'

To end the session, we all stood in a circle holding hands, with Paul in the middle. He recited, 'Now we are united together to develop our people. We must bring ourselves from the bondage of the system. We must stand by our pledge of unity to make ours and our fellows' lives better. We are no longer slaves to anybody. From henceforth we are human beings. Raise your hands and keep silence for one minute. Think of your commitment.' We all raised our hands, without breaking the chain, and shut our eyes as if in prayer. Paul broke the silence by shouting '*Jai Bhim*'. The Dalits responded '*Jai Bhim*' – 'Bhim' is the name Dalits have given to B. R. Ambedkar, the Harijan who drafted the Indian constitution. It reminded me of a meeting of evangelical Christians renewing their commitment to Christ, but Paul was calling on his congregation to come to their own rescue and not to rely on any god – least of all a god who apparently showed no respect for Dalits.

After the meeting I spoke to some of the Dalits. One of the biggest problems they faced was unemployment. Young men who had been educated up to pre-university level were still working as casual labourers. The government minimum wage was sixteen rupees a day, but one Dalit said, 'When we ask farmers for sixteen rupees, we are told "Are you mental?" ' One of the two graduates said Dalits found it very hard to get clerical jobs, because they could not speak English. When I asked him about jobs reserved by the government for Dalits, he replied, 'They go to the Dalits brought up in cities. There it's much easier to learn English, because people are talking it all the time. In the villages you never hear English, so all you can learn is from a book.'

We walked back through the village. The Dalits lived in lines of low mud huts with steep, coconut-thatch roofs. They had no courtyards, so their animals were tethered in the lanes dividing the lines of huts. There was a small temple, and a shop selling liquor – the Dalits have always been encouraged to drink as one of the most effective ways of keeping them in their place. But things were changing in Arasankuppam. Older Dalits told me that until about ten years ago they had not even been able to grow moustaches, wear shoes or fold their lungis above their knees. If they did, the high castes said, 'Who does that untouchable think he is, trying to look smart like us.' They couldn't sit on bullock carts but had to walk beside them. They had no access to wells but took drinking-water from canals, and they received food from their employers in the same vessels used for carrying dung. Unlike the young Dalits who attended Paul's meeting, the community elders had not taken advantage of the new-found freedom of dress – they seemed quite happy with their torn vests and thin, white cotton lungis. But they were pleased with their other freedoms. A woman who was asked what changes had come into her life cackled, pointed to her husband and said, 'Ten years ago he didn't even know that he was a man. Now he does.'

Driving back to Kanchipuram I asked Paul what had brought about the changes. 'Awareness,' he said. 'The Dalit community in Tamil Nadu has always been one of the most oppressed. That meant it took more time for them to realize that things had changed, that they no longer had to put up with the indignity of being untouchable. But you can see from that meeting that there is still discrimination. We have a lot of fighting still to do. It's ironic that much of the fighting has to be done with the leaders of the Church which came from your countries to teach us all about the dignity of man, brotherly love, equality and lifting up the poor. The trouble is that you in the West thought you were vastly superior to us. You despised us. The Indians now controlling the Church learnt from you. They despise the poor and the ignorant – especially the Dalits.'

The West obviously still thinks it's superior to India. Just before leaving Madras I was shown a poster produced by the United States Information Service to publicize an exhibition by an American sculptor, Henry Schiowitz, who had also been working in Mahabalipuram. Schiowitz dominated the poster, dressed in a white lungi. His bare chest was garlanded with marigolds and he held a cobra in his raised hand. At the bottom of the poster were Indian carvers, pygmy-sized compared with the great American, working outside their mean huts – the victims of cultural imperialism.

— 3 —

THE KUMBH MELA

The Kumbh Mela is billed as the biggest religious festival in the world, but no one knows exactly how big it is. Perhaps the gods keep records of the devotees who wash away their sins in the rivers Ganges and Jamuna at Allahabad during the festival. As far as mortals are concerned, satellite photographs, computers and the other paraphernalia of modern technology might give a reasonably accurate estimate, but they have not so far been used for this purpose. So all one can say is that the official guesstimate was that about 10 million people bathed on the most sacred day of the 1977 Kumbh Mela. There was every reason to believe that even more would come in 1989. As the official description of the preparations for the Kumbh Mela said, 'Due to increase in the population and also due to increasing interest towards religion it is expected that on the main bathing day about 15 million people will take bath near the Sangam.' The Sangam is the point where the Jamuna and the Ganges meet. A third river, the Saraswati, is also said to have flowed into the Sangam, but there is no sign of it today, nor is there any record of when or how it disappeared.

The pandits said that 1989 would be the most important Kumbh Mela for 144 years, because of the particularly auspicious position of the stars and planets. I had read the pandits' predictions and the official report on the preparations for the Mela, so I was very surprised when I arrived in Allahabad a week before the big bathe to find administrators, journalists, religious leaders and the local clergy all worried that the millions might not turn out this time.

The history of the Kumbh Mela – like the history of all things Hindu – is not entirely clear and is therefore fiercely debated by historians and theologians. Indians are said to be recent converts to the study of history, so it is perhaps not surprising that the first known reference to the festival appears to have been made by a Chinese. The renowned seventh-century traveller Hiuen Tsiang found that half a million people had gathered at Prayag, the old name for Allahabad, to bathe in the rivers and to attend on the Emperor Harshvardhan who was taking part in the Kumbh Mela. The emperor distributed his wealth among his vassals. They paid for their gifts and returned them to him. He thus raised taxes from his vassals and everyone gained merit from the giving and receiving of gifts. A similar practice continues to this day. Brahmins keep calves tethered to their stalls for pilgrims to buy. The pilgrims then return them, and the calves are sold and resold many times. 'Godan' or the gift of a cow is one of the most meritorious acts for devout Hindus.

The word 'kumbh' means an urn, and 'mela' a fair. The festival celebrates one of the creation myths of Hinduism. Brahma, the creator, was floating on the primeval ocean in a trance. When he awoke, he started to create the universe. The gods and the demons decided to speed up the process by churning the ocean. They used a mountain as the churn and a giant snake as the rope to rotate it. As the ocean frothed, miraculous gifts appeared. The most valuable was an urn of a nectar which made anyone who drank it immortal. The demons grabbed the urn, but the son of Indra, who ruled the heavens, managed to spirit it away from them. Disguising himself as a rook, he flew over the earth, chased by the demons. Some say that during his flight to the abode of the gods he rested in four places, one of which was Prayag, or Allahabad. Others say that drops of nectar fell on those four places during the flight. The son of Indra took twelve days to fly to paradise, so, as one day in the life of the gods is the equivalent of a year in the life of mere mortals, Kumbh Melas are held in all four places once every twelve years. Allahabad is regarded as the king of the bathing-places, and the Allahabad Mela is the most important festival.

I was staying in Allahabad with one of my political gurus, Sant Bax Singh – a former member of parliament. After being elected the first undergraduate president of the Allahabad University

Students Union, he went on to Oxford and then read for the bar at Lincoln's Inn. When he returned to India, he joined the multinational Lever Brothers, where he soon emerged as the most promising Indian executive. Sant Bax Singh's father was a raja, so ruling came more naturally to his son than managing. He rejected the prosperous life that Lever's offered him and came back to Allahabad to become the member of parliament for one of the nearby constituencies. Sant Bax Singh fell out with Indira Gandhi because he openly challenged her practice of nominating the officials of the Congress Parliamentary Party instead of allowing MPs to elect them. To spite him, she promoted the career of his younger brother, Vishwanath Pratap Singh. At the time of the Mela, Sant Bax's political career was in the doldrums while V. P. Singh, after quarrelling with Rajiv Gandhi, had emerged as the opposition candidate for the premiership. But Sant Bax Singh was not overshadowed by his younger brother and was still able to summon the leading citizens of Allahabad to meet me.

The first person to arrive was Ramjee Dwivedi – the former mayor of Allahabad, a prominent Congressman and a member of the committee advising the organizers of the Kumbh Mela. Ramjee was Mr Allahabad – he knew everyone and could fix anything, which is always very important in India. It was Ramjee who first expressed doubts about the official estimate of the number of people who would come to bathe on the big day. To my horror, he put the blame for this on the BBC, claiming that we had said that two lakhs (200,000) people would be killed in a stampede. I explained to Ramjee that this must be a rumour. It is a doubtful tribute to our credibility – particularly the credibility of our Hindi service – that Indians who want to strengthen rumours often say, 'I heard it on the BBC.' There have been several election candidates facing defeat who have tried to revive their supporters' morale by telling meetings that the BBC has predicted they are going to win. Ramjee agreed it was quite possible that there had never been a broadcast forecasting that 200,000 people would be killed in a stampede and went on to say, 'The rumour might well have been floated by the officials running the Mela. They have deliberately overestimated the number of people who will come so that more money is budgeted for the Mela. Now that they have eaten that money, they have to explain why so few people have turned up.' Although he was a Congressman, Ramjee had no qualms about criticizing his own administration, because he happened to be out of favour at the time. The Congress Party is always in a state of civil war.

'How do you know that there will not be many people?' I asked.

'We have already had two bathing-days and the figures were well below the estimate on which the budgets were based. Now you can go to the Mela yourself and you will see that there are not very many people there. I will take you and show you everything. I know everything that has happened.'

The next day I entered the sprawling fair with great trepidation. I had been in many situations where the BBC was unpopular, but never had we been accused of an offence against the gods, and that was surely the charge against us now. I hoped that perhaps Ramjee had been exaggerating and that the Mela was indeed filling up. There were now only six days left before the big bathe.

We came first to the temporary stables of the mounted police, then drove past the neat khaki tents of the police lines, on to a secular fair complete with Ferris wheels, a roundabout offering 'Jambu Jet' rides, a talking dog and a snake circus whose ringmaster boasted that he played with death. There was a great deal of noise and very little business. Next came government exhibitions, including one showing the achievements of the campaign that Rajiv Gandhi had launched to clean up the Ganges. Then we saw the high fences of corrugated iron hiding the tents of the commissioner of Allahabad and the deputy inspector general of police.

'I will take you to see their tents later,' said Ramjee scornfully. 'Then you can compare them with the accommodation they have provided for the pilgrims. If you are living in a five-star hotel and you throw me into a slum, how will you hear my crying for help?'

Leaving the administration's headquarters, we drove to the top of a long embankment built to keep the Ganges and the Jamuna out of Allahabad during the monsoon floods. From here we could look down on the very heart of the Mela. It was a magnificent sight – mile after mile of tented pavilions flying the flags of different religious orders, the Ganges ahead and the great fort built by the Emperor Akbar standing on the banks of the Jamuna to the right. But the pilgrims were missing.

We drove to Akbar's Fort, where Ramjee had organized an official boat for us to see the Sangam itself. Boatmen who had rowed their shallow craft from as far as Varanasi, or Benares, eighty miles downstream, to make their fortune at the Mela were standing around waiting for customers. I asked one about business. He said, 'People do not seem to be coming this year. I think they are not coming out of fear. Everyone's life is precious.'

'What is this fear?'

'I have heard that the BBC said many people will die at the Mela.'

'But did you hear any such broadcast or news yourself?'

'No, I haven't heard that. But people here are speaking about the BBC saying there will be lakhs of deaths.'

I tried to explain that this was just a rumour, but I don't think the message went home. As far as the boatman was concerned, the damage had already been done, so what was the point of worrying whether the report was true or not?

From the jetty I could see the Sangam, where the blue waters of the Jamuna mixed with the muddy brown Ganges and, then flowed away, sadly more brown than blue, towards Varanasi. We boarded our motor launch and set off towards the confluence. Looking along the river banks, Ramjee remarked, 'People should be bathing here, but you see how few they are.'

I couldn't but agree. There weren't many pious Hindus standing praying or bobbing up and down as they ducked themselves in the Ganges – no more than one would expect to see at an important place of pilgrimage on any day of the year. We climbed out of the boat on to a sandbank in the middle of the Sangam. There was a barricade of country boats anchored by bamboo poles which provided a floating bathing-ghat, but again there were very few customers. Ramjee pointed to the far bank of the Ganges. 'There you see another big waste of public money,' he said. 'That is where they have built a helipad for the prime minister, but now he's not coming.'

'Has he been put off by the BBC rumour too?' I asked.

Ramjee was too serious a politician to take that as even a bad joke. 'No,' he replied earnestly. 'When it was first announced that he was coming, I said wait until the results of the state-assembly elections in Tamil Nadu before making up your minds whether he will come. But the administration didn't listen. I knew that if he won that election he would be in political nasha – intoxication – and would be stupid enough to come. If he was defeated, he would not dare to show his face here. He lost that election very badly and you see his visit stands cancelled.'

'Why would it have been stupid for him to come here?'

'The sadhus [holy men] are very angry with him because he has been supporting the minorities, and they think his policies are anti-Hindu. They do not even think of him as a Hindu. They say his father was a Parsi and he has a foreign wife. They had prepared 6,000 balloons with black flags to release into the air during his meeting.'

The press had other explanations for the cancellation of the prime minister's visit. The local English daily, the *Northern India Patrika*, was owned by the family of a Congress Party MP, but that was not preventing it running stories every day against the Mela administration. It was leading the campaign to prove that the administrators had grossly inflated their estimates and were now trying to blame the low turnout on the BBC. The local press in India doesn't consider it's doing its job unless it is attacking the administration, but many of its allegations are ill-founded. Some of the less reputable papers – not, I hasten to add, the *Patrika* – blackmail officials and politicians. The *Patrika* said the Mela administration had put the fear of the godmen into Rajiv Gandhi because they were afraid that he would be met with a barrage of complaints about their arrangements for the Mela

The *Jansatta*, a national opposition paper, suggested that Rajiv Gandhi may have been reminded of an unfortunate precedent. His mother, Indira Gandhi, had addressed a meeting of the sadhus at the last Allahabad Kumbh Mela, twelve years previously.

Later that year, she had been routed in a general election. The paper pointed out that Rajiv had to face the electorate before the end of the current year.

The man officially in charge of the entire Mela was the commissioner of Allahabad, Ravindra Gupta. I met him on the sandy banks of the Sangam. He was a middle-aged, balding, soft-spoken man, accompanied by two burly peons in blue overcoats, with the red sashes and brass badges which were their badges of office in the days of the raj. Immediately we were introduced, the commissioner smiled and said, 'So you have come to see if 200,000 people really do get killed in a stampede.'

I once again denied that we had ever made any such suggestion and pointed out that no journalist would put his reputation at risk by making such a preposterous prophecy. The commissioner suggested that in that case the BBC should broadcast a denial of the rumour. A senior police officer wearing a solar topi laughed, 'Don't deny it before the big bathe – that will make our lives much easier.'

The commissioner was not amused. 'You have to take this seriously,' he said. 'It's not just a matter of the people coming or not. It's also a matter of the reputation of the BBC.'

I agreed, but pointed out that it would be very difficult for an organization which did not broadcast rumours to deny them.

Rumours and constant attacks by the press and by local politicians like Ramjee were not the only problems facing Ravindra Gupta and his team of administrators. Running the Kumbh Mela is a gigantic task. It involves constructing a city in the beds of the two rivers. No work can start until the monsoon floods have receded and the sands have dried out. The monsoon before this Mela had been particularly heavy and the site of the Mela had not dried out until October. The tented city had to be complete by January. As the commissioner told me, 'Work had to proceed on a war footing.' This was one war the Indian bureaucracy did win. Thirty-six thousand acres of land had to be flattened after the floods. Spurs and embankments had to be built to prevent the Ganges changing course and so altering the whole map of Kumbhnagar, as the tented city is called. After last year's monsoon, the Ganges had divided into two channels and irrigation engineers had tried to keep the channels separate so that there would be more space for bathing. The river defeated them, and so two months before the Mela the whole map of Kumbhnagar did indeed have to be changed. Then came another threat: the Ganges started eroding one of its banks, and could easily have flooded large areas of the Mela. An urgent message was sent up-river, and the flow through the dam at Narora was reduced.

Twenty-three tube-wells had to be sunk to provide drinking-water. They had to be deep enough to prevent the rivers seeping into them and polluting the subsoil water. One hundred and ten miles of water pipes and thirty-one miles of drainage had to be laid. The Public Works Department had to construct nine bridges on pontoons lashed to the banks of the Ganges. Forty mallahs or men of the fisherman caste watched each bridge day and night in case the moorings gave way. Every bridge had between seventy and eighty pontoons. The army was asked to construct a Bailey bridge across the Jamuna.

Twelve miles of steel plates had to be laid to provide motorable roads in Kumbhnagar, and another twelve miles or so of unmetalled roads had to be levelled. Thousands of acres of land had to be covered with tents to provide housing, offices and of course pavilions in which the religious leaders would give their discourses. There was also the threat of cholera. The medical officer who had the unenviable task of keeping the pilgrims healthy told me that he was providing 10,000 'seats' a day in trench latrines. The seats had to be covered with lime, bleaching-powder, and anti-fly powder when they became unhygienic. This is apparently known as 'ramming' the trenches. Of course new trenches have to be dug to replace the rammed ones. The medical officer had also provided 4,000 flush lavatories and 700 commodes. I asked whether all the citizens of Kumbhnagar used the lavatories he had provided. He replied, 'Well, strictly speaking it's illegal to ease yourself anywhere else, but then any law to survive needs mass support, and that by the common man not by the superior people.'

In order to cope with those who didn't obey the law, the

medical officer had laid on what he called 'picking squads' who had instructions to remove all the faeces by 6.30 a.m.

Kumbhnagar needed its own police force, more than 7,000 strong. The official note on the policing arrangements read, 'Special emphasis will be given to motivate the policemen on duty to exhibit exemplary behaviour and courtesy towards the general public. In view to ensure this aspect policemen with clean records have been deputed for Kumbh Mela duty.' Deputy inspector general of police Trinath Mishra had been chosen to command this exemplary force. A big, burly, pipe-smoking man who spoke excellent English, he appeared to be a highly anglicized member of the élite Indian Police Service – surely, I thought, not an appropriate officer to be in charge of an event as essentially Indian as the Kumbh Mela. I was to be proved wrong. When I got talking to D. I. G. Mishra I found that he had been a senior officer at the last Kumbh Mela. His predecessors had left inadequate notes about their arrangements and the problems they faced and so he set out to make a close study of the Mela and to record his findings meticulously. That had led to a book on the Kumbh Mela which was on sale this time.

D. I. G. Mishra helped me to find my way through the maze of religious organizations attending the Mela – more than 800.

'The akharas', he told me, 'are the focal point of the Kumbh Mela – the big draw, with their naked sadhus. They are the gymnosophists, the warriors of the faith. They have the right to march in processions to the central point of the Sangam to bathe on the big days, and they guard that right jealously.'

That is not surprising, because the Allahabad Mela is the most important gathering of Hindu holy men. The akharas are monastic orders of militant sadhus. Historians are not entirely clear about their origins, but they are related to the ascetic orders founded by the great Hindu reformer the Shankaracharya. He lived in the eighth or ninth century and is often credited with the final defeat of Buddhism in India, although some scholars argue that Buddhism was already on the way out. The Shankaracharya learnt from his enemies and introduced the Buddhist tradition of monasticism to strengthen the sinews of Hinduism.

The akharas are said to have defended Hindu ascetics against attacks from militant Muslim fakirs, or holy men. Some of them also hired out their services as mercenaries. As with all good soldiers, there was considerable rivalry between the different regiments, which often led to fights. The British administration put strict restrictions on the movement of the akharas' naked sadhus, or nagas, but even Victorian prudery could not prevent them marching at Kumbh Melas. The administrator of the 1906 Kumbh Mela had had to order a cavalry charge to break up a battle between the nagas. D. I. G. Mishra was to have his own difficulties with these quick-tempered ascetics, although he had taken the precaution of separating the camps of the akharas who followed the god Shiva from those of their long-standing enemies who followed Vishnu.

The akharas were now changing, as Mishra explained to me.

'Most of the sadhus now wear clothes. They are also out to recruit a better class of person. For many years now there has been intense rivalry between them to attract good scholars, because they realize now that faith must be tempered with reason. They are also anxious to get older people with influence. Everyone has to deal with government – even sadhus – and for that you need influence.'

'But do many influential people take sannyas [renounce all worldly ties] nowadays? Surely they don't want to give up their modern lifestyle.'

'Oh yes, plenty do. I think I will take the robe when I have finished with the police.'

'Will you join an akhara?'

'I think I will go for one of the modern organizations.'

The great reformer the Shankaracharya formed four monasteries – one in the north, one in the south, one in the east and one in the west – to be bastions of the faith. Each is still headed by a shankaracharya, and three of them had come with their followers to the Mela. A fifth shankaracharya, whose claim to enjoy the Hindu equivalent of apostolic succession is disputed, was also there.

There were hundreds of other holy men and organizations

whose pedigrees were not as good as the akharas' and shankaracharyas' but who all had their disciples. Gurus known in the West, like the Maharishi Yogi, were well-represented at this Mela, and so was the Hare Krishna movement. One thousand seven hundred other religious organizations applied for places at the Mela for the first time. Mishra said, 'We decided the best way to deal with them was to say we would charge for all the facilities they got. We didn't hear from them again.' The Mela is, of course, a wonderful opportunity for religious organizations to recruit and raise funds, but the competition is very stiff.

Mishra also had to deal with the wandering sadhus, the mendicants who were not attached to any akhara or other religious group. They camped near the free kitchens set up by some of the organizations. Mishra was rather dismissive of the mendicants: 'They normally become viraktas or wandering sadhus', he said, 'because they have lost their families or are frustrated with life. But there are some genuinely spiritual people among them.'

According to Mishra most of the pilgrims came for only one of the big days, but he estimated there were also some 100,000 kalpvasis, pilgrims who came for a longer stay and who took a vow to bathe three times a day in the Ganges, to eat just one meal a day – and that uncooked or cooked by their own hands – and to spend their time meditating and reflecting on the state of their soul.

Mishra told me that he was about to umpire a dispute between the three akharas which followed the god Vishnu. They were arguing with each other over the election of their leader. Two of the akharas had chosen one sadhu and the third another. The dispute had to be resolved quickly, because the leader would be surrounded by special pomp and splendour during the procession of the akharas on the big day. I left the deputy inspector general to judge this spiritual contest and set off to find out more about the Mela for myself.

Hindu sages have said that to learn you have to be like a honey-bee, flying from flower to flower to extract the nectar which will eventually make up the honey of knowledge. D. I. G. Mishra had given my nectar-gathering a good start, but as a civil servant he could not talk about the politics of the Mela and of Hinduism.

The Vishwa Hindu Parishad, or World Council of Hindus, which coordinates the activities of many organizations, was present in strength at the Mela. It was leading controversial campaigns to convert Muslims and Christians, and to pull down mosques which it claims were built by Muslim rulers on the sites of Hindu temples they had destroyed. I went to see its president, Shivnath Katju, a retired judge of the Allahabad High Court. His father had been a leading member of Pandit Nehru's secular government.

Katju was small and frail and looked every one of his seventy-nine years. He told me, 'The Council was formed twenty-six years ago to defend Hinduism. In spite of our independence, Hindus are still under serious attack. The government is always out to appease the minorities, especially the Muslims. We suffered during the Muslim days and we are still suffering now.'

'But you have freedom to practise your religion. You are not persecuted in any way.'

'Well, I don't think you are right. There is this issue of the temple in Ayodhya, where our god Lord Ram was born. The Mughals built a mosque there, and it's clear they did so by destroying a Hindu temple, because there are Hindu columns inside the mosque. Images of Ram and Sita his wife have sprung up there. We can only peep at them through locked doors. Ram is under house arrest. If the government doesn't let us build a temple on this site, it will become a very serious political issue.'

I said, 'The government has suggested compromises which could defuse the issue. Wouldn't it be better to accept one of them rather than risk communal riots?'

'That', replied the retired judge firmly, 'is the problem. Because we are the majority, we are always being asked to make sacrifices to placate the minorities. We can't go on like that.'

Although its president insisted that the Vishwa Hindu Parishad was not inciting religious hatred, the sadhus and saints who gathered for a special meeting under the Parishad's banner did just that. The stage in the vast tented pavilion on Kumbhnagar's main road was crowded with holy men wearing saffron, lemon-yellow, dark-red or white robes. Some were old and frail; some young, sleek-skinned and prosperous. Some were lean and intense, and some rather stout and somnolent. Thousands of people sat shoulder to shoulder on straw strewn on the floor of the pavilion, and thousands more stood outside listening to the speeches on loudspeakers. They shouted, 'Long live Mother India. Long live the holy place where Ram was born. Long live our mother the cow!' and many other Hindu slogans. Women stuffed notes into collection boxes tied to posts supporting the pavilion; the men seemed less generous. A thin sadhu with a greying beard ranted over the loudspeaker system: 'The Muslims stole all our temples. They stole our land. There is Inglistan for the English, Pakistan for the Muslims, there should be Hindustan for the Hindus. Now is the time to fight back. We should undo partition and make our beloved Bharat Mata, Mother India, one again. We will make every sacrifice to achieve our sacred end, to defend Hinduism, and to restore Bharat Mata. Raise your hands if you are ready to sacrifice your lives for Lord Ram!'

Thousands of hands were raised and thousands of voices shouted '*Bhagwan Ram ki jai*' – 'Victory to our god Ram!'

A portly white-bearded sadhu bellowed hoarsely, 'This holy place where we have gathered was known to Hindus as "Prayag". It was the Muslims who called it "Allahabad". It's our misfortune that after independence our governments, out of their greed for Muslim votes, have refused to restore the name "Prayag". We must stand and fight for Hindustan.'

Suddenly the crowd became restless. A murmur went round the pavilion: 'The baba is coming.' The sadhus on the platform tried to recapture the crowd's attention by shouting slogans. Marshals ordered people to sit down, but no one heeded them. All eyes were on a wooden platform built just above the right side of the stage. A young man wearing just a white loincloth and a sacred thread, his hair matted and his forehead marked with the tilak of Vishnu, came through the curtains, dusted the platform and spread a white sheet. The sadhus on the stage gave up: the legendary Devraha Baba was about to make his entrance.

It was said – although inevitably some disputed it – that this would be the first time that the hermit had appeared on a public platform. Silence decended on the vast audience as we all excitedly awaited the sage, who was reputed to be 300 years old. The curtains were drawn back slightly and an old man, bent double, shuffled to the front of the platform. The crowd exploded with shouts of '*Devraha Baba ki jai!*' – 'Long live Devraha Baba!' The holy man was naked except for a deerskin he held loosely round his waist. His thighs were emaciated, his skin was blackened by the sun, his eyes were rheumy with age, his hair was matted; but, surprisingly, his beard was quite neatly trimmed. He sat down hurriedly and raised both his hands in blessing. A woman near me stood up and folded her hands in devotion, ignoring the tugs at her sari and the cries of 'Sit down, we can't see.'

When the crowd had quietened, a former head of the state police force who had turned sadhu – it seems to be a tradition in Uttar Pradesh – read out a statement on behalf of the baba. That, I thought, would be that. But the crowd was not satisfied. They shouted, 'We want Baba's blessing. Baba speak to us.' A model of the temple of Ram which the Vishwa Hindu Parishad planned to build if it succeeded in getting that mosque destroyed was brought to the baba, who laid hands on it. The baba, still sitting, pulled himself to the edge of his platform, clasped a microphone and started speaking in a quiet but remarkably clear voice. He told the now silent crowd, 'Protecting this temple of Ram is holy work. You protect your religion and it protects you. My platform from which I give my blessing every day is the platform of the Vishwa Hindu Parishad. They have my blessings. I want everyone to cooperate with their work.'

Then he turned to his young disciple and said in a whisper caught by the microphone, '*Bahut hai*?' – 'Is that enough?' The disciple's reply was inaudible, but apparently he thought not, because the baba started to talk again, this time about the need to protect cows. After a few brief sentences he again turned to his disciple and asked, '*Bahut hai*?' He was told to exhort the crowd to worship Ram by reciting his name. After a few sentences on that theme, the baba again lifted his hands in blessing. Every woman there seemed to be standing with folded hands. The baba scurried off his platform, and the crowd started to melt away – much to the disappointment of the other saints, many of whom still had plenty of fire and brimstone in their bellies.

There is nothing that Hindus respect more than austerity in others, no matter how much difficulty they may find in practising it themselves. Austerity was one of the keys to Mahatma Gandhi's success. The Vishwa Hindu Parishad knew the value of Devraha Baba's support for their cause. I hoped it might be possible to gather some more nectar by learning about the life of the legendary ascetic, but, when I reached the baba's camp, I found that it was not only the Parishad that was taking advantage of his austerity.

The baba had established his camp about a quarter of a mile from the nearest tents, right on the edge of the Mela. Inside the gateway, a ruffianly guard with a ferocious black moustache told me that, until the great man emerged from the Ganges and began his daily audience, I could not meet any of his associates. I waited with some 300 devotees in front of the baba's small thatched hut standing on stilts about six feet above the ground. After half an hour, the aged hermit, again covered only by his deerskin, scuttled like a crab out of the door of his hut on to the edge of the platform. He lifted his hands in blessing while his henchmen urged the crowd to buy copies of a commentary on the Bhagvat Purana, a scripture dedicated to Vishnu, on sale in one corner of the camp. The baba obligingly touched the books and blessed them. This greatly encouraged the sale of the commentary, to the considerable profit of the publisher, as the book was expensive by Indian standards. Inevitably an impious thought crossed my mind: I wondered what was in it for the baba's disciples.

One villager had the impudence to light up a biri in the presence of the baba. It was snatched from his mouth by one of the baba's guards. Another guard, seeing a man wearing shoes, pointed to me and said, 'Look, that Englishman has taken his shoes off and you, an Indian, show such disrespect to the baba.'

While the devotees were thronging around the saint's platform, I found two of his disciples. I asked them to tell me about the baba's routine. One who was a printer – not, apparently, the printer of that commentary – said, 'The baba lives and is everywhere. He has no fixed place, but always stays by riverbanks. He is an ageless man who has travelled all over India on foot. Everyone claims that the baba comes from his area. Some say that he was born of water. He takes bath in the river four or five times every day.'

'Why does he live on a platform?'

'Because he says that the public are infected with worms which he will get if he stays on their level. The baba's memory is like a computer – people will tell you that he remembers what they told him thirty years ago.'

'Some people say he's 300 years old. How old is he really?'

'No one knows exactly what exercises he does, but he has mastered age and will die only when he wants to. He is a sidh yogi [an ascetic whose mastery of the yogic arts is so great that he has attained supernatural powers and transcended them] – all the time he is practising the yoga position of Udyan Band, which means his stomach touches his back.'

'What does he eat?'

'Air. He doesn't even eat fruit. You see, any great yogi can extend his tongue from inside until it touches the top of his head. That's where the nectar is situated, and one drop of nectar is all you need to live for a very long time.'

I couldn't help wondering what happened to all the baskets of fruit which were being given to the baba as offerings.

'Is it true', I asked, 'that Indira Gandhi used to come to see the baba?'

'Yes, she came several times.'

'What about Rajiv?'

'No. He will come when his heart is cleaner.'

When I returned to my jeep, the battery was flat. There were plenty of volunteers to help push it, but the clutch wouldn't engage and I had to abandon it. Until then it had been running perfectly. As I started on the long and dusty walk back, I was reminded of a friend of Sant Bax Singh's. He had told me that all those who travelled to the baba in good faith had a safe journey. Was I being given a reminder about the dangers of cynicism?

It's very hard not to be cynical about the Brahmin priests who attend to the immediate physical and spiritual needs of those who come to bathe in the Sangam. The lesser priests are known as ghatias. They set up stalls on the river edges, or ghats, where they look after the clothes of the bathers, help them with their toilet when they come out of the river and say a brief mantra to complete the process of purification. Shri Ram Mishra was an elderly ghatia who said his family had been ghatias here for generations. He claimed to have looked after Mrs Gandhi when she bathed in the Sangam. He sat cross-legged on a low wooden platform. A piece of sacking draped behind him kept out some of the sand and dust. He had small bowls of the powders and pastes necessary for replacing the tilaks and sindoor – the vermilion indicating a woman's married status – washed away in the river. There were mirrors and combs too. A woman bather put twenty-five paise – about one penny – into a basket in front of the ghatia and gave him a handful of potatoes. He gave her a piece of sacred grass to hold, poured a teaspoonful of Ganges water over her hand and mumbled a brief blessing.

Although they are only small-time businessmen, the ghatias are well organized. The joint secretary of their union came up to see what I was doing. When I explained, he said, 'Oh, so you are the person who has done us down by that broadcast.' I explained yet again that it was just a rumour. He replied, 'Well, broadcast a message so that people do start coming – business is bad.' I tried to convince him that that would just make matters worse.

A hundred yards or so behind the ghatias were the pandas, who are big businessmen. Each panda was identified by a huge flag. These Brahmins act as family priests, maintain their clients' genealogies, arrange for their stay at Melas and perform ceremonies for the souls of their dead. Rajesh Kumar Panda was writing up the latest developments in the family of a peasant from central India. The family trees are kept in long, thin notebooks whose yellow pages are bound in red.

'Ram Swarup had two sons, so what were their names?' he asked brusquely.

'Om Prakash and Shiv Ram.'

The priest scribbled hurriedly.

'Have they married? Do they have any children? Hurry up. Can't you see how busy I am?'

When he had updated the genealogy, he turned to me and asked my business. After getting through the inevitable rigmarole about the rumour, he demanded twenty-five rupees for explaining the role of the pandas. When I agreed, he told me that his was a family business, like the business of the ghatias. All pandas have a district of India in which they ply their trade. Rajesh Kumar's was Jabalpur in central India. He visited his clients there, selling Ganges water to those who had not visited Allahabad recently and encouraging them to be more regular in their bathes. At the back of his stall was a capacious tin trunk full of his client's registers of birth, marriages and deaths, each one wrapped carefully in a cloth. Rajesh Kumar took me outside his stall to see his flag, which depicted the monkey-god Hanuman trampling on a demon. Many of the pandas had chosen one or another member of the Hindu pantheon for their flags, but there were secular emblems flying above the stalls too – there was a steam engine, a train complete with a guard carrying a green flag, a fish, and a plough and oxen.

'Now you see how my clients will recognize me,' he said. 'They ask where is the Hanuman panda, and they are directed to my flag. Now pay me my twenty-five rupees quickly – I must get back to my clients.'

A group of pilgrims with shaven heads were sitting in a circle on the sand in front of the panda's stall. Two scruffy young men dressed in trousers and sweaters were moving round the pilgrims asking them how much they were going to pay for the ceremony for their dead. An old man was proving particularly recalcitrant. 'Come on, make your commitment,' said one of the pandas irascibly. 'Don't waste my time.' Another pilgrim wanted to offer only twenty-five rupees. The panda told him, 'That's not enough. Other people have given 101.' Eventually the pilgrim handed over fifty-one rupees. The panda pocketed the cash and was turning away when his client asked anxiously, 'Aren't you going to bless me?' The panda bent down, patted his head and said a brief mantra. The pilgrim touched his feet. The priest laughed and said, 'Now you've had your blessing on the cheap.' The pandas were very skilled operators – they knew exactly when to upbraid, when to cajole and when to give up to get the most out of their clients without losing any of them.

The pandas make no attempt to hide their venality, but I discovered that even a man as educated as Trinath Mishra, the deputy inspector general of police, used their services. He told me a story about his own family panda. 'After my father's death, the panda demanded money for a bicycle for him to ride in the next life. I complained that it was beneath my father's dignity to ride a bicycle – he only ever travelled by horse or elephant. Of course that was a stupid mistake – the panda immediately demanded the price of an elephant. When I refused, he insisted on the money for the bike, saying that my father's body would be lighter now, so he would find it easier to cycle.

'Priests in all religions are rogues', D. I. G. Mishra went on, 'but they have their function. They are middlemen, in between you and God. Such middlemen are everywhere. If you want to travel by rail, you have to take a ticket from a booking-counter – the clerk is a middleman. What is the state but a middleman between individuals and society? Someone has to perform the rites for the dead. My ancestors knew that the pandas were villains, but they used them, so what right have I to show disrespect to my father by robbing him of these rites?'

The pandas feed on the carrion of superstition and justify the Indian élite who write off Hinduism as backward, priest-ridden mumbo-jumbo – a brake on progress and development, the gods of the twentieth century. In this century, Indians like the Nobel Prize winner Rabindranath Tagore, the philosopher president Sarvepalli Radhakrishnan and, of course, Mahatma Gandhi have shown the wisdom of Hinduism. Hinduism has, in the words of R. C. Zaehner, the former professor of Eastern religions and ethics at Oxford, 'established itself firmly in world opinion as one of the greatest and most profound religions of the world'. But in the same chapter of his book, *Hinduism*, he expresses concern about the future of the religion:

In Europe the Reformation gave birth to the Counter-Reformation, and the old Church succeeded in purging itself of the old abuses and in recreating itself in a new image. Hindu orthodoxy at present shows no signs of such a renovation: it has lost its hold on the towns and, in the opinion of many, it is only a question of time before it loses its hold on the villages, for one of the paradoxes of Hinduism has always been the yawning gap which separates its higher manifestations from the frankly superstitious and magical practices that go to make up the religious fare of the rural masses. With the spread of Western education right down to the lowest strata of society and the progressive industrialization of the country the whole religious structure of Hinduism will be subjected to a severe strain; but such has been its genius for absorption and adaptation that it would be foolhardy to prophesy how it will confront this new and unprecedented crisis.

At the Mela, I found little or no evidence that Hindu orthodoxy was purging itself.

I tried the shankaracharyas, but they offered little or nothing. The shankaracharya of Puri, I was told, was a renowned scholar, but when I went to hear him preach he was challenging all comers to disprove his contention that sati, or widow-burning, was sanctioned by the Hindu scriptures. The shankaracharya of Kanchipuram was denouncing family planning, and the shankaracharya of Dwarka was performing complicated and esoteric rituals.

I turned to the akharas, the stars of the Kumbh Mela. Their camps were guarded by ferocious sadhus who seemed to know only two words: 'Get out.' As sadhus had already broken one television crew's camera and had threatened another crew with bows and arrows, I was not inclined to argue with them – especially as they had almost certainly heard the 'BBC' rumour. I did find some 300 men preparing to be initiated as sadhus, sitting in a group behind the akharas' compounds. They wore just a small cloth tied tightly between their legs. Three barbers were shaving their heads and beards, using cut-throat razors without benefit of shaving-soap. Some of the initiates were squatting with their back to the road, shaving their own pubic hairs. Fully clad sadhus wielding silver staves were keeping the chattering holy men in order and moving on the curious like me. From a safe distance I noticed that most of the novices were young men, although there were a few who were probably taking sannyas. One young man was deformed. They all seemed happy and relaxed, not in the least solemn like Christian novices or ordinands.

One part of the Juna akhara – said to be the most ferocious of them all – was open to the public. I passed through the gate with some trepidation and found two lines of tents with a small temple at the end. Some sadhus were sitting outside their tents; others were asleep inside. Near the temple, a naked sadhu was sharing a silver chillum or pipe of hashish with two Europeans. Another naked sadhu, his body smeared with ash and his eyes closed, was sitting motionless in the lotus position in front of a trident, deep in meditation. A few small coins had been thrown on to the blanket spread out in front of him. A more prosperous ascetic was sitting on a leopard skin, talking to a small group of villagers. There was a constant stream of villagers passing in front of the tents. Suddenly I heard shouts of 'Fire!' Turning my head, I saw clouds of black smoke billowing up from a straw hut behind the tents. Saffron-robed sadhus clambered on to the roof of the hut and threw buckets of water over the flames. The fire began to sputter and died down before it could spread. Fire is one of the great hazards of the Mela because of the countless open hearths, the acres of straw spread for bedding and the miles of canvas tents. A vast tented pavilion had burnt down two days earlier.

The burnt-out hut was in the next-door camp, which belonged to the Niranjani akhara. A special police station had been set up to keep the peace between the different akharas. The officer in charge, Ravi Shankar Mishra, rushed to the Niranjanis, and in the general chaos I managed to get past the ferocious watchmen too. I found a group of saffron-robed sadhus sitting on a raised platform covered with a thatched roof: the administrative headquarters of the akhara. I could hear the leaders of the akhara and the police shouting at each other by the burnt-out tent. The sadhus told me to take my shoes off and come and sit with them. By good fortune they were BBC listeners, so they were anxious to hear about the rumour and invited me to drink tea. When I asked what the trouble was, one of the younger ascetics said angrily,

'Those Juna sadhus smoke hashish and throw the burning ash into our camp. They started the fire.' Another sadhu said, 'Those people are all thieves and ne'er-do-wells. They are always causing trouble.'

The argument with the police died down and the secretary of the akhara, Mahant Rama Krishna Giri, came round the corner with Superintendent Mishra and his party. The mahant, or priest, was a sadhu wearing a full beard and a turban tied like a Sikh's. He had the strong, good-humoured face of a Sikh farmer too, but he was dressed in the saffron robes of a Hindu ascetic and had a Hindu tilak on his forehead. He and the police came on to the platform and discussed the fire. The superintendent sided with the Niranjanis and agreed to set up another watch-tower so that he could keep a closer eye on the Juna sadhus. The topic of conversation then changed to religion. I found myself listening to a discourse on the *Mahabharat*, one of the great Hindu epics, by Superintendent Mishra. It appeared that the administration had indeed chosen the Mela police force with great care, and that they were all men of God. The papers later reported that the Niranjani and Juna sadhus had actually drawn swords, but I saw no sign of this.

When the police had left, I asked the mahant what the purpose of having akharas was now that there was no longer any need for armed sadhus to protect Hindu ascetics. He replied, 'The akharas are still needed to protect our religion. There are lots of new religions – more than before. They are all propagating their beliefs. We through our mahatmas help to keep people aware of Hinduism, otherwise Christians encourage people to leave their religion. They offer them economic benefits. We have our mahatmas in the villages. They hold assemblies and run classes telling people how to live, how to protect their country and their religion. We go to the villages and teach children, "Awake, awake, dwellers in the land of Bharat, protect your religion and country."' His voice got louder and louder, and he shook his clenched fists as he got carried away by evangelical fervour. 'For the sake of your country, for the sake of your religion, wake up, wake up dwellers in the land of Bharat,' he shouted. 'Wake up to defend Bharat. Be holy and live by the traditions of your faith. Serve the humble and afflicted. To serve the people is to serve God.'

The mahatmas are itinerant preachers, travelling for eight months every year and staying in a monastery for four. The Niranjanis have centres all over India, which are governed from the headquarters in Allahabad. They are administered by an elected committee of sixteen members.

The mahant was not best pleased when I suggested he must be collecting a lot of money at the Mela. 'We do not beg,' he said firmly. 'So many people nowadays say sadhus are beggars. We are not. Food, drink and all necessities are provided to all our sadhus by the akharas. We also provide food and shelter for the destitute. So, if we help beggars, how can we be beggars ourselves?'

'But where does all the money come from to run such a big organization?'

'If anyone wants to make a donation, we accept it. But we don't beg. We also have property left to us from the days of the rajas and the maharajahs.'

'Do you have a strict routine?'

'Yes. We get up at four in the morning. We pray, calling on the name of Shiva, then we bathe in the Ganges. During the day there are other prayers, rituals, but we spend much time in social service, office work, etc. In the evening we again remember God and go to bed at ten o'clock.'

'In the middle of all that, many of your sadhus find time to listen to the BBC.'

'Apparently,' laughed the mahant.

'I can understand your preaching and your social work, but surely the naked nagas are an anachronism.'

'We do have nagas. They do nothing but puja [acts of worship] and bhajans [hymns]. They are people who have made sacrifices: they have given up everything – they do not even touch money – and they all have to live together. There is no need for the nagas now, but we keep them because we want our old traditions to survive. They should not be destroyed but preserved.'

'In the West there is a great shortage of vocations to religious orders. Do you have a problem?'

'We get plenty of bad people coming to us,' the mahant chuckled. 'There are plenty of khana [food] wallahs. They think: if I wear the clothes of a sadhu, people will give me all I want and I won't have to work ever again. They seem to think that an ashram means aish [pleasure] and aram [rest]. There is definitely a shortage of people who want to become real sadhus.'

'Do you recruit young boys?'

'Lots of childless people promise to give a son to the ashram if their prayers are answered, but such boys will not stay here unless they are mentally suited to the life. Then some young men also join, and of course there are people who come to us to take sannyas.'

'Will you take people from any caste?'

'The recruits must be Brahmins, Kshatriyas or Vaishyas [the three 'twice-born' or upper castes – priests, warrior-rulers, and traders/farmers].'

'So you would not take Harijans, for instance?'

'No. Being sadhus is not their traditional occupation according to our scriptures.'

'But isn't that practising caste discrimination?' I asked.

'If that's a tradition, it's a tradition. Harijans have plenty of other things to do – especially nowadays. They are the most pampered people in India, with reservations for jobs everywhere. Why should we reserve positions for them in our akhara?'

There didn't seem to be much progress we could make on that point, so I moved on to the background of those who were allowed to join the akhara.

'You will never find that out,' said the mahant. 'All our sadhus should be free of all family ties. A sadhu is not even allowed to tell you where he comes from. They must be prepared to work for the good of their religion and country.'

'In the Juna akhara I saw sadhus smoking hashish. Do you allow that?'

'You haven't seen any hashish-smoking here,' shot back the mahant.

'How many sadhus will there be in your procession?'

'We have about 5,000 robed sadhus and 200 nagas here. We have as many as 22,000 sadhus in ashrams all round the country.'

The mahant was very busy: it was a festival day and, as the secretary of the akhara, he had to organize food for thousands of people. While we were talking, he gave instructions to the munim, or accountant, squatting behind a low desk and to the others milling around the akhara's headquarters. The munim was making entries in a big ledger as sadhus came and handed over or withdrew money. Some supplies ordered yesterday appeared to have got lost, and the tractor-driver who was meant to have brought them could not be found. Volunteers from outside the order, wearing big saffron rosettes, were sent to look for him. The mahant was hoarse from shouting orders, and so I left him to more important matters than satisfying my curiosity.

The Mela seemed a little more crowded, but there was still no sign of the millions for whom the administration had catered, and the big bathe was now just three days away. I talked to a retired postmaster who had taken the full vows of a kalpvasi. He said, 'I am very happy because everyone is worshipping the Almighty. There is a fine atmosphere, because everyone is worshipping Lord Ram.' A family of five was sitting at the side of the road eating stale chapattis and puffed rice. The head of the family was a farmer from a village about 100 miles away. He was looking for the sword-sign panda who operated in his district. He thought the priest would help him with accommodation, but he didn't know how to find him. A stationmaster, fresh from his bathe in the Ganges and with a large V-shaped tilak on his brow, had been humiliated by the late running of the special train in which he had travelled to the Mela. There was also a retired schoolmaster in the full garb of an ascetic – saffron-coloured cotton robes and a string of sacred rudraksha beads. He had recently taken sannyas, and had found immense peace and happiness in his new life. 'I used to read in books about all the pilgrimage and historic places in India,' he said enthusiastically. 'Now I am seeing them for myself. I even visit mosques and churches, and I believe that you should respect their rules, so I cover my head if I go into a mosque. I stay in ashrams and I am given food and donations, but I never beg.'

There was no question of begging when it came to Vibhav

Bhushan Uphadhaya. He was a former attorney general of the state of Uttar Pradesh, still a lawyer with a prosperous practice in the Allahabad High Court, and a friend of my host, Sant Bax Singh. Sant Bax had introduced him as a man who combined a very sharp mind with traditional beliefs. Vibhav Bushan's tent was in the centre of the Mela and large enough to have an ancient green Ford Prefect parked in the forecourt. He welcomed me warmly, and I sat down to gather more nectar for my honey. The loudspeakers blaring the messages of the religious organizations were competing with the public-address system broadcasting appeals from pilgrims who were lost. 'Shri Naresh Yadav, from village Ramgarh, district Gaya, Bihar, please come to the Congress Party's lost-and-found bureau where his wife and family are waiting for him. Will Ram Adhar from Moradabad, Uttar Pradesh, please come to the Congress Party's lost-and-found bureau to collect his son.' The Congress Party had cornered the lost-and-found business because of its value as subliminal publicity.

I asked Vibhav Bhushan why he had chosen to set up his tent in the middle of this cacophony when he had a substantial house in Allahabad.

'I would like the Mela to be more peaceful, but the commercialization and loudspeakers are neither here nor there. The object of coming here is that you can take your baths easily and you hope the whole atmosphere will be charged with religious feelings.'

'But is it?'

The lawyer roared with laughter, 'Well, you hear an awful lot of discourses, bhajans and religious drama on the loudspeakers.'

Vibhav Bhushan came from a religious family. He could remember his grandfather as a sannyasi. He himself was a strict vegetarian and teetotaller, but his Brahminical code did not ban tobacco. Sitting cross-legged on a collapsible chair, surrounded by the joint family he headed, the elderly lawyer looked very much a patriarch. His fine head of silver hair, bushy eyebrows, neat moustache and even the hairs protruding from the lobes of his ears seemed to have been deliberately cultivated to give an impression of severity – an impression he doubtless put to good use when prosecuting on behalf of the government. But his eyes gave him away: they were lively and alight with humour.

'Religion in India', he told me, 'is not what you in the West understand by religion. We believe that it is dharma, that is to say our duty: how we should conduct ourselves from birth to death. The Kumbh Mela is one of the rituals of dharma. You come here because you have faith in dharma and its rituals, not because you hope to get faith. Without faith you cannot really expect to understand the Mela.'

'Can I expect to understand Hinduism at all?' I asked.

'I don't think so. You in the West have gone too far away from religion. You have suffered from an overdose of individualism. You can't face the simple fact that a man is conditioned by the nature and circumstances of his parents. When your parents conceived you, they bequeathed you some qualities and denied you others. Now of course you can build on those qualities in many different ways, but the fact remains that certain limits are put on you from the moment of your conception.'

Vibhav Bhushan drew deeply on his cigarette. The smoke set off a coughing-fit. His whole body shook. He held up his hand to prevent me interrupting and went on, 'I know you think that Hinduism is weighed down by fatalism because we put so much emphasis on the family and the caste into which we are born. I think that is just facing up to reality.'

'Surely you would accept that caste is outdated.'

'No, I would not, if caste is seen in its proper perspective. The main point of caste today is marriage. I want my son to marry a Brahmin girl. Why shouldn't I? She will share our attitudes and views. Here we have a concept of families, not individuals. There are eighteen to twenty people in my family, messing in one kitchen. You should approve of joint families, because they are socialist units – perhaps even communist,' Vibhav Bhushan laughed. 'Supposing I'm earning more and my brother is struggling. In the West I will be better off than him. In a joint family I will have the same standard of living.'

'But can this system really last?'

'I am afraid that society at the top levels is breaking up, not at the bottom. Nowadays, Indians – the better-off Indians – don't seem to accept anything unless it has the stamp of the West on it. For instance take yoga, which is entirely Indian. It has now become popular again among the élite because it has been taken up in the West. Western society seems to me to be entirely based on personal or individual achievement That is not the religious view of life.'

The lawyer's wife said, 'Life has always changed. Things are not the same now as they were in the time when Ram was king or when the Shankaracharya preached. What we have to find is the dharma for today, and it's quite possible that someone like Krishna has been born already to bring about that dharma.'

'Yes, I agree,' said Vibhav Bhushan. 'All you can do with the materialism of today is to keep your cool, keep your philosophy, and do what you have to do to exist in society. Our ways have survived for thousands of years. You are children of today.'

'Do you think that we are living in the Kalyug, the dark age that Hinduism talks of?'

'Oh, I don't know about that. We have a saying in our villages: "The bullock that died was always the best." Look at my son. He's still a student, but he's spent the whole month in the Mela.'

'I didn't know whether I would enjoy it,' Vibhav Bhushan's son Anu said, 'but I have, and I've learnt and thought a lot. When I told my friends I was going to spend the month here, they thought I must be coming to do business, that I must have set up a stall. They couldn't believe I was interested in the religious aspect of the Kumbh Mela. What have I missed by being here? Just a few evenings eating junk food and drinking coffee with them. If you like, I'll take you to some of the people you won't have seen.'

I set off with Vibhav Bhushan's son to see more of the variety of Hinduism on display in this religious bazaar.

We stood in a queue to see Baba Bhutnath, the Lord of the Spirits. Hindus attach great importance to a darshan, or view, of a saint or a holy image. Outside the baba's tent there was a line of gaudy statues, including one of the decapitated goddess Kali holding her own head in her hand. Inside, the baba sat cross-legged on a platform, waving an object which looked like a metal snake over the heads of the devotees filing past him. His hair and beard, dyed red with henna, were the same colour as his robes. When Vibhav Bhushan's son had seen the baba two days before, his hair and beard had been black.

Baba Bhutnath was a Tantric. Tantra is the school of Hinduism which lays stress on action rather than renunciation. Tantrics believe that man can overcome desires and fears only by experiencing them thoroughly. Some practise sexual yoga. Tantrics have a tradition of secrecy which has led to frightening stories about their rituals. Some modern sadhus who claim to have adopted the Tantric way make good use of the mystery and fear surrounding the cult to promote themselves as miracle-workers. During the Kumbh Mela, a battle was going on between Baba Bhutnath and Chandraswamy, a sadhu with high-level political connections. They were rubbishing each other's miracles in the pages of the newspapers.

Among the many sadhus performing spectacular feats of tapasya, or penance, were Balyogi Baba, who was reputed to have been standing on one leg for eight years, and Baba Jagu Das, who was lying on a bed of thorns. In sharp contrast to them was Abhilash Das, the mahant of an ashram of devotees of the fifteenth-century mystic poet Kabir. His was a deliberately low-key operation which had particularly impressed Vibhav Bhushan's son. Abhilash Das had close-cropped greying hair and wore simple white robes. He was quiet-spoken but laughed a great deal. When I asked him about asceticism, he replied, 'We say it is madness to perform tapasya by standing on one leg, or sitting surrounded by five fires like some sadhus do. Neither do we believe in miracles. There are plenty of religious liars here, and a religious liar is a bigger liar than any lawyer or politician. If a politician says a mouse has turned into a monkey, no one will believe him. If a mahatma says it, people will.'

The pavilion of the Kabirpanthis, as the followers of Kabir were called, was one of the cleanest and best-kept I saw in the Mela. They were the extreme Protestants of Hinduism, rejecting idols and caste. Members of any caste and believers of any religion could become members – I was introduced to a young Indian Christian who had just joined the ashram. The mahant was not even bothered about bathing in the Ganges on the great day. 'The tap is just as good,' he told me. The Kabirpanthis had come to the Mela to propagate their faith, not to participate in rituals.

On the morning of 5 February, the day before the great bathe, Sant Bax Singh came into my room flourishing a newspaper and saying, '*Bach gae*' – 'You've been saved.' He proceeded to read out the front-page editorial from the Hindi-language *Amrit Prabhat*, entitled 'The Triumph of Faith'. The editorial began, 'In spite of the fear of imaginary calamities, in spite of all kinds of rumours, people have flocked from the north, the south, the east and the west, by train, bus, taxi, tractor and on foot to the sacred soil of Prayag to take a holy bathe in the Sangam on the occasion of Mauni Amavasya.' The local press had helped to spread those rumours and fears of imaginary calamities.

I dressed hurriedly and set off to check the editorial. A river of humanity was flowing towards the Sangam. All traffic had been banned. Village women anxiously held each other's saris so that they didn't get separated. Men carried sacks, suitcases and even tin trunks on their heads – they contained pots and pans and everything else needed by the self-sufficient camper. The pilgrims walked in silence, looking straight ahead. There was no panic, no pushing – just a slow, steady progress. A woman bent double with age was being led by her daughter. They both wore their saris tied between their legs, in the fashion of the west coast. There was a group of hawk-nosed men with the bright turbans of the desert state of Rajasthan tied loosely round their heads. There were barefoot girls from the tribes of central India with thick silver anklets. There were pilgrims from the Himalayas too – Nepalis with checked caps, and women from the Indian state of Himachal Pradesh, their hair tied in scarves. There were Bengalis from the east, the men wearing flowing dhotis and embroidered shawls. Only the south of India seemed to be thinly represented. Most of the pilgrims had come in groups from their villages. The occasional girl dressed in jeans or man in terry cotton trousers stood out, even in that crowd.

All the pilgrims had already walked several miles from the bus stands and railway stations. Some were resting before starting on the last stage of their journey, the walk over the embankment into the Mela proper. A wife was massaging the thin, vein-bound legs of her husband. An old man in a torn army jumper was sitting peacefully under a bridge. He had been a soldier with the raj and had taken sannyas thirty-five years before. He couldn't remember the name of his regiment.

There was no question of tents for all these pilgrims – most of them just squatted wherever they could. By evening, the Mela was shrouded in the smoke of thousands of cow-dung cooking-fires, which stung my eyes and brought back memories of many evenings spent in Indian villages.

Commercial and religious activity in the Mela had reached fever pitch. The roads were lined with stalls selling piles of brightly coloured powder for marking foreheads and partings, sacred threads, cassettes of the words of the sadhus and their music too. A man was selling magic rings. The board beside his stall read, 'Do you have bad health? Is business bad? Has anyone cast a spell on you? Are you worried by court cases? To preserve yourself from all these worries, wear this ring and get the benefit.' Next door a stall was offering a more orthodox means of warding off evil: strings of brown rudraksha beads offering the protection of Lord Shiva. Empty whisky bottles were on sale for two rupees, to carry away the holy water of the Sangam. For the children there were spirographs and ingenious plastic toys which were catapulted into the air and spun down to earth like helicopters. All sorts of vegetarian food was available, and barbers were doing a brisk business shaving pilgrims' heads.

The crowds filed slowly past the stalls, stared through the gates of the akharas, and filled the pavilions of the holy men whose fairground lights flashed and loudspeakers bellowed. The Ram and Krishna lilas – musical performances of the lives of Ram and Krishna – were particularly popular. A vast blue clay statue of Shiva dominated one bank of the Ganges. Some pilgrims squatted quietly by the river performing puja with small clay saucers full of burning ghi. They tried to float them down the Ganges, but the river was so low that most got stuck in the mud, shining in the dark water like stars in a night sky. Under one pontoon bridge, night-herons stood silent and still, oblivious of the cacophony and the crowds, their heads jutting forward, waiting to pounce on their prey.

I decided to see how some of those I had met earlier were preparing for the great day. In the camp of the fierce Juna akhara, sadhus were sitting around fires with their disciples. The sadhu I had seen two days ago was still meditating in front of his trident. Another ascetic, this time naked, held his arm in the air. I don't know how long he had been performing this tapasya, but his arm was withered and his fingernails curved round like talons.

In the friendly Niranjani akhara, thrones were being prepared for the mahamandaleshwars, or scholar ascetics. The greatest of them were to sit in magnificent howdahs covered with beaten gold and silver. Elephants had been banned after the stampede of 1954, and the howdahs – seats for mounting on an elephant's back – were now fastened on farm carts and would be pulled by devotees. The thrones of the lesser scholars were still being hammered together. They were made of wood and covered with tin and other decorations.

The secretary recognized me and introduced me to a senior sadhu, Mahant Brij Kumar Puri. He was eighty-nine but was confident that he still had many more years to live. 'If a sadhu dies before he's reached a hundred then he's not a sadhu,' the old mahant said. 'Our age increases because of yoga and because we are at peace. I will be bathing tomorrow in spite of my age.' Brij Kumar certainly looked as if he had plenty more life in him.

Inside the akhara police station, I found Superintendent Mishra and his colleagues discussing the policing of the processions. 'One gazetted officer like me has to go at the front of each procession and one at the back,' he told me. 'They will have twelve mounted constables and 100 members of the armed police. These akhara-wallahs can't stand anyone going across the path of their processions or getting mixed up with them.'

A smartly dressed man came into the police station and asked the way to the tent of one of India's biggest industrialists. He also asked for a constable to accompany his car, explaining that he was a VIP, a former minister. Mishra said quite politely, 'I don't care if you are the prime minister – I can't allow any cars into the Mela. I am afraid you will have to walk.' The VIP realized that for once he couldn't pull rank and walked away without any argument.

Then I moved on to the ghatias and pandas. The joint secretary of the ghatias was a much happier man than when I had last met him. He clasped me round the shoulders and said, 'In spite of the BBC, the crowds are very good. Before your rumour we had expected to get 10 million people bathing. From the crowds tonight, I think we'll get even more.'

The panda Brijesh Kumar was even more euphoric. 'Business is in top motion,' he cried. 'Ten thousand of my pilgrims have arrived.'

My last call was to be on the Uphadhaya family, but the canvas fence around their tent was closed, so I assumed they were asleep. They had planned to bathe early.

I too had taken a tent that night. It was in the press camp, but the noise of the Mela made it impossible to sleep. I was up before dawn and took my place in the army of pilgrims still moving slowly and steadily into the Mela. On the other side of the road, the first of the bathers were already returning home. I had to take a police sergeant with me to persuade his colleagues that I was allowed to move out of the stream of pilgrims and make my way to the Niranjani akhara.

The procession was lining up inside the akhara, and naked nagas, chattering excitedly, were looking out for gatecrashers. I hurried past them. The disciples of the mahamandaleshwars were manœuvring their raths, or chariots, into position and unfurling the banners which announced the great scholars' names. Most of the scholars were already on their thrones. I was surprised to see three women mahamandaleshwars. One, who had adopted the name 'Mother of the Power of Yoga', had been a college teacher for thirteen years before she became a sannyasi. She had been declared a mahamandaleshwar fifteen years ago and had since then founded schools of yoga in America as well as India.

A sadhu was distributing ceremonial flywhisks to the disciples who were standing behind the scholars' thrones. A naked sadhu was running hither and thither trying to find a marigold garland. The finishing touches were being put to a richly caparisoned horse which was covered with a deep-red blanket embroidered with silver and mirrorwork depicting two giant peacocks. Last-minute instructions were given to the kotwals, or policemen, of the akhara. They were wrapped in scarlet shawls and carried silver staves. Their orders were not to allow any strangers into the akhara and to ensure that nothing was stolen from the sadhus' tents when the procession moved out. The gold image of Subramaniam, the six-headed son of Shiva who was the akhara's deity, was carried out of the temple on a palanquin. He was followed by a palanquin carrying the Sun God, the deity of the Niranjani's sister akhara. Mahant Rama Krishna was striding up and down the procession moving everyone into line and sorting out disputes about orders of precedence. An elderly sadhu, apparently unmoved by all the excitement, was warming his hands over a fire and mumbling mantras. Eventually the police officer in charge of our procession received clearance on his walkie-talkie for us to move out, and we started on the march to the Sangam with the sadhus and the lay supporters of the Niranjani akhara chanting 'Hara Hara Mahadev', names of Shiva.

I kept close to Mahant Rama Krishna, in case the naked nagas objected to me. He was the sergeant-major of this parade of the saints, ensuring that it moved on at a brisk pace. A party of laymen dressed in white robes were marching in two neat lines; Rama Krishna ordered them to bunch up. The disciples pulling one of the raths were told to move at the double. Rama Krishna was very proud of his procession. He said, 'You've only seen half of it. There's a lot still inside the akhara.'

Suddenly the procession came to a halt. Rama Krishna ran up to the front to find naked sadhus arguing with the police. Even the police horses had been unable to hold back the crowds who had burst through the barriers on to the procession route. The sadhus shouted, 'Get the public out of the way.' A young robed ascetic turned on a photographer and asked, 'Who told you to join our procession?' The photographer replied insolently, 'No one.' The young ascetic shouted, 'Break his camera! Break his camera!' An older colleague restrained him – 'No. Let him go. Don't let's have any bad blood.' Fortunately the photographer managed to duck under the crowd-control barriers before the naked sadhus could vent their wrath on him. Police reinforcements were brought up and managed to clear the route. An elderly sadhu carrying two flags like a railway guard waved the green one and the procession moved off again. A naked sadhu mounted on a pony, beating a frenetic tattoo on kettledrums led the akhara to the Ganges. Two other naked sadhus danced with abandon, twirling wooden staves like demented drum majors. The trumpets, trombones, euphoniums and sousaphones of the bands blared martial music. It should have been 'When the Saints Go Marching in', but it wasn't. The crowds folded their hands and bowed their heads as the raths of the mahamandaleshwars rolled past. Bengali pilgrims welcomed the saints with their own special ululations; others shouted 'Victory to the eternal dharma, long live the sadhus!'

When the road started to slope down towards the Ganges, the naked nagas broke ranks and ran shrieking with joy into the Sangam. They splashed each other like children playing and rubbed the sacred water into their bodies, but they didn't stay in long. Their robed colleagues followed, many of them wearing just the shorts which serve as underpants. The crowds again broke through the barriers, and it was soon impossible to see who were sadhus and who were not. One of the naked drum majors danced ferociously – it was a miracle that no one was hit by his stave. A young sadhu forced his way through the crowd, leading my 89-year-old friend Mahant Brij Kumar. This venerable old man stood up to his waist in the muddy river and poured water over his chest, smiling beatifically. A man and his wife pleaded with my police sergeant to look after their son so that they could bathe. 'He's ill, he's ill,' they implored. 'We want to take a bathe to make him better.' But the sergeant refused to take charge of the boy. In that crowd there was no knowing when or where the parents would emerge, and the sergeant could well have been landed with responsibility for taking their son to the Congress Party's lost-and-found bureau.

By this stage we were having the greatest difficulty in keeping out of the water, so the sergeant suggested we beat a retreat to the police watch-tower to get a safer view of the bathing.

The watch-tower was surrounded by pilgrims trying to hand in notices about their lost relatives, to be broadcast over the loudspeaker. We pushed through them only to find our way blocked by a police lady sitting firmly on the middle of the ladder leading to the first platform of the two-tiered tower. 'It's dangerous,' she said. 'There are too many people up there already. You can't come up.' My sergeant insisted, and she let us edge past her. The tower shook ominously as we scrambled on to the lower platform.

Across the Ganges, the sun had just risen. It was shrouded by the morning mist rising from the rivers and the dust thrown up by millions of pilgrims who had spread like a black cloud covering all the banks of the rivers. It was impossible even to guess how many millions there were. An armada of small craft was ferrying the more privileged pilgrims to bathe from the boats anchored in the middle of the Sangam. Below, the police were still struggling to clear the area reserved for the akharas. The last of the Niranjanis were making their way back to reform their procession. The police horses were called in again, and the crowds were forced to give way.

Sweepers cleaned the ghat in preparation for the Juna akhara, whose naked nagas were already approaching. When the nagas saw the cameramen on the watch-tower, they stopped, brandishing their weapons and roared, 'No photographs!' All the cameras were lowered with alacrity – none of the press fancied withstanding an attack by those ferocious holy men. Some nagas ran straight into the Ganges; others crouched to ease themselves before entering the sacred water. There must have been at least 500 of them. Their bodies were smeared with ash, their long hair was matted and their beards were unkempt. One elderly naga's beard came down to his ankles. They were followed by the initiates, with their skimpy loincloths and shaven heads. Then came the mahamandaleshwars, sitting under their gold-embroidered parasols. They descended from their raths, solemnly disrobed and went down to the river with their disciples. This time the police managed to keep the crowds behind the barriers. The nagas ran back from the Sangam whooping with joy and cartwheeling on the hard sand. The initiates came back shivering – they had not yet mastered the yogic skills to keep themselves warm. The mahamandaleshwars returned to their raths, and the procession moved off again. Some disciples struggled to pull their master's rath up the hill. The police allowed the crowd to break through to help them on their way.

The Juna akhara should have been followed by the Vaishnavites, but I heard over the police radio that they would not be coming. Apparently the deputy inspector general of police had failed to resolve their electoral dispute and so they could not agree who was to be given pride of place in their procession.

I made my way back to the press camp with the pilgrims who had bathed and were on their way home. I had never been in such a peaceful crowd. There was no frenzy, just the calm certainty of faith: the knowledge that what had to be done had been done.

The vast majority of the pilgrims were villagers. Their faith gave them the courage to ignore the ugly rumours and the fortitude to travel in overcrowded trains and buses, to walk for many miles and to sleep in the open. Yet the villagers are being told that their faith, which means so much to them, is superstition, and that they must be secular. The élite for the most part ignored the Kumbh Mela, but those who did come travelled in cars and slept in tents.

Two days later I went back to the commissioner's tent. He told me that 27 million people had bathed during the previous three days. I was not entirely convinced that the methods he had used to count the pilgrims were scientific, but even the querulous local press said that millions had eventually turned up. The commissioner admitted that he had been worried at one stage. Looking back on the Mela, he said, 'The press and some politicians were on at me about overspending, and the Mela did seem to be rather empty when you arrived. I should have realized that there was an unusually long gap between the first two bathing-days and the big one, so the momentum was bound to die down.'

'What about the BBC, then?' I asked.

The commissioner smiled. 'Perhaps your coming stopped that. Actually, I now think it was just part of the campaign to discredit me.'

There was only one serious accident within the Mela during the bathe and that was caused by the family of one of Rajiv Gandhi's ministers, Mrs Rajendra Kumari Bajpai, who, with her son Ashok, controlled the Congress Party in Allahabad. The police had arranged separate embarkation and disembarkation jetties for the pilgrims who were allowed to travel by boat to the Sangam. They knew that if boats returned full to the embarkation jetties they would be swamped by waiting pilgrims. The Bajpai family, however, insisted on returning to the jetty they had set out from, and the very accident the police had feared occurred. One of their boats was swamped by pilgrims and capsized. Two of their servants were drowned.

No other country in the world could provide a spectacle like the Kumbh Mela. It was a triumph for the much maligned Indian administrators, but it was a greater triumph for the people of India. And how did the English-language press react to this triumph? Inevitably, with scorn. The *Times of India*, the country's most influential paper, published a long article replete with phrases like 'Obscurantism ruled the roost in Kumbh', 'Religious dogma overwhelmed reason at the Kumbh', and 'The Kumbh after all remained a mere spectacle with its million hues but little substance.' The *Times of India* criticized the Vishwa Hindu Parishad's politics, but made no attempt to analyse or even to describe the piety of the millions who bathed at the Sangam.

I spent my last evening in Allahabad discussing politics and religion with Sant Bax Singh. His seven years in England and his Oxford education have not turned him into a brown sahib. That night he was wearing his usual crumpled kurta and pajamas lacking any suggestion of shape or fashion. The small room in which we sat was sparsely furnished, undecorated and badly lit. We drank Indian whisky, although many would have expected the son of a feudal landlord, a raja, to drink Scotch. Sant Bax's English is perfect, but he frequently broke into Hindi, which was not too easy to understand through his pan-filled mouth. He tutted irritably when I suggested that the millions who had attended the Mela and the speeches they had heard might justify the élite's fear of a revival of Hindu fundamentalism.

'Look, you know perfectly well that the vast majority of those who have bathed at the Sangam will go away and vote for secular parties like the Congress or my brother's Janata Dal, so where is the question of a threat to secularism? Actually, this debate about secularism is a Western debate, because in your part of the world religion blocked reason and science. Debates here have never been religion versus non-religion – that has been brought here by you. As far as we are concerned, as Mao said, "Let a hundred flowers bloom." '

'Would you say', I asked somewhat tentatively, 'that bathing in the Ganges is like a sacrament – an outward and visible sign of an inward and spiritual grace.'

Sant Bax chuckled. 'That sounds like the *Book of Common Prayer*.'

'The catechism,' I replied.

'Well, we don't have a catechism, Creed, prayer-book or Bible, but I would basically agree with your definition. The needs of an Indian, or any human being, are the material plus something else. For the pilgrims, the Ganges washes away all sins; Krishna lived on the banks of the Jamuna and made the greatest love ever made; beyond both sin and love is wisdom, and that is what the invisible River Saraswati represents. All this they have at the Mela. A bathe fulfils an inner need without the need of a psychoanalyst, so why shouldn't they bathe? There is no clash with modernists or scientists unless they themselves are fundamentalist and say, "If you don't subscribe to us totally you are a heretic." After all, how did those millions of people bathing on one day hold up India's progress? If they weren't doing this, what should they have done towards industrialization or fulfilling World Bank targets? The trouble is that these so-called enlightened people talk about a person's belief and then condemn the chappie but suggest nothing to replace those beliefs.'

That is the danger of aggressive secularism. It is a barren creed which can cause great offence to religious people. If secularism leads Indians to think their rulers are, in the words of that speaker at the Vishwa Hindu Parishad meeting, ‘ashamed to call themselves Hindus’, the villagers will start to support communal parties. Khomeini was a backlash against the Westernized shah of Iran.

— 4 —

THE REWRITING OF THE *RAMAYAN*

What is the recipe for a successful television series in India? Apparently you take a story which everybody knows, so that there is no suspense. You remove any hint of sex and reduce violence to electronic gimmicks acceptable in a video parlour for nursery children. You slow the story down to a crawl. You use archaic language which the actors even find difficult to speak, let alone the audience to understand. You deliberately choose unknown actors, although India is a country where the star system is very much alive and kicking. These were some of the principles which guided Ramanand Sagar and four of his five sons when they set out to write, produce and direct the great Hindu epic the *Ramayan* for television. Over seventy-eight weeks in 1987–8 they showed the trials and tribulations that the god-king Ram faced to rescue his wife Sita from Ravan, the ruler of Lanka.

This television phenomenon, as it was to turn out to be, was produced in the Vrindavan Studios near the small town of Umargaon on the west coast. The studios – half-finished concrete buildings – face the sea, separated from the beach by a windbreak of conifers and a strip of green turf. Umargaon is about four hours' drive from Bombay, the film capital of India and home of the Sagars. They chose this remote site to be away from the pressures of Bombay, particularly the crowds and the VIP visitors. They did not install a telephone, so secretaries of VIPs were unable to ring up to inform them that 'Shri so and so, MP for such and such, will be visiting your studio at a certain time. Please ensure suitable reception and that he meets all important actors and actresses.' Another advantage of the location is that, once there, the cast has to stay: there is no way that they can put in a couple of hours on the *Ramayan* set and then go off to work on another film, as is the custom in Bombay, where a star can be contracted to appear in as many as thirty films at the same time.

In two days at the Umargaon studios I had plenty of time to discuss the apparent commercial nonsense of the decisions Ramanand Sagar had taken. Walking around the studios, Subash, the son who was in charge of production, said, 'We chose unknown actors because we wanted people to think of them as the gods. We didn't want people saying, "That's Amitabh Bacchan, that's Dharmendra, that's Mandakani." ' Over a vegetarian lunch – only vegetarian food was served in the studio canteen during the shooting – I met Moti Sagar, Ramanand's youngest son and one of his co-directors. He explained to me the language of his father's *Ramayan*.

'It is deliberately written in an epic style. If it had been colloquial, the impact would have been lost. These are gods you know, and not human beings.'

When it came to violence, the Sagars relied on crude electronic tricks, especially in the great battle between the armies of Ram and Ravan, which turned into nothing more than a video comic. The protagonists never came near each other – they shot electronic arrows sparking like fireworks and sending out highly coloured rays. After protracted flights, the arrows would collide in mid air, spit at each other and then return to their quivers. When the time eventually came for someone to die, his enemy's arrows would slowly dismember him. An arm might be sliced off first – the viewer would see the whole limb flying away. Then perhaps another arm would soar into the sky, then the head, then the torso. Moti Sagar was not apologetic about this.

'There again, don't you see, we couldn't have the gods behaving like ordinary Hindi film actors. All that disham disham, that crude violence with people kicking each other in the crotch, punching them and throwing them over their shoulders. This had to be something quite different.'

'But were you confident that the audience would want to see something as essentially unreal as your violence?'

'We were, but we knew that we would be attacked by the élite. After all, the *Ramayan* is about everything that the élite doesn't like, considers awful – religion, superstition, women obeying their husbands, dynastic rule.'

The Sagars' judgement proved right. The popularity of the *Ramayan* itself became legendary. At first I thought it was just an attempt to imitate Hindi movie versions of the epic on television. Ram struck me as sickly and Sita as simpering. But after a few episodes the taxi-drivers from the rank opposite my house would knock on the door every Sunday morning to ask if they could watch the *Ramayan*. They had never asked to see any other television programme, and their enthusiasm made me take it more seriously. I became a fan – to the disgust of almost all my friends, because of course it's fashionable to rubbish the Sagars' *Ramayan*.

Then reports started appearing in the press about the impact of the series. An electricity substation was burnt down by viewers enraged that a power cut had robbed them of one episode. New cabinet ministers asked for their swearing-in ceremony to be delayed so that they could watch the *Ramayan*. As one cynic said, 'The last thing a politician would normally do is to delay his swearing-in, for fear that the PM might change his mind.' A bride was missing at the auspicious time for her wedding, because it clashed with the *Ramayan*. (History does not relate whether the pandit who had set the time relented and conducted the wedding ceremony after that week's episode was over.) A councillor in Maharashtra suggested that the municipality should hold a special condolence meeting to mourn the death of Ravan, the king of Lanka. The wife of a senior Indian bureaucrat told me that one of India's great transcontinental expresses she was travelling on was delayed while the passengers and crew sat on the platform at Gwalior watching the *Ramayan* on the station's television monitors. A cooperative society of women who make poppadams took out half-page advertisements in the national press when the *Ramayan* ended, saying,

For seventy-seven weeks, Sunday mornings of great many families were adorned with the atmosphere of *Ramayana*, brought alive by the galaxy of mythological characters, reliving the times millenniums back. Here is a day to say goodbye, to that blissful nearness. Yes, that immortal world will no more be before our eyes. But down the memory lane this world will accompany us with all its splendour and shine.

Like so many other great epics, the origins of the *Ramayan*, or *Ramayana*, are obscure. It is generally accepted that it was composed some time between 1500 and 200 BC, giving a wide margin for error. Its author is believed to have been the sage Valmiki, who was inspired by the god Brahma. Valmiki's was the first of many *Ramayans*. The author R. K. Narayan, in the introduction to his own English version, *The Ramayana Retold*, says the epic has been 'the largest source of inspiration to the poets of India throughout the centuries. India is a land of many languages, each predominant in a particular area, and in each one of them a version of the *Ramayana* is available, original and brilliant, and appealing to millions of readers who know the language.' R. K. Narayan also says, 'I am prepared to state that almost every individual . . . living in India is aware of the story of the *Ramayana* in some measure or other. Everyone of whatever age, outlook, or station in life, knows the essential part of the epic and adores the main figures in it – Rama and Sita.'

The *Ramayan* is the story of the eldest son of the king of Ayodhya. He goes into exile voluntarily with his wife Sita and his brother Lakshman because the king has promised the throne to Bharat, the son of his second wife. Ram accepts this without any ill will. During their exile in the forest, Ravan, the king of Lanka, disguises himself as a hermit and kidnaps Sita. Ram and Lakshman, with the help of the monkey-god Hanuman and an army of monkeys who build a bridge across the sea to Lanka, defeat Ravan and his army of demons. Sita is rescued, but her troubles are not over: she has to pass an ordeal of fire to prove that she has remained faithful to Ram. Eventually Ram returns in triumph to Ayodhya, where his younger brother, who has never ascended the throne, welcomes him.

The story of what happens after Ram ascends the throne is not normally included in traditional performances of the epic, and some scholars have questioned its authenticity. In this final section, Ram is disturbed by reports that his subjects have not accepted the return of Sita. They say that she was defiled during her captivity in Lanka. Ram sends her into exile, where she bears him twin sons, Lav and Kush. Years later, Ram and Sita meet in the forest and he tries to persuade her to return, as she has now proved her chastity beyond doubt. Sita refuses and calls on her mother, the earth, to swallow her up. This last story was not originally scheduled to be included in the television *Ramayan*, but India was so upset when the epic came to an end that the government asked Ramanand Sagar to start work on Sita's second exile. This was in production when I visited the Vrindavan Studios in October 1988.

For centuries, Ram has been seen as the ideal man, and Sita as the ideal woman. In the introduction to his translation *Eternal Ramayana – the Ramayana of Tulsi Das*, published in 1883, F. S. Growse, a member of the British Indian Civil Service, wrote, 'All may admire, though they refuse to worship . . . the affectionate devotion of Sita, that paragon of all wife-like virtues; and the purity, meekness, generosity, and self-sacrifice of Rama, the model son, husband, and brother, "the guileless king, high, self-contained, and passionless," the Arthur of Indian chivalry.' Ram is believed to be one of the ten incarnations of the god Vishnu, and Ram Rajya – Ram's rule – is always talked of as the golden age of India. Each year, in the Dussehra festival, the defeat of Ravan is celebrated as the triumph of good over evil, and in countless towns and villages the story of the *Ramayan* is staged in what are known as Ram Lilas. Lessons relevant to contemporary life are drawn from the events depicted in these performances, and so the *Ramayan* is being continually adapted. Yet intellectuals have asked angrily, 'How dare Ramanand Sagar write his own *Ramayan*?'

Ramanand Sagar certainly has written his own *Ramayan*. He has based it on Valmiki and Tulsi Das, but it is very much his own. I watched him in the small room which serves as his bedroom and study in the Umargaon studios, working on the script for the evening's shoot. 'Each person who wrote the *Ramayan* had his social exigencies to cope with,' he said. 'In the time of Tulsi Das, the worshippers of Vishnu and Shiva were fighting and so Tulsi Das had the two gods worshipping each other. I have also tried to bring in our times. You see, when the people of Ayodhya tell Ram's half-brother Bharat that they want him to be king, he says, "A month ago you chose Ram, now you have accepted that he should go into exile and have chosen me." The lesson I have drawn is that it's a great privilege to have the vote, but the vote must be safeguarded – otherwise people will have kings foisted on them by palace intrigues.'

I asked Ramanand Sagar whether this was a reference to Rajiv Gandhi's succession. His mother, Indira Gandhi, was often said to have presided over a darbar or court. Ramanand Sagar laughed and said, 'I'll leave you to work that one out.'

Some of the fiercest critics of Sagar's *Ramayan* have been the feminists, who have accused him of portraying Sita as being meek and submissive – the very qualities which they say have led to the plight of Indian women. Two feminists, Kamla Bhasin and Ritu Menon wrote in the February 1988 issue of the magazine *Seminar*:

> Eternal mythologies like the *Ramayan* are revived and popularised via state controlled media at the mass 'entertainment' level, and the negative values they convey regarding women find more than adequate reflection in textbooks and children's literature at the 'education' level. With Sita as our ideal, can sati [widow-burning] be far behind? It is this overarching ideology of male superiority and female dispensability that sanctions sati and leads to its glorification, and accepts the silent violence against women that rages in practically every home across the country.

That statement, suggesting that raging violence is tolerated in practically every home, is surely an insult to Indian women.

When I was in Umargaon, Ramanand Sagar was wrestling with feminist problems in the last section of the *Ramayan*. He was thinking of placating the feminists by making Sita take the decision to go into exile herself.

'Sita notices that Ram can't take any decision, and so she asks him what is wrong. He replies that people are saying that she is not pure. She tells him that the people are fools, but Ram says, "They are our people." Then Sita says, "I will not stay and bring disrespect on this great family." Ram's brother Lakshman then tries to pacify her by saying, "We will cut their tongues out." So Sita then replies, "That's the men's way of doing things. We have ways of making people feel ashamed so that there is a permanent change in them." Eventually, after her exile, the people of Ayodhya go out and beg her to come back. She tells them, "You do not deserve me," and asks Mother Earth to swallow her up. So she is the winner, not the loser as the feminists seem to think.'

Ramanand Sagar has certainly not turned Sita or any of Ravan's wives into sex objects. I don't know what the feminists would have said if he had stuck more closely to Valmiki's description of Ravan's court:

On opulent carpets sprawled
Hundreds of ravishing women
In colourful dresses, drowsed
With wine-drinking
And with love-making . . .
Jewels scattered
During dancing and drinking –
Dresses crushed,
Deprived of earrings,
Like overburdened mares
Hastily disburdened . . .

Ravan lay, savouring
The sugar-wine breath
Of his wives; some, in stupor,
Kissed the lips of co-wives
Again and again,
Thinking they were Ravan's;
And the co-wives, passionately
In love with Ravan,
Returned the kisses, imagining
They were kissing their lord.

It's also highly unlikely that such scenes would have passed the censor.

Ramanand Sagar always refuses to accept the credit for his *Ramayan*. He told me, 'I have no credit. All credit goes to Hanuman – he could have picked up any other person like me and told him to do this.' Whatever the divine inspiration, there is no doubt that the human agent for the television triumph is Ramanand Sagar. The small, stout, bald, Pickwickian figure does all the writing and much of the directing, and supervises the editing and the production. That is no mean achievement for a man of seventy-one. He rules the studio with a kind but firm hand – everyone calls him 'Pappaji' or 'Daddy', and he calls all the cast by their epic names.

The critics write off Ramanand Sagar as a failed Bombay film-producer, but he has many successes to his name. His family had at one stage amassed a fortune in Kashmir. His son Moti said, 'My great-grandfather's children used to skim coins across Dal Lake like other boys skimmed stones.' But then there was a family row, and Ramanand Sagar's own father was left with nothing. When he died, his wife and the young Ramanand went to live with her parents in Lahore, where Ramanand was educated. His grandparents found a girl for him to marry but reneged on the deal when they learnt of another candidate who would bring a larger dowry. Ramanand apparently refused to break off the original engagement and was thrown out of the house. The future film mogul earned a living selling soap by the roadside and cleaning cars. He caught tuberculosis and spent a year in a sanatorium in Kashmir, where he wrote a diary which was serialized in a Lahore literary magazine and made his name as a writer. When he came out of the sanatorium, he got a job as a journalist and built himself a comparatively prosperous life.

That all disappeared with partition, when Lahore became part of Pakistan. Ramanand Sagar fled to India, where he eventually made his way to Bombay to start another literary career. He wrote a much praised novel about the brutality of partition, called *Aur Insan Mar Gaya* ('And Humanity Died'), and a play which led on to the script for the first hit by Raj Kapoor, who was to earn the title of 'the Great Showman' and dominate the Bombay film industry for nearly thirty years. Ramanand Sagar became a film-producer too. As he said to me, 'I have had some of the biggest hits, and some of the biggest flops.' It has to be admitted that his last two films fell into the latter category. But that's all behind him now. He told me, 'I won't make any more commercial films now.

I will continue to do devotional work. The next project may well be the life of Lord Krishna.'

When I arrived at the studio, Pappaji was directing an outside scene – Ram seated on a chariot with Sita beside him, driving in triumph through the streets of Ayodha. One of Ram's brothers sat opposite, and the other two stood behind him. Squatting on his haunches on the front of the chariot was the giant figure of Hanuman, the monkey-god. The chariot was pulled by two reluctant and distinctly seedy ponies. Their rich caparison did not hide their humble origins – they were local tonga or trap ponies. Some of the soldiers of Ayodhya had to push the chariot from behind, to keep the royal party rolling steadily forward. Ahead of the chariot rode a few villagers on ponies with lances in their hands – the household cavalry of Ayodhya. The shot showed Ram passing a large pillared building whose steps were crowded with beautiful maidens throwing marigold flowers over the royal couple. On the other side of the street, young men mingled with soldiers shouting, '*Raja Ramchandra ki jai*' – 'Long live King Ram Chandra!'

Subash Sagar said to me, 'You see the costumes? They are all made out of silk. There was a lot of gold around in those days, so we have to make everyone look very splendid.' Ram was dressed in a brilliant yellow dhoti with a red embroidered border. Strings of pearls hung over his bare chest, and on his head he wore a pointed gold crown which from a distance seemed to be shaped like a bishop's mitre. The crown was, I think, made of papier mâché, but it glittered in the bright lights. Sita's sari was pink with a silver border. Her head was covered with a matching long, pink headscarf or dupatta, embroidered with silver. The soldiers' uniforms were purple and gold, and the citizens of Ayodhya were in their brightest and best.

All this magnificence was hidden from Ramanand Sagar himself, who was sitting inside a thatched hut directing from a monitor screen. His directions were relayed by a number of strategically placed loudspeakers. 'Give Sita some reflector.' 'Lakshman, are you ready? Did Lakshman hear?' A voice came back from the set: 'Lakshman is eating a biscuit.' Ramanand Sagar again: 'Look,

Hanuman is happy. Stay happy, Hanuman!' I don't know how anyone could have been happy crouched in the uncomfortable position that Hanuman was in. 'Roll camera. Throw flowers. Move chariot. Come on – get hold of those ponies, move the chariot.'

The cameraman, who had once worked in the news department of the government-controlled television, filmed all this from a high platform sheltered from the sun by a black umbrella.

The chariot was the main problem. The red and gold velvet parasol covering Ram and Sita kept getting caught in the branches of a banyan tree. When the chariot did move, it went so slowly and steadily, in spite of its creaking axles, that no impression of movement showed in the close-ups. Ramanand Sagar ordered a platoon of the Ayodhya army to shake it up and down. Ram and Sita obligingly bounced on their seats.

For all the splendour of the scene, a measure of economy was exercised. The extras and some sweepers picked up the marigold flowers between takes, for reuse. The set which was now Ayodhya had not so long ago been Ravan's capital, Lanka. The maidens came from Surat, the nearest sizeable city, because they were cheaper than Bombay film extras.

Madhu Jain, one of India's most sensitive journalists, wrote off Ramanand Sagar's *Ramayan* as 'moving calendar art pictures'. There is truth in her criticism. The Ram I saw resembled the stereotyped deities pictured on the gaudy calendars that hang in almost every shop in India. Sagar argues that that's how people see their gods. He told Madhu Jain, 'Transporting everyone to that golden age, I have brought the college boy from the disco culture to the *Ramayan*. College boys don't say "Hi" any more, they say "*Jai Shri Ram ki*" – "Long live Shri Ram." ' Madhu Jain didn't quarrel with that. Nor did she quarrel with Ramanand Sagar when he said, '*Ramayan* has achieved national integration. Young people in the south started learning Hindi to be able to understand the dialogues.' The venerable Calcutta daily the *Statesman*, in an editorial, described the acting in Ramanand Sagar's *Ramayan* as 'barely adequate' and the technical aspects of the production as 'nothing less than shoddy'; nevertheless, the paper could not deny the popularity of the serial and ended its editorial by saying, 'Ultimately it was the victory of good over evil, perhaps a message which has both appeal and relevance in the contemporary context.' To me, it would certainly seem to have relevance in a country which has become as cynical about its politics as India.

Later that day I saw the trouble that Ramanand Sagar had taken with at least some aspects of his production. He had moved into the main studio, which had been transformed into Ram's court. Vashisht, who had been the royal family's guru for the last forty generations, was addressing the king. Because the script was written day by day, Sudhir Dehlvi, the actor playing Vashisht, had not had time to learn his lines properly, so they were written down by hand in large letters and held up by a technician, a human teleprompter, sufficiently far away to be out of shot but sufficiently near for Vashisht to read. Even then he had a great deal of difficulty with the archaic language of his speech. After five or six attempts the reverend figure, clad in a saffron robe, muttered through his silver beard, 'These words are driving me crazy, they're so difficult.' But Ramanand Sagar would not let him give up – he told the guru, 'You are a great scholar, and the people can't see a great scholar mispronouncing even one word.'

Ramanand Sagar had told me that his *Ramayan* was relevant to today. Certainly there were parts of Vashisht's speech and Ram's reply which were relevant to modern Indian political life. Vashisht told the king that his family had survived in power for so many generations only because they had retained the confidence and loyalty of their people. Speaking of the former heads of the dynasty, Vashisht said, 'They ruled not because it was their right to rule, but because they were the servants of their people. You must give your people confidence that you too will live up to the noble traditions handed down by your forefathers – the traditions of courage and fortitude, of devotion to the path of duty set for you by our religion, of austerity and, if it should be required of you, of sacrifice.'

Modern India has seen the birth of many dynasties. At the top, of course, there is the dynasty founded by Motilal Nehru, Rajiv

Gandhi's great-grandfather; but at other levels too sons move in with their fathers as if they were joining the family business. In fact one of the most common complaints you hear in India is that politics has become a business. Very few Indian politicians now remember the lesson which Vashisht taught Ram and which Mahatma Gandhi tried to teach his contemporaries: the lesson that the people of India like their leaders to be austere. Ram, in his reply to the guru, said, 'To become a king means to become a sannyasi, an ascetic. Nothing remains that is the king's. Everything belongs to the people, to the nation. He who cannot sacrifice everything for his country has no right to ascend the throne as king.' Yet all too often nowadays the Indian politician adopts the attitude that everything which belongs to the state belongs to him.

Minor kings, ministers, army officers and Ram's colleagues from the war sat below the throne, looking like calendar gods too. Jamvan the bear, who was one of the generals of Ram's army, was clearly uncomfortable in the heat of the arc lights. He scratched at the furry costume which covered him from head to foot. During breaks, he took off his claws and sipped water through a straw, unable to get a glass to his lips.

Ramanand Sagar did lose his patience with one of the minor kings who had to make a speech asking Ram to accept the offerings brought to him by all the other rulers who had offered to join him in the battle against Ravan. The elderly actor, who had been waiting all evening for his brief moment of glory, stood up, puffed out his chest and delivered his words. Clearly not satisfied with the impact, he asked the director, 'Shall I make my speech with more dignity, because after all I am a senior member of the court?'

Ramanand Sagar replied, 'Make it how you like, but stop swaying around the place.'

It was nearly midnight when Hanuman the monkey-god made his appearance. Dara Singh, the six feet two and a half inches tall former world heavyweight wrestling champion who plays Hanuman, is, at fifty-nine, still in splendid condition. He needs to be because, as Dara Singh explained to me, 'Hanuman is a working god.' In the *Ramayan*, he lifts up a Himalayan mountain, leaps across the Straits of Palk to Lanka and sets fire to Ravan's capital with his tail. In 'real life', Hanuman is perhaps the most popular god in northern India. He is powerful and accessible – the ideal god to go to if you are in trouble. An actor less impressive than Dara Singh could never have played the role. In 1957 Dara Singh filled the Albert Hall in a world championship bout with Lou Thesz of the USA, although he admits that half the spectators were Indians. He learnt to wrestle in the traditional mud and clay pits of Punjab, turning professional when he went to Singapore, where some of his family were in business. His career as a professional wrestler lasted for thirty years. While he was in training, he ate enormous quantities of chicken, milk, almonds and ghi. At that time he weighed 250 pounds. Now he eats less and is down to 230 pounds, keeping himself trim with yoga, but he still advertises his favourite Punjabi 'Milkfood' ghi on television.

Dara Singh told me that his acting career began when he was approached to play the title role in a Hindi film called *King Kong*. Despite its name, this was inspired by Tarzan and was about 'a man of the jungle'. He was reluctant and told the producers that he was shy and couldn't act. They replied, 'Never mind acting – we want your strength and fight.' Since then, Dara Singh has starred in 110 pictures, playing roles like Hercules, Samson (as whom he wrestled with elephants) and Alexander the Great.

Ramanand Sagar had made the most of the ex-champion's physique, dressing his Hanuman in just a scarlet and saffron loincloth, an armlet, several necklaces, large gold earrings and a gold crown. A tail like a bent pipecleaner strapped on his back and clay protuberances on his nose and both lips produced the required simian appearance.

That evening Hanuman had to bow low before Ram and Sita, who were presenting him with a pearl necklace for the invaluable assistance he had given in the battle against Ravan. With tears in his eyes, he told them he would rather have the divine royal couple living in his heart. Ramanand Sagar insisted on retake after retake. During each break, the make-up man wiped the sweat off the wrestler's torso and adjusted the protuberances on his nose and lips which had slipped out of position. Eventually Dara Singh, who had been crouching in extreme discomfort for over an hour, gave up, saying, 'I've dried.' The director called a halt, and we all left the studio for a nightcap. It was by then forty minutes past midnight, and Ramanand Sagar had still not written the script for the next day.

Over a glass of whisky I asked Dara Singh how the public reacted to him now that he was identified with the popular god Hanuman. He said, 'I have added more fans. Religious people never see feature films, but they have seen *Ramayan*.'

'Do people actually think of you as a god?'

'So many innocent people have seen pictures of Hanuman that when they see you in that dress they really feel it. They touch your feet and they want blessings. In the name of God I give them blessings, but not as a person.'

In spite of his success, Dara Singh is still a modest man with a trace of that shyness which made him a reluctant actor. But when he relaxes he is excellent company. I asked him, 'What about the élite? What do they think?'

'Oh, the élite. They never mix with the innocent people who live in the villages – that is Indian culture. The élite are Western, and they don't meet the villagers.'

'You are strictly speaking not a Hindu, because your family are Sikhs. What do Sikhs think about Hanuman and the *Ramayan*?'

'There was some trouble in Punjab when the Sikh extremists threatened villagers that they would be killed if they watched the *Ramayan*. They stopped for a bit, but after one or two weeks they were watching again.'

Earlier I had asked Deepika, who plays Sita, how the public reacted to her. She replied, 'People definitely treat us differently – not like other film artistes. They feel that anyone from *Ramayan* is someone from outside. They look on us as a god or goddess. At functions, really grown-up people come and touch your feet.'

Deepika, in true film-star tradition, wouldn't reveal her age, but I would guess she was little more than twenty-two. Playing Sita was her first big break, but some film magazines have said she will never be able to play any other role because she will always be seen as the wife of Lord Ram. Sita said she had already had other offers of roles, but she was being choosy. 'I'd of course like to be one of the most successful actresses in Bombay, but I'd like to be something different – not the typical heroine.' Perhaps that's a wise ambition, since Deepika is a little too squarely built for the modern Bombay heroine.

I think the greatest success of Ramanand Sagar's *Ramayan* was Ravan – he was certainly my favourite character. His walrus moustache, his bloodshot eyes and his pot belly made him all too human – especially in comparison with the overdone divinity of Ram. When Ravan ranted against Ram in his magnificent bass voice, he was every inch a furious and frustrated ruler. He also inspired sympathy, especially in the scene where he refused to accept that his favourite son, Inderjit, had been killed in battle. Arvind Trivedi, who played Ravan, is a mild, middle-aged man who lives in a small flat in an unfashionable suburb of Bombay. His life has none of the glamour of the film star – in fact he is proud of not being one. He told me, 'I have done more than 10,000 performances on the stage, because you see I have my own Gujarati-language theatre company in Bombay. That's how I make my living. Of course I had acted in films and television before, but I am basically a man of the theatre.'

Trivedi had worked with Ramanand Sagar before, and so he approached him for a part in the *Ramayan* – the small part of the boatman who ferried Ram across a river. He asked about this role twice. The second time, Ramanand Sagar said, 'Let's see – there are other roles.' But Trivedi decided not to mention the matter again – after all, he had his pride. Then, out of the blue, he was summoned to Umargaon from Ahmedabad, where he was filming. When he reached Bombay airport, there was a car waiting for him. 'I was surprised', he said to me, 'they had sent a car for such a small part – just a boatman. But when I arrived at the studio I was told to make up for Ravan. When I got to the dressing-room, there were already ten fully got-up Ravans there. I was given a dialogue. It's not difficult for me to learn dialogue, because of my stage experience. I was the last man in, and when Ramanand

Sagar saw me he shouted, "My Ravan is selected!" I said, "But let me say my lines." Sagar refused to listen to them. He said, "I know your talent. I just wanted to see what you look like in this costume." '

Trivedi had great sympathy for Ravan. He said, 'Ravan is a hero – more than a hero, more powerful than a hero – but he didn't have any good guru and it is very difficult to digest power. Ram had Vashisht. Anyhow, you may not know that Ravan had a very good reason for stealing Sita. It was to revenge his sister, who had fallen in love with Ram and his brother and wanted to marry one of them. The brother cut off her ears and nose. Even a small man wouldn't suffer that, so how could I?'

'But didn't Ravan realize he was going to be defeated because Ram had Hanuman on his side?'

'Ravan is a brave man. Once he has spoken, he sticks to it – even if it is a mistake. He is conscious of what people will say if he shows weakness. He never says he has done the right thing by taking Sita. He says to himself, "I may have done the wrong thing, but I will not go back on my decision." He knows Ram is stronger than him, but he thinks, "If I kill Ram I will be famous, and if I die by him I will also be famous." '

Trivedi must be the first actor to have made Ravan universally popular. When it was clear that the end was near, groups of women descended on Umargaon to plead for Ravan's life. According to Trivedi, 2,000 people turned up at Heathrow Airport to welcome him when he arrived on a visit to Britain. In the holy city of Ujjain in central India, a woman asked him to bless her child. She said, 'I have called him Lankesh, the lord of Lanka.' Although Ravan had been dead for three months, Trivedi was still receiving fan mail – hundreds of letters a day. I was struck by one from a Christian woman from southern India:

My father who is 82 years of age was not watching TV. But after the episode in which he heard your voice he started watching *Ramayan*, and after Ravan's death he stopped. Your acting was excellent and we were happy that you were a brave man. As for Ram, your traitor brother had to tell him all the secrets to concur [sic] you. So I can say you are greater than Ram.

May our Lord Jesus and Mother Mary Bless you and keep you Healthy and Happy,

Yours affectionately,

Mrs Philomena K.

The film critic Aruna Vasudev, who has written a history of the Indian film industry, once told me, 'You can no longer call India a secular country after the *Ramayan* has dinned home its Hindu message week after week.' But all the evidence suggests that the *Ramayan* was enjoyed by believers of all the religions in India. Mrs Philomena was of course a Christian, and Christians are a rather passive minority. The same certainly cannot be said about the Muslims: their leaders vie to outdo each other in their militancy, yet they did not create a controversy about the *Ramayan*. In fact, the *Ramayan* is the only even remotely sensitive television series which has not created a serious row, and there is plenty of evidence to suggest that many Muslims enjoyed the series.

I asked Bashir Khan, the Muslim actor who played one of the generals of the monkey army, whether he had been criticized for playing a role in a Hindi epic. He said, 'I did get some letters telling me that I had forgotten Allah, but most people approved. In fact my friends told me that they hadn't been interested in *Ramayan* until I played a role, and then they got interested.'

'But didn't Hindus object to a Muslim playing a role in *Ramayan*?'

'On the contrary, they are very pleased that a Muslim should accept playing the role of one of their lords.'

Ramanand Sagar has had many letters from Muslims, praising his production. One of them came from a lecturer in southern India, who wrote:

My Lord, please send me a recent photo of yours. I want to keep it in my house. You see how people cause bloodshed in the name of religion. The communal disturbances of Meerut, Delhi and other places are the mischief of politicians. To tell you, really common people have no time to think and quarrel in the name of religion. Ours is a prominently Muslim area . . . but on Sundays all Muslims, old, young and children, eagerly see *Ramayan*. My brother's wife is an illiterate lady. She is very orthodox. But she will never miss *Ramayan*. She wept like a child when

Dasarath [Ram's father] lamented the departure of Ram. Such is the impact of *Ramayan* on the minds of people, irrespective of religion . . . Your name will shine and shine like the morning star in horizon. God bless you. You live for hundreds of years as our sages lived and lift Hinduism to the top once again.

It must surely have been the gods of Hinduism who were responsible for the weekly miracle of *Ramayan* getting on the air. It was a production-line job, with one week allocated for each episode. During the first run of the series, each episode was shot from Monday to Thursday, edited on Friday and dispatched to Delhi perilously close to the transmission time of 9.30 on Sunday morning. For the last hour-long episode, which included a grand musical finale with Ramanand Sagar himself appearing as a heavenly figure, the cast shot for seventy-two hours continuously.

From what I saw, however, the production line started and stopped in the most erratic manner. I arrived on my second morning at the studios expecting to see Ramanand Sagar directing Ram in a continuation of the 'return to Ayodhya' sequence. There was no sign of life inside the studios or on the outside set. The door of Ram's small room was firmly padlocked. Eventually I was told that Ram had been allowed to go back to Bombay, since Ramanand Sagar had not managed to write the script for the day's shooting. That meant I missed my interview with Ram. I finally located the director sitting cross-legged under a banyan tree in front of a garlanded picture of the goddess Durga. Beside him stood a Brahmin reciting Sanskrit mantras for the first of the nine days of the festival of the goddess of destruction. A temple bell for summoning the goddess hung on a rope from a branch. Actors, technicians, cooks and cleaners stood in a semicircle around Ramanand Sagar. Although Durga was the consort of Shiva, the markings on the forehead of the Brahmin showed that he belonged to a sect which worshipped Vishnu. In Christianity that would be rather like asking a Protestant pastor to celebrate the Mass, but devotees of Shiva and Vishnu do not allow their differences to come between them. In this respect Hinduism is a generous and broadminded religion, as it is indeed in its attitude to other faiths.

Ramanand Sagar is a great believer in the efficacy of religious ceremonies. After the puja, or worship, he said to me, 'When you are in Delhi, you are living in certain snobby circles who are not with the people. They feel ashamed of going to a temple. They think you look archaic if you do that. There is nothing wrong with going to a temple.'

'But when you go to a temple or do puja like you have done today, and your prayers are not answered, don't you lose faith? There seems to be so much pessimism, gloom and depression in India these days. What are your gods doing about that?'

'I was at one stage depressed. I have now become optimistic that there is a future, otherwise the gods would not have made me make *Ramayan* and have made it produce such an impact. It's not a film success, it's devotion – in the same way that devotees of Mahatma Gandhi used to touch the rails after the train he was travelling in had passed.'

'But what difference is all this devotion going to make?'

'Well, the new generation will be devoted to the gods instead of all the irreligion you see nowadays.'

Ramanand Sagar's religious enthusiasm did not go down well with Bhaskar Ghose, the director-general of Doordarshan – Indian television. Ghose is a member of the élite Indian Administrative Service, but he is a civil servant with a difference. He is a talented theatre actor and director himself, and he took a personal interest in *Ramayan*. The first four episodes arrived well in advance of transmission. When Ghose saw them, he was horrified. He told me, 'There was far too much ritual and not nearly enough story. He had used the worst extras he could get, because he was doing it on the cheap. The infant Ram looked half-starved. Some of the dance sequences were ridiculous. When I told Sagar this, he was not amused. He said, "No one has ever spoken to me like this." But he did cut some of the ritual and dances, and marginally improved his extras.'

Ghose had his next row with Ramanand Sagar when it became clear that the story was not going to be completed in the fifty-two episodes Doordarshan had contracted for. By now the director knew he was on to a winner and had every reason for wanting to stretch the *Ramayan* as far as he could. 'He really had me by the short hairs,' Ghose admitted. 'He sent me each episode just two days before transmission, and so I couldn't control the pace.'

The director-general threatened to double the charge for broadcasting the programmes if Sagar didn't let him have them one month in advance, but Sagar's contract enabled him to get round that. Eventually Ghose granted an extension of twenty-six episodes on the understanding that the story would be complete by then. When it came to a further extension, to cover Sita's second exile, Ramanand Sagar went directly to the minister, who overruled the director-general and sanctioned yet another twenty-six weeks' worth of the epic.

In spite of the defeats he had suffered, Ghose had the honesty to admit to a sneaking admiration for Ramanand Sagar. 'By the end,' he told me, 'I came to rather like the old bean. His great success was that he presented the thing as a Ram Lila. If you see people when they are at a Ram Lila, no matter how rustic the performance is, they are rapt. You are really involved in the enactment – it's a kind of expiation of everything inside you. It doesn't matter how many times you see it. It's like reciting a mantra – the more times you say, "*Ram nam satya hai*" – "Ram's name is truth" – the more you are spiritually uplifted. In the villages, you can't say that the Ram Lila is entertainment, because entertainment is much more sophisticated than that nowadays. It's part of a ritual.'

It was not on artistic, or even religious, grounds that the minister of information and broadcasting, H. K. L. Bhagat, agreed to an extension of *Ramayan*. He took a political decision, realizing how unpopular he and the government would be if Sagar let it be known that he had refused to extend the programme. At the same time, the minister was determined to get as much mileage as he could out of the *Ramayan*'s success. The Indian government is facing what economists call an 'internal debt crisis', which, to put it more simply, means that it's chronically short of rupees. So, one way that Mr Bhagat could win points for himself was by raising more money from the *Ramayan*. This he did by sharply increasing the transmission charges.

The other main concern of Mr Bhagat – as of all politicians – was to win votes. Here a unique opportunity presented itself. At the height of the *Ramayan* fever, the Congress Party faced a series of by-elections. Rajiv Gandhi's reputation as a vote-winner was at a low ebb following a series of electoral reverses, so the prime minister's reputation as well as the party's was on the line. The most important by-election was in Allahabad, the home city of Motilal Nehru, the founder of the ruling dynasty. Allahabad had been represented by the prime minister's close friend the film superstar Amitabh Bacchan, but the opposition had linked Bacchan's brother's name with alleged scandals over international defence contracts. Although the opposition could prove nothing, Bacchan ended his brief political career so as not to be an embarrassment to Rajiv Gandhi.

The stakes in Allahabad had been upped by the opposition nominating Rajiv Gandhi's former defence and finance minister, V. P. Singh, as their candidate. He had resigned from the government and had then been expelled from the Congress Party because he didn't believe that the alleged defence scandals were being seriously investigated. V. P. Singh – who, incidentally, came from near Allahabad – had by the time of the by-election emerged as the potential prime minister most widely acceptable to the fractured opposition. He had to be stopped at all costs, thought Mr Bhagat and other senior Congress leaders. So Arun Govil, the Ram of the *Ramayan*, was wheeled out to speak on behalf of the party. But the magic of the *Ramayan* did not work: the Congress candidate was trounced. Film stars are normally very successful in Indian politics, but perhaps Ram's wife Sita had been right when she said to me, 'People definitely treat us differently – not like other film artistes.'

The advertising agents and their clients made no attempt to hide their motives for supporting Ramanand Sagar's divine extravaganza: they saw it as a heaven-sent opportunity to sell their products. Television in India is intended to be primarily a 'tool of development', but the government has allowed the medium to become almost exclusively middle-class, promoting a consumer society whose products most Indians can't afford to consume. The *Ramayan* was preceded by fifteen minutes of advertising. Lovely ladies washed their hair with expensive shampoo, young lovers cavorted hazardously on scooters, macho males advertised the latest suiting materials and smiling children guzzled instant noodles. Not only were the products beyond the range of most Indians, they were also for the most part alien to their lifestyle – the noodle-eating nuclear family instead of the traditional joint family; the woman immodestly flaunting her glossy shampooed hair; the suits so much less comfortable than the loose cotton clothes still worn in Indian villages.

The advertisers make no secret of the fact that they use television to target the middle classes. Colgate-Palmolive was one of the companies which sponsored the *Ramayan*. Its advertising account is handled by Santosh Ballal, of the agency Rediffusion. He told me that 80 per cent of the multinational's products in India were sold to the middle classes. Advertising agencies are not worried about the dangers of creating a demand for products that most people can't afford – of undermining traditions which still hold the lives of the poor together. 'We create the lifestyles, we create the aspirations. Whether the viewer achieves the aspirations is his problem, not mine,' says Ballal. It might be argued that a government and a party which claims to be socialist should care about the impact of advertisements – especially the advertisements before a programme so popular as the *Ramayan*.

For all Ramanand Sagar's insistence that his *Ramayan* is not a film success but a divine phenomenon, he too has not been above taking advantage of its success. When he was granted his extensions, he raised the price for the advertising sponsors who pay for the production. Santosh Ballal said, 'It was blackmail. The programmes became uneconomical, but we decided to continue because of their power.' In an office in a Bombay studio, Prem, another of Ramanand Sagar's sons, was launching video cassettes of the *Ramayan*. The cassettes are coloured saffron – the holy colour of Hinduism. There are twenty-six cassettes in the series, and each one has a different picture from the *Ramayan* on the front. The cassettes are imported from Singapore – always a strong selling point in India. Prem told me, 'We are making a quality product – purely quality-based – which people will want to buy for itself, so we can defeat the video pirates. They will never be able to bring out a cassette like this.'

When I asked whether the consumer might not prefer something cheaper, even if a little nastier, Prem Sagar replied, 'We believe that people will be buying these cassettes to keep, like they might buy the *Encyclopaedia Britannica*. They are not just buying a cassette: they are buying the *Ramayan*.'

'So it will be something like the family Bible used to be in our tradition.'

'Exactly.'

Along with the cassettes, Prem was also marketing the other by-products which accompany successful television programmes everywhere – books, calendars, pens, key-rings, stickers and all the rest. He would not say what sales he had achieved so far, nor what his target was – none of the Sagar family would give any details of the finances of the *Ramayan*. Rediffusion said the price they paid Sagar was 'a secret between the agency and its client'. The minister of information and broadcasting told Parliament that the sponsors had paid Doordarshan 10,350,000 rupees – that is, more than £2 million.

The Sagar family own a large share of the Natraj Studios where Prem has his office. Although Ramanand has said that he is going to restrict himself to devotional works in future, the studios are still open to all. When I went to meet Prem, a nightclub scene was being filmed on one of the floors. The singer was Mandakani, a star who shot to fame by bathing near the source of the Ganges in a flimsy white sari which left little to the imagination. In this nightclub, she was dressed in a clinging sequined dress and a platinum-blonde wig. Another disco number was being rehearsed on the next floor, this time in the smoke-filled den of a smuggler. A male chorus wearing silver shorts and glittering eyeshadow gyrated around a young starlet in a bra and the briefest of brief gold and red loincloths – a far cry from Sita.

Bombay is India's most westernized city. When I was there *No Sex, Please, we are Hindustani*, *Run for your Wife* and *Cabaret* were playing in the theatres. In video libraries, the most popular cassettes were *Dallas* and *Dynasty*, which I was told could be delivered to your door. The bookstalls were full of glossy magazines. There was *Savvy* for women, and for men there was

Debonair – the nearest India gets to *Playboy* (and it's not very near).

Bombay unashamedly worships Mammon. A young journalist told me, 'Everyone in this city wants to join a foreign bank, work on the stock exchange or be an advertising executive. The civil service, the police and the other government jobs no one wants, because you are not making money.'

But there are some Bombay-wallahs who reject that culture. One is Iqbal Masood, a former income-tax commissioner who is now a distinguished film critic. I knew that he disapproved of the *Ramayan*, but after my visit to Umargaon I wanted to find out exactly why.

Iqbal Masood believes that the *Ramayan* is part of a government plot. 'They wanted a model which would be religious and keep people glued to their sets. You see, now they have already started showing the other great Hindu epic, the *Mahabharat*, and they have given Ramanand Sagar another extension to make that doubtful portion of the *Ramayan*. The tendency of the minorities to break away is watched with great alarm. Here is something which is very Indian and makes people submissive.'

'But what about your community – the Muslims – and the other minorities?'

'You see, people like you can't understand the Indian Muslims. They are influenced by the passive attitudes of Hinduism, whatever their politicians might try to say. The minorities were the most ardent fans of the *Ramayan*.'

'But isn't it a good thing if the *Ramayan* is bringing people of different faiths together? Surely India has enough communal trouble.'

'I don't agree. All religions are useless to the philosopher and useful to the magistrate. Here you have a prime minister talking about bringing India into the twenty-first century and he puts on this television series which teaches you to lie back and rely on miracles. That will induce a submissive temperament. If you are going into the twenty-first century you want technology, not Hanuman lifting up a mountain. There are no "works" in Sagar's *Ramayan*, only "faith". You know, it's possible that if the *Ramayan* had been given to a modern director, and a sensitive one, a relevance to modern life could have been established. Sagar didn't attempt to relate religion to life and problems today.'

'My feeling is that Sagar's *Ramayan* has succeeded because, in spite of whatever faults it might have, it is very Indian, and people are looking for that.'

'What is Indianness today? The basic thing in India today is mediocrity. It has never been so mediocre as it is today. I feel stifled by the mediocrity. All our genuine intellectuals live in the West. We need another infusion of the West here. The freshness has gone out of this country, because people stopped reading and thinking thirty years ago.'

When I suggested that India had perhaps had too much of the West imposed on it and needed to get back to its own roots, Iqbal Masood laughed and said, 'You are an idealist.'

By the time of the Dussehra festival, I was back in Delhi. There was a traditional Dussehra image of Ravan in the small park opposite my house. Thirty feet high and made out of coloured, shiny paper wrapped around a bamboo frame, it was secured with ropes and tent-pegs. This Ravan had a cardboard black moustache shaped like Arvind Trivedi's, and round earrings. He carried a raised sword in one hand and a shield in the other. I asked the taxi-drivers who had first made me interested in the *Ramayan* whether there had ever been a Ravan in the park before. 'No,' they replied. 'Usually there are only a very few Ravans in the big parks, but this year they are everywhere, because of the television.'

There are Sikhs and Hindus on our taxi rank. They had all loved Ramanand Sagar's *Ramayan* because it was so Indian. Dilip, a young Hindu from the Himalayas, said, 'It made me proud to see how great my country was.' A Sikh, Manjit Singh, told me, 'I was interested because I learnt about ancient history. Some parts of the story I had never heard. They have shown the whole story on the television, but they never do in the Ram Lilas. I am thirty-eight, and this is the first time I have seen it in full.'

'But some people have said it went very slowly – the story, I mean. Didn't you get bored?'

'No. It was like a novel you couldn't put down.'

Across the road, a large crowd had gathered to watch the death of Ravan. Drums were beating and fireworks exploded. Five young men – two Sikhs and three Hindus – picked up flaming torches, marched seven times round the demon king and then set him alight. The fireworks stuffed inside Ravan exploded like machine-gun fire, the crowds cheered and a mushroom of smoke formed above his crown. Just four years ago I had seen smoke rising from the market behind that park as Hindus killed Sikhs and burnt their property in the dreadful riots which followed Indira Gandhi's assassination.

— 5 —

OPERATION BLACK THUNDER

Operation Blue Star, the Indian army's clumsy attack on the Sikh Golden Temple at Amritsar in June 1984, shook the foundations of the Indian nation. It deeply wounded the pride of the Sikhs, the most prosperous of India's major communities. It strengthened the cause of those Sikhs campaigning for the setting up of a separate Sikh state – Khalistan – and gave them a martyr – Sant Jarnail Singh Bhindranwale, the fundamentalist preacher who had fortified the Golden Temple complex and died defending the shrine. It caused Sikh soldiers to mutiny. It led directly to the assassination of the prime minister, Indira Gandhi, and to the worst communal violence since the partition riots of 1947. What particularly 'hurt the Sikh psyche' – a phrase I must have heard a thousand times – was the attack by tanks on the Akal Takht, one of the two most sacred shrines in the complex. The Akal Takht symbolizes the temporal authority of God, while the Golden Temple itself symbolizes his spiritual power.

Before Bhindranwale fortified the Golden Temple complex, it had been a place where only those entirely devoid of all spirituality could fail to feel something of the presence of God. The reflection of the Golden Temple shimmered in the water of the pool in which the temple is set. The sound of the sacred music, sung with verve but without vulgarity, and backed by the light, quick beat of the tablas, reached to all corners of the complex. Venerable Sikh priests with flowing white beards sat reading the Sikh scriptures in the Akal Takht. Pilgrims stood praying immersed to their waists in the water of the pool or prostrated themselves before the shrine. Families walked round the marble pavements or parikrama surrounding the pool, children chattering away happily. In India, awed silence is not necessary for prayer or worship, but the Golden Temple complex never degenerated into the noisy bazaar which tourists have made of so many cathedrals and temples. There was never any attempt to extract money from visitors – Sikhs were too proud to do that, and voluntary donations proved more than adequate.

Loving the Golden Temple as I did, I was deeply shocked when I entered the complex just after Operation Blue Star. Heavily armed soldiers in battle fatigues had replaced the pilgrims. There was a sullen silence. The walls were pockmarked with bullet holes. Squash-head shells fired by tanks and designed to destroy by sending shock waves through their targets had pulverized the frontage of the Akal Takht, leaving hardly a pillar standing, blackening marble walls and destroying plaster, filigree and mirrorwork decoration more than 200 years old. The floors of the shrine were carpeted with spent cartridges. The white marble of the pavement outside was stained with blood.

For months before Operation Blue Star there had been no secret about the fact that Sant Jarnail Singh Bhindranwale, with the assistance of a retired general of the Indian army, was turning the Akal Takht into a fortress. I filmed the fortification of the shrine three months before Blue Star. If Bhindranwale had been removed when he first started his fortifications, the Akal Takht would not have been destroyed and all the disasters which flowed from that would have been avoided. Yet, just four years after Blue Star, Indira Gandhi's son Rajiv allowed Sikh separatists to fortify the Golden Temple again, and was eventually forced to order another operation by the security forces to get them out.

The cause of Operation Black Thunder was the same as that of the earlier Blue Star: once again the prime minister and the politicians of the Sikh religious party, the Akali Dal, had both failed to rise above considerations of their own immediate petty political gains. Within a year of coming into office, in July 1985, Rajiv Gandhi had signed an imaginative and effective accord with the Akali Dal. The accord survived the assassination of Sant Harchand Singh Longowal, the Akali leader who signed it, and was enthusiastically endorsed by the success of the Akali Dal in the elections for the Punjab state assembly later that year, only to be scuppered by Rajiv Gandhi. He failed to implement the accord, I believe, because he was persuaded that it would spell disaster for his party in the neighbouring state of Haryana.

Haryana was unhappy about the accord because it gave the city of Chandigarh to Punjab. The city was shared as the capital of both states. Haryana also believed that the division of river waters agreed to under the accord was unfair. There was fear in the Congress Party that the opposition in Haryana would capitalize on the discontent over the accord and defeat the Congress in the next state-assembly election. A defeat in Haryana, Rajiv Gandhi was warned, would have a domino effect throughout the party's stronghold in northern and central India – the Hindi belt as it is always known. So Chandigarh was not given to Punjab and the accord with the Akalis was put in cold storage.

A few weeks before the Haryana state elections in June 1987, Rajiv Gandhi again sacrificed the interests of the Sikhs for short-term political gains by dismissing the Akali chief minister and imposing central-government rule in Punjab. This crude gesture to Haryana chauvinism did not produce the expected gains: the Congress Party was routed in the assembly elections. In the general election two years later, the Congress Party met a similar fate throughout the Hindi belt. Sacrificing the Punjab accord had not prevented the dominoes falling.

Rajiv Gandhi does not bear the sole blame for the collapse of the accord and the return of central-government rule in Punjab: the Akali Dal leaders had also let down their community again. Before Operation Blue Star they had been arguing among themselves, pursuing their own petty interests rather than presenting a united front against Bhindranwale, who was as grave a threat to them as he was to Indira Gandhi. This time some Akali leaders had deserted their own government because it was not headed by a member of their faction of the party. This fatally weakened the Akali chief minister, Surjit Singh Barnala, and gave Rajiv Gandhi an excuse not to implement the accord and to dismiss the Punjab government.

The collapse of the Punjab accord strengthened the separatists, who argued that it proved that Bhindranwale had been right when he said that Sikhs were slaves of a Hindu government. Rajiv Gandhi followed his mother's example by failing to take resolute action against this new threat. Sikh separatists were again allowed to occupy and fortify the Golden Temple, and there is no telling how long they would have been allowed to stay there if they had not shot a senior police officer on 9 May 1988.

On that morning, police pickets surrounding the Golden Temple sent a wireless message to their deputy inspector general, S. S. Virk, asking what they should do about some Sikh separatists who had now started building fortifications outside the temple complex. Virk, who was himself a Sikh, had just returned from investigating the killing of six people in a village outside Amritsar. Such killings by Sikh militants had become an almost nightly affair. Virk had been given strict orders by the government that his men should not open fire on the militants inside the Golden Temple unless the separatists shot a policeman or came out of the complex and flaunted their arms, so he decided that he should go immediately to the Golden Temple to see whether these new fortifications justified opening fire or asking for new orders.

At the temple, Virk was told that young Sikhs were building a wall which would provide them with cover to cross into a four-storeyed building outside the shrine. Possession of that building would have given the Sikh militants a firing-position overlooking four of the paramilitary police pickets surrounding the complex. As he and his colleagues walked down the alley which ran behind the room which the militants used as the office of Khalistan, the young men building the wall fled into the temple complex. Virk ordered policemen to demolish the wall. Suddenly a paramilitary policeman on guard in a picket overlooking the alley shouted, 'Look out, look out – extremists are aiming at you.' Virk bellowed, 'Take cover!' As he himself was running for cover, a bullet from an AK47 rifle hit him. He fumbled in his pocket for a handkerchief, pressed it to his jaw to staunch the flow of blood and ran on. When he reached a safe place, he lifted the handkerchief and blood and splinters of bone fell on to his uniform.

By this time, heavy firing had broken out between the militants and the police pickets, so Virk couldn't get away for five minutes. When the way seemed to be clear, his colleague Suresh Arora, the senior superintendent of police of Amritsar, borrowed a scooter from one of the local residents and drove off with Virk on the pillion. Just before the hospital, the scooter had to stop at a level crossing, so the two officers got off and walked the rest of the way.

When Virk reached the hospital, doctors found that his jaw was badly broken but his life was in no danger. He wrote an order which was broadcast to the pickets over the police wireless. It read, 'I am all right. Continue firing and keep up the pressure on the extremists in the temple.' S. S. P. Arora returned to the temple complex to supervise the firing.

Dinesh Kumar, the journalist who reported for the BBC from Amritsar, was inside the temple with some colleagues when the firing started that morning. He suddenly found himself surrounded by young Sikhs firing AK47s, ammunition pouches hanging from their necks. One man shouted, 'We've got that bastard Virk. He's dead.' The others shouted '*Khalistan zindabad!*' – 'Long live Khalistan.' Three pilgrims scuttled across the causeway leading from the parikrama to the Golden Temple. The police fired on them, ignoring the danger of hitting the Sikhs' most sacred shrine, but the pilgrims somehow reached the sanctuary. A sewadar, or temple servant, hiding in front of the Akal Takht was less lucky.

The journalists and some pilgrims eventually managed to reach a room with a telephone. Dinesh Kumar rang the police headquarters and was told, 'We are doing something.' But nothing happened and he prepared to die, writing a letter to his girlfriend which he hoped would be found when his body was recovered. Then the telephone line was cut.

There was no longer any point in waiting for instructions from the police, so the journalists decided the best thing was to make for the main gateway. They reached it running from pillar to pillar along the verandah. At the main gateway they halted – no one wanted to run over the open ground in front of the temple in case the police opened fire. Eventually two people did pluck up courage and ran. When they got out safely, they came back to call the others.

The security forces surrounding the Golden Temple were a frustrated lot. For more than a month they had watched as separatists inside the temple complex built fortifications. First the separatists had sandbagged windows and arches, and then, when that provoked no response, they had built brick walls. They had constructed battlements on the top of two towers known as bungas which were higher than any of the police positions. One of these looked down on to the headquarters of the police surrounding the complex, in a building called the Brahambuta Akhara, which belonged to a Sikh sect. To add insult to injury, the saffron flag of Khalistan flew from prominent points of the complex. The police were sure that Sikh militants were once again using the Golden Temple as the headquarters and communications centre for a campaign of terror. They had received many complaints maintaining that extortion, torture and murder were everyday occurrences inside the complex. Several bodies had been found in the drains outside the complex. But the police were not allowed to do anything: they were ordered just to stand by, as mute and humiliated spectators.

Two weeks earlier I had been standing with a sub-inspector of the paramilitary Central Reserve Police on top of one of the buildings overlooking the Golden Temple. He was a big man with a hard face and close-cropped grey hair. His medal ribbons showed that he was an army veteran re-recruited into the police. I pointed to the saffron flag flying from the clock tower and asked him what he thought of it. 'Sahib, it is very bad for our izzat [honour],' he replied. 'These bastards, they are making us look fools. All the people in these alleys jeer at us when we are on patrol and ask, "What are you doing about the temple? Are you just waiting for the army to come and do your job again, like you did four years ago?" But what can we do? We don't have any orders. We could take those bastards out any time if only we were allowed to.'

With the wounding of Virk, there was a very real danger that the discipline which had been restraining the frustrated police would break down and that they would attack the temple complex, orders or no orders. Fearing this, Sarabjit Singh, the soft-spoken Sikh who was district commissioner of Amritsar, rushed to the temple, but he could do nothing to restore discipline. He told me, 'Firing seemed to be coming from everywhere. I found that AK47 fire was coming from the temple and the police were replying with light machine-guns. No one seemed to have any orders. I stayed for half an hour, but no one was in a mood to stop firing.' A police officer admitted that his men were enraged, and it was not possible to stop them firing.

When Sarabjit Singh got back to his office, he put the walled city surrounding the temple under curfew. Operation Black Thunder – the second battle of the Golden Temple – had started.

Senior superintendent of police Arora rang his headquarters in Chandigarh and got through to Julio Ribeiro, the former police officer who was now in charge of the Home Ministry in the Punjab government. Ribeiro had until recently been the head of the Punjab police force. He had made his name as an outstandingly successful commissioner of the Bombay police and had then been sent to Punjab when the morale of the police there collapsed because of the casualties they had suffered and their failure to make any impact on the Sikh militants. Ribeiro, although a Christian from Goa in western India, had succeeded in reviving the morale of the predominantly Sikh Punjab police and was respected by its officers.

Arora said to Ribeiro, 'Virk has been shot and all my boys are mad. You know that Virk is very popular and I can't promise to control my boys. They are demanding to go in and take it out on those bastards. Too much has happened. They've had enough.'

Ribeiro insisted that the young police officer must control his men and keep them out of the temple complex. He promised Arora that some action would be taken, but only after he had consulted the central government in Delhi.

Attacking the temple complex was not a decision that Ribeiro or anyone in the Punjab government could take – the possible consequences were far too grave for that – so he spoke to the home minister in Delhi, to the minister for internal security and to the secretary of the Home Ministry. It was agreed that commandos from the National Security Guards – a new force raised by Rajiv Gandhi to be the SAS of India – would be flown to Amritsar and that Ribeiro would go there himself the next morning to make an assessment of the situation on the spot.

Ribeiro got back to S. S. P. Arora in Amritsar, told him what had been agreed and repeated his order that under no circumstances must any attempt be made to enter the temple complex. Arora said, 'I'll do what I can to control the situation. I hope it'll be possible, but I have already told you my boys are in a foul mood.'

That night, both sides kept up the firing. The next day – Tuesday – Ribeiro arrived in Amritsar. He did indeed find the police in a foul mood. All his officers favoured entering the temple complex as soon as possible. They claimed that the Sikh community would rise in anger if the shrine was kept under attack for too long. Only the district commissioner, Sarabjit Singh, maintained that there would be no reaction in the countryside. He later explained to me, 'I was confident there would be no reaction if we went against the separatists in the Golden Temple because I had been going out into the countryside and talking to people. People used to come to my office too, and I had been asking them. I was sure they had no sympathy for the separatists, because of the indiscriminate killings and all the other things that had been happening. The militants were alienated from the people. Short of signing a legal statement on stamped revenue paper, I could guarantee the government there would be no reaction.'

K. P. S. Gill, the man who had succeeded Ribeiro as director-general of the Punjab police, had also arrived in Amritsar. It was to be Gill, not Ribeiro, who would dominate the scene from now on. Ribeiro and Gill were very different. Ribeiro was a tall, bespectacled man with a white fringe of hair round the back of his bald head – an avuncular, mild-mannered figure. He was a devout Catholic and smiled a lot. His relations with the press were excellent, and journalists had built up his reputation for using his brain rather than the brawn preferred by most Indian police officers – they called him 'Supercop'. But there was a hard side to this apparently soft man. It was Ribeiro who had started the bullet-for-bullet policy, as it was known in the Punjab: he gave the police powers to fire if they were fired on. These powers were sometimes used by officers to disguise the shooting of young men they had arrested but knew the paralysed courts would never convict – 'false encounters' as they are known in India.

K. P. S. Gill was not afraid to be known as a hard man. He was a Sikh himself and very proud of it – always wearing a khaki turban when in uniform. A man of few words, to those who didn't know him there was something sinister about this tall, thin police officer, with a white beard and an aquiline nose which dominated his face. He had returned to the Punjab with a reputation for ruthlessness won during his handling of earlier violence in the state of Assam.

Gill and Ribeiro, who was in effect his minister, disagreed about policing policy. Ribeiro told me, 'Gill is being far too harsh. He thinks only of fighting terrorists, not of fighting terrorism. The police are turning the people against them, and you can't fight terrorism unless the people are on your side.'

Gill felt that he had a better understanding of the Punjab police force than an outsider like Ribeiro. When I asked him about the allegation that he was too harsh, he replied, 'We have seen the morale of the Punjab police force collapse before. We don't want that to happen again. But I can assure you it will if senior officers don't back up their juniors. They believe that we must keep up the pressure on the militants, and they are the ones who are getting shot at, so I have to support them.'

Ribeiro and Gill had disagreements during Operation Black Thunder, but they have different memories about those disagreements. Ribeiro claimed that Gill supported his officers' demand to go into the temple immediately. But Gill maintained that he too told his men that there was no fear of a Sikh uprising. He said, 'I knew that 1988 had been a bad year for the extremists. They had started killing farmers, there had been rapes in the villages, there was the continual extortion of money. The militants had destroyed their own constituency, and the Khalistan movement had lost what support it might have enjoyed in the countryside. The men accepted my reassurance that action would be taken at the appropriate time and in the appropriate fashion.'

Whether Gill wanted to go into the temple complex immediately or not, no decision was made that day. But Gill's assurance that action would be taken was confirmed by the arrival of a contingent of the National Security Guard, which had been practising an assault on the temple complex for several months. One senior police officer suggested that the snipers who were part of the National Security Guard contingent should at least pick off any of the separatist leaders they saw moving around the complex, but the brigadier commanding them refused to allow that without clearance from Delhi, so Ribeiro, Gill and the governor of Punjab flew to Delhi to seek orders from Rajiv Gandhi.

While the police were waiting for instructions from Delhi, District Commissioner Sarabjit Singh was making the civilian arrangements for what he believed would be a long siege. His first problem was to arrange for a regular supply of food and other essential commodities in the area under curfew. By the second day, he told me, his arrangements were working well and he was able to assure Gill that the townspeople would be fed no matter how long the siege continued. Gurjeet Singh, a young Sikh lawyer who lived in one of the alleys surrounding the temple complex, was not impressed by the arrangements, however. He told me that his family did not receive any supplies from the government during Operation Black Thunder.

The second problem that Sarabjit Singh faced was the pilgrims who were stuck inside the temple. Virk had been shot on the day when Sikhs celebrated the accession of Guru Hargobind, who had built the Akal Takht, and so Sarabjit Singh was worried that there would be an unusually large number of pilgrims inside the temple because of the festival. Police intelligence assured him that fear of the militants had been keeping devotees away from the temple for some time now; nevertheless, Sarabjit Singh did not want to risk a repeat of Operation Blue Star, which also started on a Sikh festival day. In that operation, pilgrims were still inside the complex when the battle proper started. Many were killed, and those who survived were rounded up and roughly treated by the army. Some of them were arrested and held without trial for nearly five years – a major cause of the anger in the Sikh community.

Gill agreed to a brief cease-fire to get the pilgrims out – brusquely overruling suggestions that this too should be referred to Delhi – and this was announced over loudspeakers. Sarabjit Singh told me, 'About 750 people came out. We were not prepared to transport so many, because the CID had told me there were only about 150 to 200 inside. But we were able to rustle up some police buses and other transport. I was afraid that some of the young men might be activists, so we separated them from the others and took them for questioning. We took the women and children to the kotwali [police station], where we gave them bananas and sandals because they had left their shoes at the gate of the temple when they entered.'

The police did indeed find that some of the young men who had taken advantage of the cease-fire had been sent out by the militants to incite violence and to arouse anger against the Golden Temple operation. Later, it also became apparent that not all the non-combatants had taken advantage of the cease-fire.

Rajiv Gandhi chaired the lengthy and difficult meeting in Delhi that night. Once again Ribeiro and Gill differ about what happened. According to Ribeiro, the director-general of police insisted that Operation Black Thunder must be completed within the next two or three days. Gill told me he had never urged the prime minister to 'go in and get the terrorists', but he did warn against 'being over-cautious'. The central-government Intelligence Bureau was wary after the mistakes made in assessing the situation before Blue Star was launched; it insisted that great caution should be exercised this time, because the morale of the militants was very high. Gill totally disagreed with the assessment of the morale of the Sikh separatists, but he did accept that there were lessons to be learnt from Blue Star, and so it was decided that this time all operations should be conducted in daylight and that extremely accurate covering fire should be provided for forces assaulting any part of the temple complex.

The Gill plan, as Rajiv Gandhi described the arrangements

which were eventually agreed, provided for the phased occupation of the temple complex. The army's lack of knowledge of local circumstances and customs had been a major disadvantage in Operation Blue Star, so it was agreed that Black Thunder should be a police, not an army, operation. For the same reason, command was given to Gill as the head of the Punjab police force – not to Brigadier Nanda, who was commanding the National Security Guard contingent and whose commandos were to provide accurate sniping and support fire and to be the storm troopers if it was decided to go into the temple. In spite of being in overall command, however, the director-general of police was given virtually no autonomy. He had strict orders not to start on any phase of his plan without first clearing it with Delhi. The meeting broke up at five a.m.

When Gill got back to Amritsar, his first priority was to prevent any of the separatists escaping from the temple complex. He did not want a repeat of the fiasco of what was officially known as Black Thunder One, the operation the last chief minister of Punjab, Surjit Singh Barnala, had mounted, only to find that all the militant leaders had fled. The police were ordered to step up the firing at the complex, so that the Sikhs inside couldn't move. The security belt surrounding the temple was tightened, and the curfew in the old city was strictly enforced – or at least those were Gill's orders.

According to Gurjeet Singh, the young lawyer living near the temple, Gill's curfew was nothing like as strict as the army curfew during Blue Star. 'During Blue Star,' he said to me, 'the army used to shoot on sight anyone in the street. We were not allowed out for twenty days. They searched every house in the area regularly, and if they found a saffron turban like the militants used to wear they would shoot any young man in that house. When some militants did escape from the Golden Temple, the army forced some residents of this area to strip as a humiliation. The officers were not so bad. The jawans, the soldiers, were terrible.' The young lawyer was convinced he would have been arrested if he had not been able to speak in English to the officers and persuade them that he was not a militant.

Black Thunder was much more relaxed, however. 'During Black Thunder,' Gurjeet Singh told me, 'the Central Reserve Police used to apologize for searching our house, saying it was their duty. We used to give them tea and biscuits. When we came out of our houses, the police used to beg us to go back, saying, "We will be snubbed by our officers." The atmosphere was quite relaxed. We spent much of the time playing cards on our verandah.'

Thursday saw the only anger in Amritsar against the siege of the Golden Temple, and that was a somewhat contrived anger. Jasbir Singh Rode, the head priest of the Akal Takht, led a march on the Golden Temple, but the police had no difficulty in rounding up the few people he had managed to muster. This strengthened Gill's conviction that there was no need to fear any public reaction to a long siege.

Gill had other worries, though. When he had been in Delhi, he had received the clear impression that, come what may, he would not be allowed to send the commandos into the heart of the complex, and this worried him. He told me, 'We were concerned about how we could disengage if the pressure tactics didn't work and they didn't surrender. We couldn't go in and get them, but we had to be able to end the operation with our honour intact. The only thing that I could think of was that we would claim we had shot those who shot Virk and so our mission had been accomplished. That was one reason why I was anxious to get the snipers from the National Security Guards into action, picking off anyone who moved on the parikrama.'

Gill maintained that Brigadier Nanda, the commanding officer of the commandos, worked closely with him. The two had played cricket together as young men, and this apparently helped. Ribeiro had stayed behind in Delhi to act as liaison officer with the control team Rajiv Gandhi had set up. This was headed by the young minister for internal security, P. Chidambaram – a Harvard-trained lawyer with very little political experience: one of the new school of Westernized young men whom Rajiv Gandhi found it easier to work with than the traditional Indian politicians. According to Ribeiro, Nanda refused to order his snipers to fire until he got orders from

Delhi – they didn't start picking off people moving around the parikrama until Ribeiro flew back to Amritsar with Chidambaram's clearance.

On that Thursday, Gill not only started the sniping at the militants but also completed the first phase of the operation to clear the temple complex. Under the Gill plan, the complex had been divided into three sectors. Gill believed that he had been given permission to capture the outer sector – the pilgrims' hostels and offices on the other side of the road running along the eastern wall of the complex. Gill was very anxious to move in there to prevent any escapes from the complex itself and to get new vantage points. He met with no resistance from the hostels and offices, but Delhi was not amused, as Gill told me.

'I had to fly to Delhi that night to explain myself. The minister for internal security, Chidambaram, argued that it was not in the original plan. I said it was, and I had only gone ahead a little quicker than anticipated. But the job was already done and so no one could say much. I flew to Delhi almost every night of the operation to report progress to Chidambaram, and sometimes to Rajiv Gandhi himself.'

'Surely,' I asked, 'you must have found all the back-seat driving from Delhi very frustrating? You were meant to be in command of the battle.'

'No, I accepted it,' Gill replied. 'After all, whatever you journalists may think, Operation Black Thunder was not a battle: it had a major political dimension. If anything went wrong, it would have had very serious political consequences, so the political leadership had to be involved.' Gill smiled and went on, 'Of course, you wouldn't believe me if I said there were never any differences of opinion.'

Satisfied that the capture of the strategic road between the hostels and the complex proper would prevent any militants escaping, Gill told Sarabjit Singh that the curfew could be lifted in most of the walled city: it was enforced only within a radius of 400 yards of the complex. This was done before the director-general of police left for Delhi again on Thursday night.

Gill had another reason for feeling confident. Telephone lines to the rooms around the parikrama had been kept open, and Gill was able to speak to one of the separatists. By the tone of the man's voice, he judged that morale was collapsing. But Gill's confidence was misplaced: while he was in Delhi, ten to twelve people tried to escape. Two were shot and the rest ran back into the temple complex. From then on, night curfew was imposed in the whole of the walled city.

One of the decisions taken in Delhi was actively to encourage the press to witness Operation Black Thunder. This was in sharp contrast to Operation Blue Star, when we had all been bundled out of Punjab. Gill explained this decision to me: 'We were particularly anxious to have television there because we were genuinely afraid that the militants might blow up the Golden Temple. If they did and it was filmed, then everyone would be able to see what had happened and no amount of propaganda could have saved them.'

The governor of Punjab told me the decision to encourage the press to watch the operation had been taken by Rajiv Gandhi himself. He had apparently told Gill, 'I want Sikhs to see that we are not committing any excesses. I also want to be able to see for myself that you don't commit any.'

There was some resistance to this decision, as the police and the National Security Guard were not used to operating under press surveillance. In fact the National Security Guard were so shy of publicity that they had disguised their men in police uniforms. These difficulties prevented us seeing the next stage of the Gill plan – the capture of some of the outer buildings of the complex itself.

Ribeiro told me there was another disagreement over the capture of those buildings. At about midday on Friday, Gill apparently phoned Ribeiro to complain that the commandos were refusing to accept his orders to occupy the buildings and so he was going in with his own police. Ribeiro told him he must wait for clearance from Delhi and contacted Chidambaram, who gave the go-ahead. The commandos captured the langar – the canteen where free meals were served to all those who came to the Golden Temple – and the Gurdwara Manji Sahib – a large hall used for public meetings by the militants and the Akali Dal. Three members of the security forces were wounded during the capture of the langar and the gurdwara – the only casualties the security forces suffered during the whole operation.

On Saturday I was taken to the top of Gill's headquarters for my first ringside view of Operation Black Thunder. It was not exactly a comfortable experience, as I had to run across an open roof to get to the police posts, which were just a few yards from one of the bungas or towers still occupied by the Sikh separatists. The police were firing intermittently, but fortunately there was no response from the towers.

While I was in the headquarters, the police made another attempt to get all the remaining non-combatants out of the complex. Sarabjit Singh knew that some were still stuck inside because Baba Uttam Singh, the burly Sikh elder in charge of the reconstruction of the Akal Takht, had told him that some of his craftsmen were still missing. I watched Baba Uttam Singh announce a temporary cease-fire through a loud hailer and appeal to his craftsmen to come out. The deputy commissioner had offered to allow the baba to go into the complex to rescue his men, but had warned him that there would be nothing the security forces could do about it if he were held by the militants. The baba turned that offer down. When he made his appeal, the militants shouted from the bunga near me, 'We will only allow them out if the baba himself comes to get them.' But I saw two elderly men and one woman scuttle out of the east gate of the complex and totter across the road to the safety of the hostel opposite. The militants fired on them, injuring the woman. Only two other people – also elderly – came out that day.

Gill decided the time had come to step up the pressure. Snipers had already softened up the bungas; now the National Security Guards were ordered to bring up their Carl Gustaf rocket-launchers to fire at the defensive positions. The onslaught was kept up all night. Staying in the Ritz hotel, perhaps a mile away as the crow flies, I could see tracer bullets criss-crossing the sky above the Golden Temple and hear the deep staccato stutter of heavy machine-guns, the sharp crack of the snipers' PSG German rifles and the occasional rocket exploding. Searchlights shone down on the complex. Gill told me, 'The intention was psychological: we wanted to make them feel what they were up against.'

Sunday was the worst day of the siege for Gill. In the early morning, fire broke out in the clock tower above the main entrance to the parikrama. Gill admitted, 'I was a very worried man. It was very hot and dry: the fire was very unpredictable – especially in an old building like that – but, when we contacted the boys on the telephone, they would not allow us to bring up the fire brigade. If that fire had spread to the parikrama, it would have been a terrible thing. Fortunately, the fire burnt itself out.'

'Do you know whether the fire was started deliberately, in an attempt to destroy the temple and discredit you?' I asked.

'I honestly don't know, but I suppose that's possible. We never discovered how it started. It could have been a short circuit. Anyhow, however it started, I can tell you I was very worried while it was raging, but luck was on our side – the fire just burnt out.'

Later that morning, Gill's luck seemed to be holding. Sarabjit Singh came to the operational headquarters and made another appeal to the militants to surrender. To the delight of all in the headquarters, 148 people walked out from the east gate of the parikrama with their hands above their heads, crossed the road and surrendered to the police in one of the hostel buildings. Many of them were young men – clearly Sikh separatists.

Sarabjit Singh didn't allow his excitement to show. He calmly announced an extension of the cease-fire, in the hope that more would surrender. His instinct seemed to have been proved correct when another group of people emerged from rooms on the far side of the parikrama with their hands above their heads and started walking in single file following the directions he was shouting over the loudspeaker. But then their leader turned sharply and walked through the gateway which houses the Golden Temple treasures and along the causeway leading to the shrine itself. The rest of the group followed. Sarabjit Singh shouted, 'Turn back turn back. Keep on the parikrama or you will be shot.' But the snipers had strict orders not to fire at the Golden Temple itself, and so forty-eight people were able to take sanctuary there, knowing that the security forces would never be allowed to attack the shrine.

Gill was not there at the time – he had been called away to meet Ribeiro, who had arrived from Chandigarh. As soon as he was told that some militants had moved into the temple itself, he drove straight back to his headquarters.

Occupation of the temple, Gill told me, was the worst possible thing that could have happened. 'We had always feared that they would somehow hole up in the Golden Temple, then there would be nothing that we could do except wait for them to come out. We couldn't possibly attack the temple. On the other hand, it would be a big defeat for us if we just went away and left them in control of it. We would find it very hard to make excuses for that. At the same time, I was very worried about what they would do if we made them desperate. They might, for instance, have blown up the shrine.'

Nevertheless Gill did not reprimand anyone for failing to prevent the militants entering the shrine. He held a long discussion with his officers, at the end of which he agreed with their decision not to open fire. He explained to me, 'It would have looked very bad if there had been bodies littering the causeway leading to the temple. Half our battle was psychological, not to upset the Sikh community. That might certainly have done so.'

Sarabjit Singh told me that some of the police officers had wanted to open fire, but he had opposed this. 'I said no. We have given a blanket cease-fire and should not break our word. I also thought that perhaps they might have gone into the temple to pay their obeisance before surrendering.'

Gill's troubles that Sunday were not yet over. When he reached the courtyard where the 148 people who had surrendered were being held, an excited junior officer said to him, 'I think Surjit Singh Penta, the man we have been looking for, is among this lot.' Penta was the commander of the Bhindranwale Tiger Force, a particularly brutal terrorist organization. He had recently led an attack on a children's birthday party in Delhi, shooting thirteen of the guests dead. Penta was still barely twenty. He had been an outstanding athlete, training to represent India, when his parents were arrested on suspicion of harbouring a terrorist. That turned him against the Indian police and drove him into the hands of the Sikh militants.

The officer pointed to a young woman who he said was Penta's wife. Gill went over to her and asked which was her husband. Penta was watching her. As soon as he saw the woman he had married only nine months before look towards him, he hurriedly stuffed his hand in his mouth, chewed on a capsule which he kept on a string round his neck and collapsed. He had swallowed cyanide. Sarabjit Singh saw him collapse and shouted for a doctor, but Penta died before medical help reached him. That was a serious setback to Gill, who had hoped to extract invaluable intelligence by interrogating Penta. Gill ordered a close watch to be kept on all the others who had surrendered and made arrangements to start interrogating them as soon as possible.

Gill's immediate aim was to find out more about the situation inside the temple. He was told that militants were still holding out in well-fortified positions in cellars below the two bungas, and that the militants' position above the clock tower was still intact in spite of the fire. Those positions had to be knocked out, just in case Rajiv Gandhi did eventually allow the security forces to go on to the parikrama.

That evening the press gallery – or perhaps I should say grandstand – was ready. It was the roof of the Guru Ram Das hostel, which overlooked the whole of the complex. I went up there during the night to watch the bombardment from close quarters. The bright beams of the searchlights sparkled on the white marble and lit every corner of the parikrama. I could see a body lying in a pool of blood outside room 14 and the notice above the door of that room saying 'Office of Khalistan'. The body was that of Jagir Singh – the spokesman of the Panthic Committee which claimed to control all the groups fighting for Khalistan. He had made many statements to the press from that office.

The temperature the next morning was up in the forties. The authorities had put up a shamiana or canvas pavilion on the roof of the hostel to give us some shade, but it didn't provide a good view of the parikrama so we had to brave the full heat of the sun. The evening before there had even been talk of a bar, but Sarabjit Singh had pointed out that Sikhs regarded the hostel as part of the

Golden Temple complex and that they would not take kindly to pictures of journalists drinking beer on its roof. Derek Brown of the *Guardian* – certainly the most mild-mannered and good-humoured of the foreign correspondents – was a bit put out when told he couldn't even smoke for fear of offending Sikh sensitivities. Eventually a little cubby-hole halfway up the stairs was identified as safe for Derek to smoke in. The only correspondent to come well prepared was Bruce Palling of the *Independent*. Always a man dressed for the occasion, he arrived on the rooftop wearing a khaki solar topi and carrying his personal water-purifier. In spite of these precautions, however, he soon turned lobster-red.

Monday was dull as well as hot. The security forces kept up the pressure with sporadic firing, but there was no response from the temple complex. The bombardment of the bungas continued, but we began to wonder whether they really were occupied. When the sun was at its height, a few of the wives who had surrendered on the day before were brought on to the roof to appeal to their husbands to surrender, but they were too nervous to carry conviction over the loudspeakers when they told the young men in the Golden Temple that they had been well treated and had been assured that no one who surrendered would be tortured.

Sarabjit Singh also tried to get Jasbir Singh Rode, the head priest who had led the abortive march on the temple, to appeal for a surrender. Rode, however, excused himself on the grounds that he was not senior enough: he said the appeal should come from Baba Thakur Singh, who headed Sant Jarnail Singh Bhindranwale's religious order, the Damdami Taksal. Baba Thakur Singh was very old and rarely spoke in public because of his frailty; nevertheless, he did agree to appeal. But he soon changed his mind under pressure from younger members of the Damdami Taksal, who told the deputy commissioner, 'This is the government's job, not ours. Baba can't do this sort of thing.' When Sarabjit Singh pointed out that the daily religious ceremonies in the Golden Temple had been disrupted, they replied, 'That may be so, but there's nothing we can do about it. You have attacked the temple.'

By Monday evening, Gill was beginning to doubt whether the

militants in the Golden Temple would surrender. They had survived two days in what must have been an inferno. The terrifying sounds of the bombardment had not shaken their resolve. Nobody knew how much food or water they had stored in the temple, but it was quite possible they had provisions for many days more. Each day that went by increased the chances of an accident which might damage the sacred shrine – the one thing Gill had been told he must avoid.

On Tuesday morning Gill decided to try another cease-fire. It was announced by his deputy, Chaman Lal, and by Sarabjit Singh, thus giving the militants the assurance that their safety was guaranteed by the operational command and the civil administration. While the announcement was being broadcast, the door of the temple facing us opened. A young Sikh came to the edge of the pool and drew water in a bucket. Snipers asked, 'Shall we fire?' Gill replied, 'No – time the intervals between their going inside the temple and returning to refill the buckets.' The timings led Gill to conclude that the water was being drunk as it was drawn – that the militants had nowhere to store it.

During the cease-fire, two young men also ran down the causeway and tried to pick up a sack of flour from a corner of the parikrama. Sarabjit Singh shouted, 'Get back or you'll be shot!' The two men dropped the sack and ran back into the temple.

The cease-fire restored Gill's confidence. It was now clear that the militants had no water and were short of food. He did not believe that they could hold out for long under those circumstances. He told his colleagues, 'There will be no more cease-fires. We will leave them for twenty-four hours to let the heat get at them. Let them stew in it. We won't make any announcements at all, but we will complete the capture of the bungas. That should make a hell of a noise and make their lives even more uncomfortable.'

Shortly after the cease-fire, I saw masked commandos wearing black denims and flak jackets running towards the towers with explosives tied to the end of long poles. We heard a series of muffled explosions and saw brown smoke seeping out of the holes in the bungas. Nothing seemed to happen for some time. Then we heard a series of loud explosions which appeared to come from below the bungas. We were at first told that the commandos had fought their way into the cellars, but later Gill admitted that the separatists had fled earlier and that the commandos had found only two dead bodies.

Gill now knew that he could send the commandos into the parikrama without fear of their being fired on from the rear, but he didn't believe that that would now be necessary. He was confident that all he had to do was to let events unfold. The security forces continued firing throughout Tuesday night and Wednesday morning, although they no longer had any targets: their commanders now knew that the only militants left were those in the Golden Temple, and firing at that was totally taboo. The sharp crack of the snipers' rifles and the deep stuttering of the heavy machine-guns were now just part of Gill's psychological warfare.

It was not until the militants had felt the full force of the midday sun on Wednesday that Gill made his next move. We were woken from our torpor by the voice of Sarabjit Singh. He was standing on the roof of the langar building, looking intently at the Golden Temple and speaking slowly and deliberately over the loudspeaker. He said, 'We told you yesterday that we would give you a time to surrender today. If you have made up your minds to come out, wave cloths.'

Almost immediately, a saffron-coloured cloth waved from one of the windows of the temple. It looked like the cloth of a militant's turban. Sarabjit Singh's voice rose in excitement. 'I will give you instructions. Wait, wait.' More cloths were waved from other windows of the temple. One person waved so vigorously that he dropped his cloth into the pool. We couldn't see who was waving. Sarabjit Singh said, 'I have seen the cloths you are waving. Wait, wait. Do not move until you hear my instructions, and then follow them exactly.' The waving continued for another minute or more. Then Sarabjit Singh, who was by now very much in control of himself, said, 'Come out of the temple. Walk down the causeway and turn to the right at the end. Keep moving all the time.' The Sikhs obediently walked out of the temple in a single file. We could see one woman among them.

A continuous stream of instructions from Sarabjit Singh echoed around the parikrama. 'Walk straight on until you come to the parikrama and then turn right. Keep moving. Don't stop. Don't drop your hands. Keep going and move exactly as I tell you.' But when the file reached the parikrama, some turned left. Sarabjit Singh screamed, 'Go back! Go the other way or we will open fire!' For a moment the young Sikhs panicked. They stopped and stared like rabbits caught in the headlights of a car, not able to move. Sarabjit shouted, 'Turn round, walk back along the parikrama in the direction of the clock tower. Follow my instructions.' The message went home: the petrified militants turned around and followed those who were walking the other way round the parikrama. One stopped and bent down to drink water from the pool. Sarabjit shouted, 'Get up. Keep moving. You will be shot if you stop. We will give you water.' He kept up his commands until the last man had walked through the eastern gate of the complex into the waiting arms of the police.

Gill had rushed down to supervise the arrests. He pulled two of the men aside and asked whether there was anyone left in the temple. Surprisingly, he didn't recognize the two men as the important militant leaders Nirvair Singh and Malkiat Singh Ajnala. They said three people had still not surrendered. Gill asked them to go back to the Golden Temple and bring out the three who remained. They refused.

Eventually one young Sikh did agree to go back to the Golden Temple, provided Gill sent an official with him. The two men entered the temple, and Gill heard raised voices. Then suddenly three people walked out of the temple. One was a vast man more than six feet tall with the shoulders of an ox and a great barrel of a chest. Gill did recognize him – as Karaj Singh Thande, a former sergeant-major in the army who had deserted after Operation Blue Star. Thande suddenly staggered. The police in their headquarters in the Brahambuta Akhara opened fire in panic and Thande fell to the ground. A second man started running. The police fired on him and he fell down dead. The only one of the three to come out alive was a mentally defective young man who had been caught inside the Golden Temple accidentally. When the body of Thande was recovered, it was found that he had taken cyanide.

Ajnala and Nirvair Singh were kept separate from the rest of the prisoners. Ajnala sat on a wall wearing just a dirty lungi and nursing an ugly open wound in his shoulder. He had been shot taking part in the only escape attempt of the siege. On the day Virk was shot, Ajnala had told Dinesh Kumar that he would give 'a fitting reply' if the security forces tried to force the militants out. Two weeks earlier I had asked Nirvair Singh what would happen if the temple were attacked, and he had replied, 'We will defend it until we die. We will be very happy to die for Khalistan.'

According to Gill, thirty people were killed in the entire operation – most of them shot by the snipers. One hundred and ninety-two people surrendered. The security forces suffered only three casualties – the three men wounded in the attack on the buildings on the edge of the complex.

Gill's triumph was short-lived. On Thursday night he was trying to get a well-earned rest when he was woken to be told that Chidambaram and the home minister, Buta Singh, had arrived in Amritsar and were demanding to see him. That meeting turned into a bitter four-hour row. Chidambaram had issued orders that the filth and squalor inside the Golden Temple should be shown on the government-controlled television, to discredit the Sikh separatists. Gill had questioned the wisdom of that: he said he didn't know what effect it would have on the Sikh mind and he thought it was not worth the risk of causing offence, but the ministers overruled him. When no film appeared on television, the two ministers thought that Gill had deliberately disobeyed them and they had flown to Amritsar to discipline him. It was not until the television producer himself was found that Gill convinced the two ministers that there had been no film because the television team did not have lights.

The two ministers were also livid because Gill had allowed the temple management committee, which was dominated by the Sikh religious party the Akali Dal, into the complex to take an inventory of the gold stored there for the replating of the dome of the Akal Takht. The ministers accused him of handing back the temple to the committee without their permission. Gill argued that the temple had not been handed back. He also asked what the government would have done if the committee had later accused officials or the police of stealing some of the gold.

There was a third argument over Chidambaram's insistence that the security forces should now search the complex. Gill asked him, 'If the prime minister was so anxious to keep the security forces off the parikrama during the operation, why throw away all the psychological advantage we have won now?' Chidambaram eventually accepted that argument. A senior civil servant who accompanied the two ministers from Delhi later told me he was 'reluctantly proud' of the way Gill stood up to his political masters.

Operation Black Thunder was a major set-back to the pride and the standing of the Khalistan movement. Young men who had so often sworn to defend the Golden Temple with their blood and prided themselves on being followers of the 'martyr' Sant Jarnail Singh Bhindranwale were seen on television walking round the parikrama with their hands above their heads and surrendering meekly to the police. The desecration of the Sikhs' most holy shrine was also eventually shown on television – the brass pots full of urine and faeces, the cooking utensils, the clothes and rugs littered all over the stained red carpet, and the arms and ammunition.

Worse was to come for the cause of Khalistan. When the police first interrogated Ajnala, he confessed that two people had been tortured to death and their bodies had been buried in the rubble of the old Akal Takht opposite the residential buildings. He was taken to the mound of masonry and pointed out the position of the bodies. Labourers who were engaged to dig them out eventually discovered not just two but forty bodies. Those at the bottom were skeletons. The young militants claiming to fight for a land where the Sikh religion could flourish in all its pristine purity had defiled the relics of their shrine – relics which pious Sikhs regarded as sacred.

There had been rumours of murder and torture in the Golden Temple complex after the militants regained control of it. Here was proof of murder. Men and women had been killed because they were suspected of being police informers, because they had backed the wrong group of Khalistanis or because they had been relatives of rich men who were getting a little reluctant to respond to extortion. Gurjeet Singh, the young lawyer who lived in a lane just behind the Guru Ram Das hostel, had seen bodies thrown out of the temple and heard the screams of people being tortured. The journalist Dinesh Kumar had once been forced to watch a man roped to a pillar being whipped with a leather thong and then thrashed with a stick in what the militants called their 'interrogation centre' in the temple complex.

I visited several Punjab villages just after Operation Black Thunder. For the first time, villagers were prepared to speak openly against the militants. In one village, I was told they were a disgrace to Sikhism; in another, that they were worse than common criminals. In a third, I was told that the Khalistan movement had been created by the government to give it an excuse for persecuting Sikhs. A team of academics who also visited the Punjab after Black Thunder wrote in the independent and respected magazine the *Economic and Political Weekly*, 'It was only after Operation Black Thunder forced the Khalistanis to surrender that the erstwhile "silent majority" of Sikhs began to voice their misgivings about them.' The academics also remarked, 'The Sikhs have made it apparent through their response to Operation Black Thunder that the extremists do not speak for them. If New Delhi is seriously interested in bringing an end to the sufferings of the people of Punjab, then the present popular mood in the state offers it yet another opportunity.'

New Delhi was not interested. Rajiv Gandhi did take some cosmetic measures to woo the Sikhs, but they did more harm than good. He released some of the innocent people who had been arrested by the army during Operation Blue Star, but this just served to highlight the illegality of their detention. He also visited Punjab for the first time in three years, but only to announce some economic measures to help the state – which had the somewhat unfortunate effect of giving the Sikhs the impression that the prime minister thought they were a purchasable commodity. Some Punjab civil servants had advised that during his visit the prime minister should pray in a famous Sikh temple in Govindwal, the town where he announced the government's largesse, but the secularists in Delhi overruled that: 'There must', they said, 'be no pandering to Sikh religious sentiments.'

Chidambaram, in an interview he gave after Operation Black Thunder, blamed the continuing impasse in Punjab on the Akali Dal. He said, 'The Punjab problem has many dimensions . . . but most important is the collapse of the moderate leadership.' When asked whether the central government was not responsible for the collapse of the moderate leadership, Chidambaram replied, 'The government has always extended its support to the moderates. The collapse has come from within.'

If Rajiv Gandhi had really been interested in reviving the moderate leadership of the Akali Dal, he should have called an election for the Punjab state assembly. The lure of power would have brought the leadership of the Akali Dal together as it had done in the election Rajiv Gandhi called after the signing of the accord. The politicians who had supported the separatists would have been discredited and so would not have been able to put up a fight. There would have been the almost certainty of Punjab being ruled by a Sikh government again, with all that could have meant for the restoration of the community's confidence in the central government. But then the Punjab problem had been precipitated by Indira Gandhi's desire to break the traditional Akali Dal, in the mistaken belief that this would make Punjab a Congress Party stronghold. Rajiv Gandhi was not about to help the Akali Dal to get back in business.

Eighteen months after Operation Black Thunder when the general election was held, with Punjab still under central-government rule and no major concessions made to the Sikhs, nine out of the thirteen seats in Punjab were won by candidates supported by the separatists. They included the widow and the father of Beant Singh, one of the two bodyguards who had assassinated Indira Gandhi; a senior police officer still under arrest facing charges of involvement in the assassination; and the leader of one of the militant organizations, who was also under arrest. The moderate Akali Dal and the Congress Party were trounced.

The Punjab problem might have been precipitated by Indira Gandhi's desire to break the Akali Dal, but she had been able to get support for this because in India it is only considered respectable to believe in the total separation of religion and politics – as if that has ever been achieved in a society which is still religious. This is taken to mean that it is justifiable to destroy a religious party like the Akali Dal. Those who warned that Sikhs wishing to have a party of their own were 'communal' – a threat to secularism – have been proved wrong. If ever a party would have been justified in becoming communal, it would have been the Akali Dal after the massacre of Sikhs when Indira Gandhi was killed. But its leaders did not preach hatred, nor did the Sikh community take revenge.

India is not alone in the world in facing terrorism, nor is it the only country to have used its army to fight terrorists, but Operation Blue Star, and the military rule that Indira Gandhi imposed on Punjab after it, went far beyond anti-terrorist tactics. Her son did not use the army in Punjab, but it was always there in reserve. He did use the paramilitary police, who are now the first line of defence when the government needs to call out armed forces to perform the old colonial function of 'aid to the civil power'. There has never been any significant political protest in India against the brutal tactics used by the army and the paramilitary police in curbing uprisings or other challenges to the central government's authority, whether in the remote tribal states of the north-eastern hills, in Punjab or now in Kashmir. It is surely because politicians know that they have the ultimate sanction – the power to declare war on a section of their own people – that they do not feel bound to look for political solutions to problems. If Indira and Rajiv Gandhi had not known that they could always use the army to suppress the Sikhs, they would never have allowed the situation in Punjab to deteriorate so far that they were both obliged to mount operations against the Golden Temple.

am Chander's daughter, Rani, in
er bridal dress on the morning of
her wedding. (Chapter 1)

Ram Chander (Chapter 1)

Paul Paneereselvan of the Dalit Liberation Educational Trust talking to Dalit children in the village of Arasankuppam in Tamil Nadu. (Chapter 2)

Pilgrims at the confluence of the Ganges and Jamuna at Allahabad on the morning of the most auspicious bathing day of the 1989 Kumbh Mela. (Chapter 3)

A naked sadhu on a horse leads his akhara's procession through the crowds to the sacred confluence. (Chapter 3)

Sadhus bathing at the confluence of the Ganges and Jamuna on the most auspicious bathing day. (Chapter 3)

Operation Black Thunder. Sikh militants firing at the police from the Golden Temple on the morning that deputy inspector of police S. S. Virk was shot. (Chapter 5)

Sikh militants surrendering in the Golden Temple complex. (Chapter 5)

K. P. S. Gill, director-general of the Punjab police, briefing reporters outside the Golden Temple after the surrender of the Sikh militants. (Chapter 5)

Ramanand Sagar's Ram and Sita returning in triumph to their kingdom of Ayodhya. In the chariot with them ride Ram's brothers Bharat (to the rear) and Lakshman (right). (Chapter 4)

The communist chief minister of West Bengal, Jyoti Basu, at a party rally in Calcutta. (Chapter 6)

Roop Kanwar's in-laws lead local people through the streets of Deorala during a ceremony following the young woman's death. (Chapter 7)

The author with the artist Jangan Singh Shyam in the shade of a mahua tree on the outskirts of Jangan's village. (Chapter 9)

The author in conversation with Digvijay Narain Singh in the garden of his house in Muzaffarpur, northern Bihar. (Chapter 10)

— 6 —

COMMUNISM IN CALCUTTA

Joseph Stalin glowered down on the Soviet fraternal delegation attending the thirteenth party conference of the Communist Party of India (Marxist). This must have seemed a particularly unfraternal gesture to the comrades from Moscow. Their Indian hosts knew full well that the Soviets had come with the hope of selling perestroika; they also knew, of course, that Stalin was anathema to Mikhail Gorbachev. The host party did not intend a deliberate slight, but it was determined to send a clear message to its own cadres that, in India at least, Stalin had not been dethroned.

At first sight it might seem strange that a party which has often been described – wrongly in my view – as an Asian version of Eurocommunism should be so concerned about preserving the reputation of the dictatorial Stalin. But communism in India owes a great debt to Stalin. He may have been a dictator, but at least he was a realist when it came to India. Immediately after independence, the Indian communist movement identified the new ruling class as bourgeois compradors – agents of a foreign power – allied with imperialists. They were reckoned to be too enfeebled to stand up to an insurgency, and so the communists committed themselves to installing their system of government by force. But the compradors and the imperialists proved less feeble than the communists had thought, and the people of India did not rally to the red flag. Eventually Stalin intervened. In 1950 he summoned a delegation of three leading Indian communists to Moscow. There he questioned them about their strategy and the help they required from him. The Indian communists displayed a less than convincing mastery of the art of war and were particularly ignorant about the arms required for an insurrection and the difficulties of transporting them. Stalin pointed out that the centre of their insurgency, in the Telengana region in southern India, was too far away from any port for him to be able to help very much. He advised his Indian comrades to drop the insurgency and prepare for the elections due shortly.

The delegates took Stalin's advice, and since then the main elements in the Indian communist movement have stuck to the democratic path. In 1957, the world's first democratically elected communist government came to power in the southern Indian state of Kerala. Trivandrum, the capital of Kerala, was the venue of that thirteenth party conference.

Once communism had become an Indian movement, not a Soviet one, it was inevitable that the communists would follow the fissiparous pattern of Indian politics. They are continually in flux, with politicians walking out of one party sometimes to join another, sometimes to form a splinter group which they claim is the genuine party, and sometimes to return eventually to the fold from which they strayed.

The communists' first split was based on serious ideological differences: it was not just the result of frustrated personal ambitions, as happens often in India. What can only be described as the right wing of the party favoured some sort of compromise with the Congress Party – or at least with those whom it identified as progressive elements in that party. The left wing regarded the Congress as irredeemably bourgeois. The right wing also sided firmly with the Soviet Union in the great divide in world communism; the left leant towards China, although it did not commit itself to either side. When the split was formalized in 1964, the left adopted the title of the Communist Party of India (Marxist); the right remained the Communist Party of India.

There were to be more divisions in the movement, but these two parties remained the major contenders for the communist vote. Just to make the whole affair thoroughly Indian, the great divide within the Communist Party has never been final. That, in my view, is not at all surprising in Indian politics. Since their divorce, the Marxists and the Communist Party of India have been partners in several coalition governments in both Kerala and West Bengal, but the Marxists have been far more successful electorally than the pro-Moscow communists. The Marxists' greatest success has been in West Bengal, which they have ruled continuously since 1977, officially as partners in a Left Front but in practice as very much the dominant partner.

West Bengal is the obvious place to try to start an Indian revolution. During the independence movement, Bengal was the only state where the British faced a serious threat from terrorism. It also produced Subhas Chandra Bose, the most aggressive president the Indian National Congress elected. Mahatma Gandhi was so alarmed by the militant Bose that he prevented him taking office for a second time. West Bengal has a volatile and well-educated middle class. Caste – often seen as the greatest barrier to revolutionary politics in India – plays less of a role in West Bengal than in other major Indian states. Calcutta, the capital of West Bengal, is synonymous with poverty and squalor. I would suggest that Calcutta's bad name is not entirely justified, but there is no doubt that its slums and shanty towns should be fertile ground for revolutionaries. It is therefore strange that, with all this going for it, a party which still reveres the name of Stalin should have provided such a mild and unrevolutionary government.

I went to Calcutta just after the thirteenth party conference of the Communist Party of India (Marxist). The papers were carrying reports of a critique of perestroika by the editor of the *Marxist*, the party's 'theoretical quarterly'. The editor had complained of a certain ahistorical attitude towards the earlier years of Soviet society under Stalin's leadership'. He had doubts about 'the appeal to the market'. He was concerned about the stress on encouraging 'individual initiative and personal gain', and warned that personal holdings for peasants could not 'be a permanent feature of the socialist society'. The *Marxist*'s editor would also like to have seen 'more emphasis on centralized planning' in the documents and speeches of the last conference of the Soviet Communist Party. He warned Mr Gorbachev not to blame the economic crisis in the Soviet Union entirely on 'bureaucratism' – pointing out that the 'old spirit of socialist consciousness' had not been 'continually rekindled'.

Calcutta under the Marxists showed few signs of 'socialist consciousness' and all too many signs of 'bureaucratism'. The party appeared to have abandoned centralized planning in an all-out effort to attract private capital to revive industry in West Bengal. As for agriculture, the Marxists had clearly allied themselves with the peasant farmers. Journalists I met described them as 'kulaks' – rich peasants – although that was something of an exaggeration. Life in the capital was continuing in a distinctly *laissez-faire* atmosphere. The only place I could detect Stalin was on pavement stalls selling his picture alongside those of other non-communist heroes of Bengal and members of the Hindu pantheon.

I was born in Calcutta and spent the first nine years of my life either there or in a boarding-school in Darjeeling. Whenever I go back, I am struck by how much of the life my parents used to live still survives. The Bengal Club, which my father told me with pride was reserved for 'burra sahibs of reputable firms', has lost its Corinthian-pillared frontage but it is still a fine and well-maintained building. The membership has changed, but it's still a very exclusive club. I was taken to lunch there by M. J. Akbar, the pioneer of Indian investigative journalism, who had just published a biography of Nehru. I'm not sure that my father would have approved of journalists in his club, but he certainly would have approved of my old friend Pearson Surita, who was drinking beer from a silver tankard. He was complaining that All India Radio no longer allowed him to do cricket commentaries because his English was too pukka. AIR apparently claimed that modern Indian English-speakers could no longer understand the language of the burra sahibs. At the Calcutta Club, I was robbed of dinner because a member of our party was improperly dressed – he wasn't wearing a tie.

The Tollygunge Club where I used to be taken by my English nanny to play on the swings and see-saws has lost a little land to the Calcutta underground railway but still has spacious and immaculately kept grounds. The swimming-pool brings back memories of my father pushing me off the high diving-board, and the lawn in front of the golf-course recalls 'chokras', or boys, waving flags tied on bamboo poles to keep the kites from swooping down and removing our sandwiches. Tolly, as it is known, was being managed by Bob Wright – one of the last Englishmen still staying on in Calcutta. He is a handsome man – a broader version of the late David Niven – admirably set off by his petite and beautiful wife Anne. I sometimes feel sorry for them, since their status as the most prominent stayers-on inevitably makes them objects of curiosity – a must for every foreign visitor to Calcutta, and sometimes the butt of snide comments by foreign journalists writing predictable stories about the contrast between the survival of the raj and the dismal poverty of Calcutta.

When I was in Calcutta, the British high commissioner and his wife were the guests of Bob and Anne Wright at Tolly. One of the high commissioner's duties was to address members of the English Speaking Union. A scholarly and mild-mannered man, he complained gently about the perversion of his language in many countries. He went on to say, 'In India, too, though some try to preserve true English, there are many examples of adventurous use of the language – even in newspapers.'

The event which had brought the high commissioner to Calcutta was the annual race for the Queen Elizabeth II Cup at the Calcutta racecourse. The Queen had once presented the cup herself. The owner of the winning horse that year was the proprietor of the Great Eastern Hotel, always known as 'Maila' or 'Darling' Billimoria because he addressed all his guests by that adorative. Tradition has it that, when the Queen presented the hotelier with the cup, he replied, 'Thank you very much, darling.' Tradition, as far as I could find out, does not relate the royal reaction. The Queen has never been back to the Calcutta races.

In spite of the communists, the races are still run by the Royal Calcutta Turf Club – a club which blackballed my father when he applied for membership. A former chief steward of the club told me that that was nothing to be ashamed of. He said the club still limited its membership very strictly by operating what he called a 'six-to-one blackball'. That apparently means that six members have to vote for a member to wipe out one contra vote. Blackballed applicants are further humiliated by having their names posted on the club notice-board.

The Queen Elizabeth II Cup proved a disappointment, with a field of only three and the odds-on favourite romping home, but there was a card of seven races and the atmosphere of an oriental Ascot to enjoy. In the paddock, the ladies wore summer hats and the men wore suits or natty sports jackets. Some elderly gentlemen wore dhotis, one end tucked into the pocket of their shirts. These were acceptable because the dhoti is Bengali. The north-Indian kurta and pajamas – the uniform of politicians in Delhi – was not accepted. English as the high commissioner would like to hear it spoken was the language used in the shade of the ancient, sprawling banyan tree that still spread its tentacles over the paddock. In front of the stand, the band of the Gurkhas, clad in olive-green uniforms and pillbox hats, played music for all comers. For those with a Western taste in martial music there was 'Old Comrades', for those with an Eastern taste there was the stirring march '*Sare Jahan Se Accha Hindustan Hamara*' – 'Our India is the Best Place in the World'. For the bright young things there were hits from the Bombay movies, including 'Life is a Game of Love'. 'Game of Chance' would have been more appropriate at the Calcutta races, where the bookies looked as prosperous as they do the world over. Club servants wearing white pagris or turbans and olive-green cummerbunds padded around the dining-room at the top of the stands. They insisted on serving all three courses of the traditional lunch, although I protested that it was a little heavy for me. They showed me with pride the portrait signed by Edward, Prince of Wales – later Edward VIII – when he visited Calcutta on his ill-fated tour of India in 1921.

It would be wrong to give the impression that the races are only for the nabobs of Calcutta: they attract a large and volatile crowd in the cheaper stands who can turn very nasty if the stewards ignore their shouts of 'Objection, objection!' The stewards are obliged to give a written explanation of their decisions in the next day's racecard. On Queen Elizabeth II Cup day the punters were told that the previous week Royal Cormorant had 'received tender handling from his jockey' – presumably a polite way of saying the horse had been pulled. The jockey and trainer were fined. The Calcutta racecrowd may not exactly be the raw material of a Marxist revolution, but they are quite capable of demanding their democratic right to be informed.

The racecourse is at the southern end of the Maidan, the park which is the heart – or perhaps it would be more appropriate to say the lungs – of Calcutta. From the stands, the racegoer gets an impression of the splendour which was Calcutta, the capital of the British Indian Empire. To the left the racegoer can just see the Hooghly, the river on whose banks Job Charnock founded his city. In the foreground is the Gothic St Paul's Cathedral, with its tower modelled on that of the mother church of Anglican Christianity, Canterbury Cathedral. The Anglicans in India have outdone the rest of the Church by showing that ecumenicalism is not just a lot of theological hot air: they have merged with the other major non-Roman-Catholic denominations to form the Churches of North and South India. I was delighted to find that, in Calcutta Cathedral, High Anglican worship has survived the transformation.

Next to the cathedral stands the white marble Victoria Memorial, described by Geoffrey Moorhouse in his splendid book *Calcutta* as 'a sort of St Pancras by the Hooghly, but Classical not Gothic'. It dominates the Maidan. Queen Victoria still sits in state outside, making sure that her memorial is looked after. Unfortunately she has not been so successful in preserving the pictures inside. When the daughter of that most imperious of viceroys, Lord Curzon, visited Calcutta recently, she complained to the governor of West Bengal about the condition of some of the pictures in the Victoria Memorial. She had a certain right to do so, because her father's contribution to the preservation of India's heritage is acknowledged by all Indian scholars, no matter how anti-imperialist they may be.

In the distance, racegoers can see the tall tower erected in memory of Sir David Ochterlony, who defeated the Gurkha king of Nepal. The monument is now dedicated to Bengali martyrs.

Wide boulevards – remarkably free of traffic – cut across the Maidan. The Red Road, which was the route that imperial processions used to take, leads to the gates of the former viceregal palace. It lost that status in 1911, thirty-six years before independence, when the capital of India was moved to Delhi. Lord Curzon had never felt really comfortable in that palace, even though, by some strange quirk of history, when it had been built 100 years earlier the architect had taken Kedelston Hall, the family home of the Curzons, as his model. Sir Fredrick Burroughs, the last Englishman to live there, came from far more humble origins: he was a former railway man appointed by the Labour government in London to be the governor of West Bengal. Sir Fredrick used to boast, 'I am not a hunting and shooting man – I am a shunting and hooting man.'

Clubs, races, sung Eucharist in the cathedral, Queen Victoria – all these are signs that a past which most communist regimes would have eliminated is still alive in Calcutta. They should not, however, be taken as signs that Calcutta is still a British city. A visit to what used to be called Clive Street, at one time the commercial capital and trading centre of the second city of the empire, reminded me that the British were gone. Clive Street had been what Calcutta was really all about: it was the headquarters of the managing agencies which used to run British investments in India. The iron gates with their round shields embossed with the heads of lions still stood at the entrance to Gillanders House, the headquarters of the firm my father belonged to, but tattered tarpaulins leant against its semicircular frontage and spilled over the pavement. A road runs through the middle of the building, and I am sure my father would have approved of the notice ordering 'No horning'. But most of the office space was occupied by other companies. Gillanders is but a pale shadow of its former self. The Darjeeling Himalayan Railway, the narrow-gauge steam tramway Gillanders used to run, is now part of the nationalized Indian Railways. The coal mines and the life assurance and insurance companies Gillanders used to manage have been nationalized too. Jute is in decline, and Gillanders has lost many of its tea gardens, the only traditional industry of Calcutta which still flourishes.

The other managing agents have not fared any better. It was

difficult to tell whether the headquarters of Jardine Henderson, another of the managing agencies, was falling or being pulled down. Andrew Yule's House was in much better shape, but that agency has been nationalized lock, stock and barrel. The communists had nothing to do with all this nationalization: it was the work of the central government. What remains of the managing agencies has fallen into the hands of the Marwaris – a vigorous Indian business community once known more for their skills as moneylenders, traders and investors than for their managerial ability. They certainly have no sympathy for communism.

In Calcutta, the generally accepted reason for the decline of the British presence in Clive Street is laziness. A financial journalist said to me, 'The burra sahibs did not realize that the days of chota hazari [light breakfast], burra hazari [main breakfast], lunch and then the club had gone.' But that is at the best a very partial truth. My father was one of the hardest-working men I ever knew, and he and many of his colleagues from Calcutta became very successful industrialists when they returned to Britain. Independent India did make life much harder for the managing agencies – what with nationalization, high taxation, restrictions on the remittance of profits, work permits for foreigners and, above all, the stifling bureaucracy of a planned economy – nevertheless, I can't help feeling that the British accepted defeat too easily. Clive Street and its environs are now shabby, down-at-heel, overcrowded and ill-kempt, but it is still possible to sense – and indeed see – that it was once a great trading centre. It saddens me to think of the progress made by Hong Kong and Singapore and to compare them with Clive Street. But then India faced very different problems – particularly the problem of large-scale poverty, and Nehru chose socialism and a protected economy to deal with that – so Calcutta's trading activities were inevitably curtailed.

When the communists came to power in 1977, they found that industry in West Bengal had entered a serious decline. The old jute-mills and engineering factories had not been modernized and there had been no new investment. Many companies had moved out of the state. The communists were themselves partly to blame for this. In the sixties they had enjoyed two brief spells in power as members of unstable coalitions. They created industrial anarchy. The gherao – a particularly uncomfortable form of industrial action from management's point of view – was employed on the slightest of pretexts. 'Gherao' means 'surrounding', and that is exactly what the workers did. They surrounded the management in their offices, their factories or their yards – wherever they happened to be – and menaced them until they surrendered. The police had orders not to intervene. Then came the Naxalites, a splinter group of communists who still believed in violent revolution. They terrorized the citizens of Calcutta until the second coalition of the Marxists and other leftist parties collapsed. The Naxalites were then put down with considerable brutality by the man Indira Gandhi sent to restore order in West Bengal.

Gheraos and Naxalites did not exactly encourage investors. However, the Marxists also have a point when they blame the central government for the start of West Bengal's decline as an industrial state. The state used to enjoy a considerable geographical advantage because it was near India's coal belt, and also its iron ore and other minerals. That advantage was lost when the central government declared that raw materials for industry would be available at the same price throughout India, irrespective of freight charges.

The Marxists were sobered by their earlier experiences of power and by the years in the opposition which followed. They lost valuable cadre members in clashes with the Naxalites and in the police campaign which put them down. They had seen the Congress Party blatantly rig an election to the state assembly. Their leaders had been arrested in Indira Gandhi's state of emergency in 1975–7, and they feared that if she were ever returned to power she would end democracy in India once and for all. That is one reason for the remarkably pragmatic way in which they set about restoring West Bengal to its position as one of India's leading industrial states. The unions were told to behave themselves and to cooperate with management – even with management in the private sector. Strenuous efforts were made to persuade industrialists to invest in the state. Talks were even held with the vanguard of capitalism, the multinationals. Nationalization became a dirty word. Even the company which generates electricity for Calcutta was left in the hands of its shareholders, since the Marxists realized that it was doing a better job than the nationalized power stations.

One of the few concerns which the Marxists did nationalize was 'Darling' Billimoria's Great Eastern Hotel, but there was now talk of pulling down that historic building and putting up a modern five-star hotel with the help of Japanese capital and expertise. Not that Calcutta needs Japanese technology to run five-star hotels – the Grand on Chowringhee shows that Indians can do it perfectly well. This was the foundation of the fortune of Mohan Singh Oberoi, the father of modern hoteliery in India, who got the hotel on the cheap shortly before the Second World War because it had been closed for a year after six guests died of typhoid. Oberoi soon got to the bottom of the problem – a dead cat in the water-tank. During the war, the allied high command wanted to requisition the Grand to accommodate army officers. The army calculated it would cost twelve rupees a day to feed an officer. To retain control of his hotel, Oberoi offered to do it for ten. He calculated that he would make more than enough profit on the bar, and he proved to be right. Mohan Singh Oberoi is still alive, and I am sure he could revive the Great Eastern too.

The private sector was also introduced into public transport. Members of the Marxist Party were encouraged to become entrepreneurs by being given licences to operate buses in Calcutta. Standing in Dalhousie square, or BBD Bagh as it is now known, I watched the young drivers of these buses revving their engines to amuse themselves while their conductors yelled the destinations in a bid to attract passengers. When the buses were full they roared off to contribute more than their bit to the chaos of Calcutta's traffic, and to the noise and air pollution of a city which, while I was there, the Botanical Survey of India warned could turn into a gas chamber by the turn of the century. I contrasted those noisy, dirty buses with the trams of the nationalized Calcutta Tramways Corporation passing through the square, which is one of the two main junctions of the tram system. The trams did not pollute, and they made no noise except for the clanging of pedal-operated bells that still serve as horns. It might be an overstatement to describe the bells as musical, but they are certainly a lot more euphonious than horns.

The trams carry more than 180 million passengers a year. They are slower that the buses but are preferred by many people because their staff are comparatively polite and disciplined and the tickets are cheaper. The Marxists, in collaboration with the World Bank, have put money into the tramways, but the young managing director of the tramways felt that much more should have been done. He told me, 'Our technology is still the technology of 1900. Experts are now realizing again that trams are a very useful form of transport. They call them "light railways". I hope that we will eventually be able to upgrade Calcutta's trams to light railway.' A notice-board in his office showed that improvements were indeed necessary. The day before there had been fifteen derailments, three breakages in the overhead wires, one mechanical failure, three cases of other vehicles getting stuck on the tramlines and seven miscellaneous hold-ups. The total running time lost was nineteen hours five minutes. That apparently was not too bad a day.

There has been some progress in public transport in Calcutta. The underground, or Metro, has at last been opened – or at least half of it has: the five miles of line from outside the Tolly Club in south Calcutta to Esplanade at the northern end of the Maidan. It would be churlish to complain of the incomplete Metro, because the line to Tolly is one of the few success stories of Calcutta: it is quick, clean and punctual. Standing at Esplanade, I rather wished the service was a little less punctual because I had to tear myself away from a Laurel and Hardy film showing on the platform's television monitors. There is no question of subjecting travellers to Marxist indoctrination – but then the Metro is run by Indian Railways, a department of the central government.

Even in the field of public health the Marxists have had to turn to the private sector. The chief minister himself told a conference of doctors that the state government was encouraging the establishment of private nursing homes on condition that 30 per cent of the beds were free.

The Marxists have not touched distribution either. Stallholders have captured almost every inch of pavement in Calcutta. Perhaps as a result, I saw no queues and no shortages, the usual by-products of communism. One evening I visited the area around the university, in search of the publisher of a book on the Naxalites. Oranges, apples, grapes, bananas, cauliflowers, long white radishes and bitter spiky gourds spilt over the pavements. Carcasses of goats hung in butchers' shops. Behind the butchers there were black statues of the goddess Kali, with her grisly garland of human skulls. A cockroach was crawling over a pile of ginger in a provision merchant's shop. The merchant had sacks of five different sorts of dal, including the pink 'masoor ki' dal. For those who didn't want the bother of cooking, there were kebabs bubbling in a big, black pan. Another stallholder fried vegetables in batter to make pakoras. Fried fish seemed to be popular too. Bengalis are great sweet-eaters, and there were several shops to cater for that weakness. They sold two types of syrup-soaked Bengali sweets – white, creamy rasagallas and brown, sticky gulabjamuns – and many different sorts of sandesh, something a little like fudge. Stalls selling pan, or betel-leaf, seemed to be crammed into every spare space.

I couldn't find the publisher so I browsed in the bookstalls which line College Street. There I was not surprised to learn that cribs of the examinations for jobs as government clerks, or babus, were the best sellers. Bengal has long been famous for its babus, and a safe job in government service is the height of ambition for all but the most successful or privileged graduates. I bought the crib of the exams for recruitment into the clerical grade of the railways. I am not at all sure I would have passed the general knowledge; as for the maths, I could not understand some of the questions even after I had cheated by looking up the answers. I was most surprised by a sample essay that the editors of the crib, Messrs Khanna and Khanna, had provided. The examinee was asked to describe a railway journey in 250 words. Messrs Khanna and Khanna suggested the first paragraph of the essay should read

> Railway journeys, these days are fraught with disasters. Accidents and robberies are all too commonly associated with railway journeys and not without justification too. Overcrowding, delays filthiness, and other general inconveniences have of course come to be regarded as normal features of a railway journey. And the Indian railways is the biggerly [sic] public sector undertaking in the country and one of the biggest business undertakings in the world. While railway journey today is a nightmare and no body would undertake it unless forced to do so. It may be of interest to know how different things were not so long ago.

Ignoring the eccentricities of vocabulary and punctuation which might, one would think, lead to some 'marking down', the sentiments of that first paragraph hardly seem the way to the heart of a railway examiner.

The clerical skills of the Bengali babu make him a difficult subordinate to handle. He knows the rule book much better than his boss and can always find a reason why something should not be done. In that article on perestroika, the editor of the *Marxist* had admitted that bureaucratism in the Soviet Union had been one of the main causes of economic stagnation. In spite of that awareness, the Indian Marxists have not tackled the problem of the Bengali babu. Civil servants told me the government had become the prisoner of the Coordinating Committee, a trade union which in the name of Marx controls the government clerks. One civil servant described the start of a clerk's day. 'He will arrive at eleven thirty. He then puts down his briefcase, polishes his spectacles and drinks a glass of water. Next he will call for a cup of tea while he reads his newspaper. He will then be ready to discuss the news with his colleagues. By four o'clock he will be ready to go home.' The headquarters of the government of West Bengal is still called Writer's Building, after the writers of the East India Company. The piles of dusty files tied up with red tape, to be seen in the outer offices of every senior official and minister, indicate that the administration has not moved much beyond the days of 'John Company'. The courts are even worse: I met one litigant who had taken two years to get a copy of a court order.

Religion is also flourishing in Marxist Calcutta. I took the number 32 tram from Esplanade to Kalighat, the temple of the goddess Kali from whom many believe Calcutta takes its name. It took us almost an hour to reach the street leading to the temple. I was soon approached by a sleek, dhoti-clad Brahmin who came up to me and asked, 'Which country are you from?' I replied with pride that I was born in Calcutta, but the Brahmin was not put off. 'You will still need my help to go into the temple.' Realizing that I could hardly pass for a Hindu, in spite of the accident of my birth, I agreed and accepted the Brahmin as my guide.

As we entered, I saw the carcass of a decapitated goat being removed from what looked like an executioner's block. As if sensing disappointment, the Brahmin said, 'Don't worry, there will be plenty more sacrifices. You are bound to see one.' The Brahmin told me he was a member of one of the three original families which owned the temple. Unfortunately for him, there are now apparently about 700 Brahmins serving – if that's the right word – there. He explained that this was one of the places where the fifty-one parts of Kali had fallen after she had been cut up by Vishnu when he destroyed evil. Kali, or the black, is one of the names of the wife of Shiva: among her others are Durga, the inaccessible; Chandi, the fierce; and Bhairavi, the terrible. All bear witness to the terror she inspires and hence to the need to placate her by sacrifice.

The Abbé Dubois, the great French scholar who fled the executioner during the revolution in his own country and came to live in India as an Indian, found old men who told him that human sacrifice to placate the gods was still being practised when they were young. In *Hindu Manners, Customs and Ceremonies*, the Abbé described the theology of sacrifice thus: 'Man, overwhelmed with infirmities and misfortunes, and fully convinced that they were the punishment of his sins, imagined that he would appease and propitiate the Gods by offering them the most perfect sacrifice that he would find.' My Brahmin friend was not so lucid: he told me, 'People believe that, if they sacrifice a goat, Kali will stop bad things happening to them. The goat is the symbol of evil. It must be black or, if not entirely black, as black as possible.'

As he was speaking, a drummer started beating a fevered tattoo in one corner of the open sacrificial pen. A black kid goat, its horns coloured orange and garlands round its neck, was carried into the pen. The kid's neck was placed on the bottom of a U-shaped block and a pin was rammed home above it, to keep it in place. Without any further formality – not even apparently a prayer – the executioner, a sturdy man in a vest and loincloth, silenced the bleating kid with a scimitar, decapitating the sacrificial victim with one stroke. The penitent came forward and the executioner marked his forehead with a tilak of the goat's blood. The Brahmin turned to me and said, 'Of course not everyone comes here to offer a sacrifice like that. Most come to pray.'

We then climbed up into a pillared prayer hall, from where we could with difficulty see into the sanctum sanctorum over the heads of the eager stream of devotees filing past the image of Kali. Only the goddess's large, black, stone head was visible above the level of the floor. Her three eyes – she has a third eye in the middle of her forehead – were bright orange. Much of her face was covered with flowers. Above her head was suspended a colourful canopy embroidered with appliqué elephants. An elderly woman in a deep-pink sari came and stood next to me, bowing her head in reverence before the deity. Her husband stood behind, muttering, 'Give money here, give money there, feed this one, feed that one – these Brahmins are looting me.' My escort hurriedly drew me out of earshot and explained how the goddess was cared for. 'The head of the goddess', he said, 'is anointed with one kilo of vermilion every day, and that is used by the priests to put tikas on the foreheads of the devotees. The goddess is washed once a year by a priest with closed eyes, and the cloth that is used is distributed.'

The Brahmin was most anxious to show me the kitchen where food was prepared to be given to the poor. 'This is a highly expensive matter,' he said. 'Each day, one of the Brahmins has to provide the rice for this. It is highly critical to maintain this.' I was soon to learn how critical. As I left the temple, the Brahmin said to me, 'Give me 400 rupees. It is my turn to provide the rice tomorrow and I need the money for that.' Much bargaining ensued and we eventually settled for 100 rupees, which I was fairly sure would go into the well-rounded belly of the Brahmin, not to the poor and needy.

Although communism has not made much impact on the day-to-day life of Calcutta, discipline within the Marxist party is strict. A certain measure of self-criticism is allowed, however. Ashok Mitra, an academic economist who was for many years finance minister of West Bengal, admitted to me that his party had not provided a very radical government. 'When we came to power, we said we could not hope for any radical changes under the existing social and constitutional arrangements. We did say we would provide relief for the poor and set an example to other governments and states. We have provided plenty of relief, but we have done nothing to show the way to other governments. We could certainly have improved the working of the government, but we have not done so. For instance, not a single senior officer has been suspended.'

'Why have you not been able to improve the performance of the government?' I asked.

'Well, I am afraid we have not tackled our own clerical associations. It is strange that we have disciplined industrial labour but not the clerks. We haven't even got much out of disciplining labour. The chief minister has lobbied the multinationals and Indian industrialists pointing out that we now have one of the best climates for investment because of our labour relations, but the problem is that it's the central government, not us, which gives the licences. Also, much of the money which is invested in private ventures in fact comes from the financial institutions the central government controls.'

Ashok Mitra is an excitable, outspoken man who has spent many years in Western universities. He is not liked by the rank and file of the party, who do not feel he is really one of them. He could have returned to a comfortable place in a university after leaving the government, but he had chosen to live a comparatively spartan life in his small Calcutta flat. He hoped to resume his political career, in spite of the disappointments he suffered as finance minister – disappointments which led to his resignation officially on the grounds of poor health. One of his greatest disappointments was that the recommendations of the committee he chaired on administrative reforms were not implemented.

Mitra believed that the Marxists would have to become radical if they were to survive. 'When we came to power again in 1977, the chief minister said, "We tried to rush things in the sixties and I am not prepared to take risks again." But personally I don't feel that we can go on with this type of small-time relief. Either we must become more radical or we will become very unpopular. If when we came to power in the sixties the party had readopted the line we took at independence, we might have achieved effective radicalization. Instead we split, with the Naxalites going their own way. The trouble is that the Britain-returned barristocracy among the leadership thought the revolutionary line was foreign. It did not tally with Westminster, which was always their reference point.'

There are two strands in the leadership of the Marxists: the lawyers who learnt their communism in London in the thirties and the revolutionaries who learnt their communism in the jails of British India. The native communists have dominated the party machinery, but the 'barristocracy' has dominated the political wing. Ashok Mitra said, 'The lower orders have been overawed by the barristocracy: that's why there has been no effective radicalization.'

Jyoti Basu, the chief minister of West Bengal, is very much a barristocrat. He was educated by Jesuits in Calcutta and then went to London to train as a lawyer. He returned to India a convinced communist – just in time to be arrested by the British, the *sine qua non* of a political career at that time. I had approached the chief minister in true Indian style, through two friends known to be close to him. At first they were optimistic about the prospects of an interview, but I soon started to get indications that Jyoti Basu did not want to see any journalists because he was in the middle of delicate negotiations with other members of the politburo over strategy for the next general election. He feared that anything he said in public might be misunderstood. I had met him on earlier occasions and had always found him polite but firm – not a man to suffer fools gladly. He is a charismatic figure much loved in Bengal, but it's very difficult to explain his charisma. It certainly doesn't lie in his oratory, which has neither fire nor sparkle. He is short and bespectacled, looking not unlike one of those clerks he has failed to control. Nevertheless, Jyoti Babu, as he's known, has come to epitomize Bengal, not just the Marxists. One journalist said to me, 'Jyoti is more of an institution than a Marxist.' He has not shed all the habits of his British past. He speaks English within his family, and while I was in Calcutta he took time off to take them to a play by Stephen Spender staged under the auspices of the British Council. He is careful to live a simple life, but that does not preclude him from having an occasional drink in one of Calcutta's clubs.

Instead of seeing Jyoti Basu, I was sent to see one of the party's young ideologues, Anil Biswas, the editor of the party paper. Party headquarters is a modern building – much more modern in equipment, layout and atmosphere than the government's head offices. Biswas must have been in his early forties – a small, intense, but by no means humourless man. He felt that the Marxist government had achieved its goal 'to a small extent', but said that it was just beginning its task. He admitted that the realities of power had led to changes of emphasis in its thinking. 'In 1967, our slogan was "The government is the instrument of struggle." We gave the slogan and we haven't abandoned it, but we can't say the government is in the vanguard. Now the government is with the struggle but not of the struggle.'

I was not quite sure that I had followed his Marxist dialectics, and so I asked what the purpose of the struggles was. The editor of the party paper was quite clear on that: 'Our ultimate aim', he explained, 'is to destroy the Congress, to have a people's democratic revolution. We have to overcome many hurdles and go through many experiences. This government is one part of that experience. You must not forget that the state power in India is still in the hands of the landlord bourgeois class.'

I asked Biswas why the Marxists had not nationalized more industries. He replied, 'We are trying, but the rules and regulations of the central government are there.' The editor maintained that 180,000 factories had closed down in India because of what he called the 'crisis of the capitalist system', but went on to defend the party's invitation to capitalists to invest in West Bengal, saying, 'We are inviting capital, not capitalists. The state structure is not really suited to run industries, so the central government has to do it. If they will not, we have to invite capital from outside.'

Biswas claimed that the government's major successes had been achieved among the peasants, not the workers. The Marxists had introduced three important reforms in the countryside. They had registered sharecroppers – that is, tenant farmers who divided the crop with their landlords. That gave the farmers much greater security. They had made a determined effort to implement laws which restricted the amount of land anyone could own and to redistribute the surplus to the landless. They had entrusted the planning and implementation of development schemes to the panchayats or village councils.

These were measures that the Congress Party had put on the statute book but had not implemented. Suspecting that the same might be true of the Marxists, I went into the countryside to see for myself. I was fortunate in finding a dedicated block development officer – the civil servant who is responsible for a group of villages. He had left a comfortable job in one of the government services based in the capital because he wanted 'to do work which really mattered, not just file work'.

The block development officer said there had been real improvements since the Marxists came to power. Not only were the tenants secure, they also got a larger share of the crops. He did not agree that the Marxists had ignored the landless. 'Previously,' he told me, 'the landless had great difficulty in getting enough work. Now, because the government employment schemes are well administered, they get work for ten months a year. Of course there is some corruption in distributing the work and paying the workers, but I would say it only amounts to 20 per cent. In some states it is as high as 60. The landless have also benefited from the surplus land. I have just completed the redistribution of 350 acres taken from big owners.'

'But does that really do any good for the landless?' I asked.

'The trouble is that the land is given away in very small parcels, and that leads to inefficient farming. The best answer would be cooperative farming, but that has failed miserably in India. In

China, Mao found the same problem of small plots, lack of unity among the peasantry, helpless people, wasted land. He used the party's dictat to make the people swallow cooperative farming. In India there have been no leaders whose voices could rise above petty interests.'

The reforms in the panchayat system meant that decisions about development work – digging irrigation channels and tube-wells, building mud roads, planting trees and many other schemes – were now taken by the villagers themselves, or at least by the committee they had elected. That meant that the planning process had been reversed: instead of schemes coming down from bureaucrats on high, they now started from the bottom and went up to the bureaucrats for approval. The panchayats now also had powers to supervise the work and make sure it was actually completed. Under the previous system, the villagers had no check on officials who failed to implement schemes and pocketed the funds themselves. The block development officer approved of this in theory, but said there were problems.

'Since this new scheme, the quantity of work done has improved but the quality has deteriorated. The difficulty is that the sarpanches [panchayat leaders] who head the committees want to get as much work done as possible so that they'll be re-elected. That means they often ignore our professional advice and take up work of doubtful benefit. For instance, they sometimes have small canals dug which will adversely affect the land after a few years because they are not properly planned. The worst case is tube-wells. They should not dry up for seven to ten years, but now the sarpanches say, "If I dig tube-wells 100 feet instead of 300 feet deep, I can get three for the price of one." The trouble is, the tube-wells will dry up after three years.'

'What about corruption?' I asked.

'Of course there is some corruption. That is inevitable, because the sarpanch can choose the contractor to do the work – he doesn't necessarily have to get it done by our departments. That means he is open to bribery by the contractors.'

'But surely', I asked, 'you have powers to prevent this?'

'In theory, yes. We can refuse to accept the sarpanch's word, which means that we don't disburse funds; but the trouble is that he can appeal over our heads and we don't get the support we should do from our superior officers. That's politics for you. Most sarpanches are members of the Marxist party. The party backs them, and so our superior officers feel threatened and tow the line.'

Block development officers are sometimes called 'officers who block development'. They have an unenviable reputation for corruption, because so many of them are hand in glove with contractors. They tend to side with the dominant caste and so they do not implement government policy fairly. I was impressed by the frankness with which the Bengali block development officer spoke to me, and I was convinced that here at least I had met an honest and sincere official.

The panchayat reforms in Bengal have certainly reduced the powers of the block development officer, but they could just lead to another tyranny: the tyranny of the dominant caste. The block development officer was not unduly concerned about that. 'In Bengal, we are lucky in one respect: we do not have dominant castes like the Jats in Haryana, or the Yadavs in parts of Bihar. They are farmers with their own land. Here, many of the farmers are still tenants and we don't have large holdings. I would be more worried about the possibility of the party workers grabbing the development process for their own advantage. The panchayats are undoubtedly being used by the Marxists to provide their base in the rural areas.'

The former finance minister, Ashok Mitra, had told me that it was the presence of the party in the countryside which prevented the panchayats from being captured by vested interests. I decided to test this, although I knew I could take only a very small sample which would not make my findings scientific.

Turning off the main road, I drove along the embankment of a canal. It had once been a potholed village road, suitable at best for bullock carts, but it had now been levelled and covered with red Bankura earth which prevented the monsoon from washing away the surface. There were houses all along both banks, most of them made of mud with tiled roofs. They were shaded by banyan trees, banana plantains and date- and coconut-palms. In places the canal widened into village ponds, covered with green algae, in which men in loincloths bathed and women washed and oiled their long, black hair. Rickety, bamboo footbridges arched over the canal – I was very thankful that I was not called upon to cross one. This ribbon development made it impossible to tell where one village stopped and the next one started, so after four miles I stopped the car and got out to walk. I set out along the embankment, followed like the Pied Piper of Hamelin by a train of children.

We soon reached a small tea shop, where I asked for the sarpanch. The villagers pointed down the road towards the only brick-built house in sight. It was obviously the home of the richest man in the village, so I assumed that he would be the sarpanch. In fact there was no sarpanch in that village, just a member of the panchayat which covered a cluster of these small villages. He lived not in the brick-built house but in a much smaller one made of mud. In the narrow courtyard, a tethered cow was eating chopped green fodder out of a round earthenware manger. A young boy was sent to call Sanjay Khan, the member of the panchayat, from his fields. Indian villagers are hospitable and curious, so I knew that he would meet me. Sure enough, the boy soon returned with a short, stocky man wearing just a lungi. He had been irrigating a field of potatoes, and his dark skin was spattered with mud. The panchayat member owned only a quarter of an acre of land and had recently leased another half-acre.

Sanjay Khan had become a communist in 1964 when just out of school but had been made a fully fledged party member only in 1980. He had gone to university but that had not led to a job, and so he had worked in factories as a casual labourer, at the same time tilling his very small holding. He had to provide for a joint family of fourteen. After being accepted as a pukka Marxist, things looked up and he was made a primary-school teacher in the village. In many parts of India a schoolteacher would not stoop to work on the land, but Sanjay Khan did not regard manual labour as demeaning. He pointed out some of the improvements that the panchayat had achieved – the village was electrified, the road was covered with that red Bankura earth and 500 people had been given loans to start some income-generating activity.

I asked whether the panchayat used private contractors.

'Yes we do, because they will be loyal to us and work under our supervision. If you use government agencies, they work as and when they feel like it.'

'But doesn't that mean that the members of the panchayat can make money out of the contractors?' I asked.

Sanjay Khan pointed to his mud house and said, 'You can see for yourself. Does it look as if I'm making money? Would I work in my own fields if I was stealing the village funds? Look for yourself. This is a small and congested village. Everyone knows what everyone else is doing. How could I get re-elected if the village knew I was a thief?'

Sanjay Khan was firmly convinced that the new system was an improvement. 'Under the old system, nobody was interested in doing anything for the panchayat. You had to go to the bureaucrats to get anything done. They would not communicate. They would make you hang around and wait. Now there is not much problem – we can get things done without being harassed by the bureaucrats.'

I was interested in the fact that Sanjay Khan was a primary-school teacher, because a senior civil servant in Calcutta had told me that the party cadres were being rewarded with jobs as schoolteachers and other government posts. Sanjay Khan did not see anything wrong in that.

'I can tell you the position. Around here, about 60 per cent of the schoolteachers are Congress and 40 per cent Marxist. That shows that the Congress used to give jobs to their people, so why shouldn't we?'

The schoolteacher still studied Marxism – he showed me a history of the Bolshevik Party, a history of political theory in Russia and Germany in the nineteenth century and pamphlets by Marx and Lenin to prove it – but he maintained that no attempt was made to indoctrinate children in primary schools.

While Sanjay Khan was talking about Marxism, his mother was praying to the family deity. He laughed when I pointed out this contrast, and said, ‘The elder people are still religious. I am not, although I must admit I do remember God when I am in danger.’

After driving a few more miles along the canal bank, I came to the house of Gopal Naik, the sarpanch of that group of villages. It was built of concrete and was comparatively spacious. He employed labourers to work his land, and taught in a secondary, not a primary, school. In fact he was altogether a cut above Sanjay Khan. Perhaps for that reason I trusted him less. He had become a communist when he was a student at Calcutta University in the sixties. He admitted that there had been some corrupt sarpanches in West Bengal but said that they had been dealt with by the local party committees. When I suggested that he had been elected as sarpanch because he was well educated and comparatively prosperous, he said, ‘I have only been sarpanch for one year. I have been a member of the party for many years. Why have I only just been elected if it’s such an easy thing? My predecessor came from the Muslim community, although he was a Marxist. The Muslims have very little influence of their own here. He couldn’t have been chosen without the support of the party, and they choose people they trust.’

The sarpanch did admit that some tube-wells had gone dry, but denied that it was due to bad planning. He confirmed that, in spite of the panchayat’s Marxist members, it did employ private contractors. He did not accept that the new panchayat system helped the farmers but not the landless labourers. ‘The landless get these loans to start some business,’ he said. ‘Of course there have been cases of loans being squandered, but now we have set up loan-repayment camps and the panchayat acts as an intermediary between the borrower and the bank. We tell the landless that if they repay their loan they will get another one. We also start agitations to make sure that the labourers are paid the minimum wages.’

As I walked back to the car, a young man came up to me and said very quietly, ‘There are some people who are getting the party a bad name. I think our leaders are going to do something about them, otherwise workers like me will get disillusioned.’ He wouldn’t give me any names.

On the way back, I stopped to talk to a family of labourers squatting outside a station. They had been working on the roads and were waiting for a train back to their village. The head of the family, Bhradeswar Singh, was frail and pigeon-chested, with spindly, bandy legs. A sparse straggling beard partly covered his confused and defeated face. I asked whether he had been given a loan to start some business of his own. He replied, 'No, I asked for a loan to start a shop. I am now fifty-five and I can't go on working much longer. What will happen then? I will have to starve. That's why I asked for a loan, but I don't know why I couldn't get one. Many people of our caste have got loans, but not me.'

I suggested it might be because he was not a communist.

'I don't know much about parties. I vote for the Marxists, but how can I do more than that? I don't have time to work for them.'

That was a sad conversation with which to end my visit to the beautiful Bengal countryside, but I was not unduly depressed. Even sceptical Calcutta journalists had told me that conditions in the countryside had improved under the Marxists, and the little I had seen convinced me too. Nevertheless, it was strange that their rural revolution should be based on the ancient Indian panchayat system. Mahatma Gandhi – no communist – had hoped that the panchayats would be the basis of the revival of village life which he saw as the key to a prosperous India.

Returning to Calcutta, it took me one hour to cross the Hooghly. I could feel the 60-year-old Dakshineshwar bridge tremble as the traffic crawled across it. The first post-independence bridge over the Hooghly was started seventeen years ago, but there is still a yawning gap in the middle of it. That is partly because of arguments over the design, but it also reflects the neglect this once great city has suffered since independence – a neglect that has grown worse since West Bengal chose to vote for the communists rather than the Congress Party which controls the central government's funds. Delhi has been given three new bridges since independence, and a fourth is much nearer completion than Calcutta's new bridge.

The roads of north Calcutta were almost as crowded as the Dakshineshwar bridge. North Calcutta is the area where once lived the wealthy zamindars – the landowner class created by the British at the end of the eighteenth century. Their palaces are now falling into ruins; the lanes leading to them are lined with slums. The families living in those slums are, however, better off than the homeless squatting under the Strand Road flyover in central Calcutta, beside the railway lines leading from Sealdah Station and anywhere else where the police are tolerant or have been bribed. British Calcutta had more than its fair share of slums and squalor, but after independence the city succumbed to the pressure of population – the million refugees who fled from the then East Pakistan, a burden any city in the world would have had difficulty in bearing. The poverty of the neighbouring states of Bihar and Orissa has kept up the pressure on the city. It should be said in Calcutta's defence that even Delhi, which has a prosperous hinterland and has received the most favourable treatment from the central government, has become a city of slums. They are hidden by the glamour of New Delhi, but they are there. The miracle of all the metropolitan Indian cities is that they have not yet suffered any major ecological disaster.

Geoffrey Moorhouse's *Calcutta* quotes the British town-planner Professor Colin Buchanan, writing after a visit to Calcutta more than twenty years ago: 'This is one of the greatest urban concentrations in existence, rapidly approaching the point of breakdown in its economy, housing, sanitation, transport and the essential humanities of life. If the final breakdown were to take place it would be a disaster for mankind of a more sinister sort than any disaster of flood or famine.' The disaster has not taken place yet – largely due to the courage of the poor of India, who have an immense capacity to bear suffering.

In fairness, it has to be said that, since Professor Buchanan's jeremiad, efforts have been made to improve living conditions in Calcutta and they have had some effect, but neither the Congress Party nor the Marxists appear to have any answer to the fundamental problems of the city. That is not altogether surprising when one sees the failure of prosperous Western countries to solve the problems of their cities. A Calcutta businessman made that point to me rather forcibly at a dinner party. He said, 'When I go to London now and see the filth, the traffic jams, the crowds on the tube, the drunks sleeping in cardboard boxes and the graffiti, I am glad. When I see the buskers in the tube, I think, "Look, the white man is now begging from me." You are going our way, and about time too. Now you can keep your pity for yourselves.'

That businessman was an immigrant Calcuttan who came originally from Bihar. Bengalis don't often get upset about criticism of Calcutta – they love the city for all its faults, because it is still a bastion of their culture. Many believe that is why they like the Marxists too: that they vote for them as Bengalis, not as communists. It is true to say that the Marxists have managed to penetrate only the Bengali community in the neighbouring states, but Manoranjan Roy, the veteran Marxist trade-union leader who graduated from terrorism to communism in jail in the twenties and thirties, flatly denied that his party was Bengali. 'People only say that to sow confusion,' he told me. 'The trouble is that in Bihar and other parts of the Hindi-speaking area the feudals are still strong and we haven't been able to organize the peasantry.'

For 'feudals' I would substitute 'caste'. Caste is a very powerful factor in the backward and largely rural states of the Hindi belt, and caste and communism do not go together. But that does not explain the communists' failure in other big industrial cities, like Bombay and Ahmedabad. There Manoranjan Roy had to admit himself defeated. 'Those cities have long traditions of trade-unionism,' he told me, 'and I don't know why we have not been able to build more on that. Perhaps it's because Mahatma Gandhi got there first.'

Kerala, in the extreme south-west, is the only other major state in which the Marxists have a powerful presence. Like Bengal it has a strong identity of its own, and the Kerala Marxist Party has had similar difficulties in expanding into the neighbouring state. It has also had to make compromises – even at one stage forming an alliance with a Muslim religious party.

In spite of the compromises the Marxists have made in West Bengal and Kerala, they do have real achievements to their credit.

T. J. Nossiter of the London School of Economics has written in his recent book *Marxist State Governments in India*, 'Flawed the Communist Movement of India may well be but it has sustained its values far more successfully than any other movement or party in independent India.' Nossiter does not entirely dismiss the possibility of the Marxists becoming partners in the government of India. But therein lies their dilemma. They have already seen how far they have been forced to stray from orthodox policies in order to survive as a political force in two states of India. They therefore fear that if they adulterate their doctrine too they will end up like almost all the other national opposition parties in India – little more than rootless resting places for politicians who have not been able to realize their personal ambitions in the Congress Party. But the Marxists cannot hope to defend their identity by sticking to Stalin forever: they must evolve a theory of history and an ideology which responds to the realities of the Indian, not the Soviet, situation.

— 7 —

THE DEORALA SATI

On 2 September 1987, Maal Singh, a 23-year-old man belonging to the Rajput caste living in Deorala village in Rajasthan, fell mysteriously ill. The next day his 18-year-old wife, Roop Kanwar, together with his father and brother, took him to the hospital in the town of Sikar, the administrative headquarters of the district. He was suffering from severe stomach pains and low blood pressure. The doctors said her husband was in no danger, so Roop Kanwar returned to the village that night, but Maal Singh died in the early hours of the morning. His father reached Deorala with the body of his son at ten o'clock in the morning.

Roop Kanwar had been married for only eight months. Her wedding photographs show her to have been a beautiful young woman with a finely chiselled nose, big almond eyes, high cheekbones and a long, slender neck. In one picture she is leaning towards her husband, smiling confidently, with her head touching his broad turban.

When the body of her husband was brought to the house, Roop Kanwar asked her relatives to take it to the small room where she had lived with him. The body was laid on a mattress on the floor. She then asked everyone to leave the room and started to prepare her husband's body for the funeral. She paid her last respects to him by pressing her forehead to his forehead, her nose to his nose, and her chin to his chin. Then the young widow bathed her husband's body. Relatives had offered to help, but she had insisted on performing this ceremony herself. When she had finished this, she covered the body with a white sheet, went to the door and asked for her father-in-law.

By this time a large crowd had gathered on the verandah

outside the small room and the lane in front of it. Her father-in-law came to the door, but Roop Kanwar would not allow him into the room. She told him in a quiet but firm voice, 'I am going to be a sati.' He was appalled. He told her that the whole family would be in serious trouble with the police, pointed out that she was like a daughter to them and promised to look after her and care for her. But Roop Kanwar was adamant. Her father-in-law called a retired soldier who enjoyed respect and authority in the village. He explained the legal consequences for her family if she committed sati – they would, he said, be charged with murder. But Roop Kanwar still insisted that she would burn herself on her husband's pyre. Eventually some village elders and Brahmin priests were called. After questioning the young widow about her motives for wanting to be cremated with her husband, they pronounced that she was indeed a genuine sati. When the Brahmins left her room, Roop Kanwar had a bath herself and put on her wedding sari and jewellery.

The body of Roop Kanwar's husband was then carried out of the small room into the courtyard around which the house was built. Women were sobbing and beating their breasts, but Roop Kanwar said, 'Don't cry, don't cry. I am going to become a sati.' The women stopped weeping and stared at her. After a moment, the silence was broken by a cracked voice singing, 'I have worn my rakhri [bridal hair ornament], I have put on my necklace, I have gold earrings hanging from my ears and anklets on my feet and I am wearing my wedding chunari [long scarf or veil]. I cannot leave the man I wed. I am going to be a sati.' Other mourners took up the refrain, but their piercing voices mixed with angry shouts about Roop Kanwar's claim to be a sati – some mourners were arguing that she was too young, not married long enough or not sufficiently pious. They warned the enthusiasts who were still singing the praises of sati that they might all find themselves in a lot of trouble if they didn't stop the young widow burning herself. Their opponents proclaimed they would be cursed if they tried to prevent the sati.

A woman from the nai or barber caste grasped Roop Kanwar's wrists to break one of her bangles and place it on her husband's body. Traditionally, widows cannot wear bangles. Roop Kanwar pushed her away, saying, 'What do you want to break my bangles for? I am going with my husband. You will be cursed if you stop me.' Then a senior member of the family held up both her hands and said, 'Stop, stop! I'll find out whether she is a sati. I have an illness. I will bathe and put on clean clothes. If the bleeding stops, I will know she is a sati. If it does not, she is not.' The singing petered out, the arguments died down and everyone waited for the woman to return. Roop Kanwar sat by her husband's body muttering, '*Om sati, om sati, om sati.*' When the relative returned, she walked over to Roop Kanwar, took her chin in her hands and said, 'I accept that you are a sati.'

The mourners surged forward, surrounding the young widow and singing the song in praise of sati. Roop Kanwar said quietly, 'Please do the parikrama.' The women lined up and performed a ritual circumambulation around the body, still singing funeral songs. By this time, all opposition to the sati had collapsed. The men of the family came forward, picked up the bamboo bier and asked Roop Kanwar to lead the procession out of the courtyard.

The procession wound down narrow, sandy lanes to the small bazaar in the centre of the village. Roop Kanwar then turned back and, passing within a few yards of the family home, led the funeral procession on to the cremation ground at the other end of the village. Although Deorala is a large village, with a population of about 7,000, its old-fashioned houses are packed closely together on both sides of the lanes, which are barely wide enough for a tractor to drive through. There could not have been a single villager who did not know that a woman was going to commit sati by the time that Roop Kanwar ended her last walk through Deorala.

The pyre had been prepared in an open space surrounded by village houses. Maal Singh's body, wrapped in a white shroud but with his face uncovered, was laid on the pile of logs. Roop Kanwar started to walk slowly round and round the pyre. A few yards away, in the shade of a pipal tree, a sacred tree for Hindus, there stood three small shrines commemorating earlier women of the village who had committed sati. The air was thick with dust as thousands of villagers stamped and shoved to get a better view of the pyre. The prayers of the Brahmin priests were drowned by the beat of the drums, and by the frenzied crowd shouting '*Sati mata ki jai*' – 'Long live Sati, our mother' – and '*Jab tak suraj chand rahega, Roop Kanwar tera nam rahega*' – ' As long as there are sun and moon, Roop Kanwar, your name will live!'

Some of the relatives of the dead man urged the young widow to climb on to the pyre quickly, in case the police came and stopped the sati, but she insisted on taking her own time. Eventually she sat on the logs laid out for her husband's cremation, lifted his head on to her lap and asked her youngest brother-in-law, Puspendra Singh, aged just fifteen, to light the pyre. He walked round the pyre lighting it in different places and poured ghi, or clarified butter, on the body of his brother to help it burn. But it was slow to catch fire, and Roop Kanwar called out, 'It's a disgrace that you can't find enough wood and ghi to perform the sacrifice of a sati.' Some villagers ran back to their homes to bring more ghi, which was poured on to the fire until the flames rose and burnt Roop Kanwar and her husband to ashes. Villagers maintain that Roop Kanwar continued to pray right up to the moment her body slumped forward and was consumed by the flames.

A police constable arrived during the cremation – apparently he had been informed about the sati by the village postmaster and the patwari or land-records official. Seeing the frenzied crowd, the lone constable realized that there was nothing he could do to stop the crime – which it certainly was under the Indian Penal Code – so he went back to the nearest police station to make a report.

That was the version of Roop Kanwar's sati given by members of her husband's family, her own relatives in the village and the villagers themselves.

Tej Pal Saini, the correspondent for the Rajasthan newspaper *Rashtradoot* who covers the district of Sikar, was the first journalist to arrive in Deorala. He visited the village every day for the next week. All the villagers he questioned insisted that Roop Kanwar had committed sati of her own volition. *India Today*, a sober and highly respected magazine, also reached that conclusion. It reported, 'According to preliminary official reports and accounts given by friends and relatives, Roop Kanwar's sati was voluntary.'

The police have another version of the cremation. According to them, the sati was anything but voluntary. The police quote villagers as saying that Roop Kanwar was drugged with opium by a local doctor who was her husband's cousin. She was then dragged through the village leaning on the shoulders of two women. When they reached the cremation ground, members of her husband's family forced her to sit on the pyre and placed her dead husband's head in her lap. The flames shocked Roop Kanwar out of her drugged stupor and she struggled to get off the pyre, but she was forced back by young Rajput men wielding swords – the emblem of Rajput chivalry. Her screams were drowned by the slogans of the crowd and the beating of the drums. So, according to the police, the death of Roop Kanwar was a brutal murder and the whole village of Deorala connived at it.

To strengthen their case, the police maintained that Roop Kanwar had been having an affair and therefore could not have committed sati out of love for her husband or grief at his death. A government lawyer dealing with the case told me that the police had evidence that there had been a relationship between Roop Kanwar and Dr Magan Singh, the man who they say drugged her before she was burnt alive. The doctor was married and was a cousin of Roop Kanwar's husband, but he had been a regular visitor to her parents' house in the Rajasthan capital of Jaipur before she was married. The police also maintained that Roop Kanwar's marriage had been a disaster from the start. They said, 'She had become used to city life. She even used to go to beauty parlours and did not in the least want to go to live in a remote village. Things got so bad that her father arranged a holiday in a hill-station, hoping that she would accept her husband after that. But it did not work.'

According to the police, Roop Kanwar returned to Deorala only a week or so before her husband fell ill. There she conspired with the doctor to poison him. The police said the doctor accompanied Maal Singh to Sikar hospital, because he had contacts there and could prevent the correct treatment being given. When the young man died, his father, Sumer Singh, accused the doctor of poisoning him and threatened that he would expose the crime unless the doctor administered morphine to Roop Kanwar so that she could be forced to burn herself on the funeral pyre. According to the police, the morphine was not entirely effective, because Roop Kanwar did escape and run to a neighbour's house, but she was dragged back by her in-laws. The police maintain that the villagers thought they would 'benefit spiritually' from the sati, and so none of them intervened.

A different version of this story was published in the Delhi daily the *Hindustan Times*, attributed to 'senior citizens of this once obscure hamlet beginning to speak up albeit in hushed terms'. According to the young woman journalist who wrote the report, Roop Kanwar's husband was being treated for impotency and she was having an affair with a boy from the mali or gardeners' caste – a caste classified as Harijans. This report appeared twenty-four days after the death of Roop Kanwar and her husband and was one of a number of similar reports written well after the sati, but it particularly incensed the villagers of Deorala – perhaps because it had been written by a woman. A reporter from a Jaipur paper quoted villagers as saying, 'These girls come from Delhi in their trousers and write whatever they like about us. If they wanted to commit sati they wouldn't know which man to do it for.' An old farmer told a senior official, 'Our honour has been insulted. Women who travel all the time and spend only two nights a month with their husbands have come and said these dirty things about our women.'

The family of Roop Kanwar point out that young girls in Rajput homes are watched strictly and are not allowed out unaccompanied, so, they maintain, it would have been impossible for Roop Kanwar to have had any relationship with a man they didn't know about. They also say that she and her husband were friendly before they got married. He used to come to Jaipur and was allowed to take her to the cinema or to a restaurant, with an escort. At the same time, they deny that Roop Kanwar did not live with her husband in Deorala. This is also the view of two judges of the Rajasthan High Court, who heard a series of petitions against the government. In their judgement, they said it was 'an undisputed fact' that Roop Kanwar had lived with her husband in her father-in-law's house 'for some months'.

It was three weeks after the sati when the police made their first arrests in the case. They maintain that the delay was because all the offenders were 'absconding'. Unfortunately for the police, none of the witnesses who gave statements against Roop Kanwar's in-laws was willing to testify in court. This, the police maintained, was because they had come under pressure from the higher-caste villagers – the Rajputs, the Brahmins, and the banias – who were likely to benefit either politically or commercially from the reports that a voluntary act of sati had been committed and the consequent shrine. Now it is perfectly possible that the higher castes did get together and agree on a conspiracy of silence, and if that were so they would certainly have been able to put very effective pressure on the police witnesses, who were mainly 'servants and subordinates'. But, at the same time, 'servants and subordinates' are just the sort of people the police would find it easiest to persuade to make statements supporting their case – Indian police methods of persuasion are not of the gentlest.

There are two serious discrepancies in the story as told by Maal Singh's family: there is no record of the young man's admission to Sikar hospital and there is no adequate explanation of his family's failure to inform Roop Kanwar's parents of their son-in-law's death. It's quite possible that they feared that the parents would prevent Roop Kanwar committing sati – it's significant that failure to inform the wife's parents has been a feature of all the cases of sati in Rajasthan in recent years.

Inevitably, scholars do not agree on the origins of sati or on whether there is any scriptural authority for it. However, memorials to women who committed sati make it clear that by the tenth century some of these women were being worshipped because it was believed that Shiva's consort had entered into them. 'Sati' is one of the names given to that powerful goddess. Criticism of sati had also started by the tenth century. In Rajasthan, sati was clearly associated with a woman's duty to love and be faithful to her husband. The Mughal emperor Akbar did his best to discourage the practice. Commenting on the belief that a woman who committed sati assured her husband's salvation, he said, 'It is a strange commentary on the magnanimity of men that they should seek their deliverance through the self-sacrifice of their wives' – a sentiment that Indian feminists today strongly applaud. In the nineteenth century, the great Hindu reformer Ram Mohan Roy campaigned against sati. At the same time, the British rulers overcame their reluctance to interfere with Hindu religious customs and outlawed the practice. Ironically, the maharaja of Jaipur, whose kingdom included the village of Deorala, had banned sati before the British did. Nevertheless, stray cases continued in his kingdom and in parts of British India.

Rajput women in Rajasthan who survive their husbands are condemned by tradition to live highly restricted lives and cannot remarry. So there could have been three motives for Roop Kanwar to sacrifice herself on her husband's pyre: grief, fear of the life of a widow or religious fervour prompted by the belief that she would be worshipped thereafter. All three motives could, of course, have combined in the mind of the young widow, deeply disturbed by the loss of her husband and carried away by the intense emotion of Rajput mourning.

Many Indians refuse to believe that it is possible for a woman living at the end of the twentieth century to decide to burn herself on her husband's pyre, but I have come across one case where a highly educated Rajput woman certainly did commit sati of her own free will. On 18 October 1954, Brigadier Thakur Jabar Singh, a wealthy Rajput landowner who was the comptroller of the maharaja of Jodhpur's household, died after a long illness. His widow, Shugan Kanwar, asked for her husband's younger brother to be called from Jaipur. When he arrived, she told him that she intended to commit sati. He protested that it would do grave damage to the rest of the family, and particularly to his career as a government employee. Shugan Kanwar insisted that no harm would come to him or to any other members of the family. To demonstrate that she had the courage to commit sati, she held her hand over a diya or small oil-lamp. The flame appeared to cause her no pain, nor did it mark her hand. The next day a vast crowd assembled to watch her lead her husband's funeral procession, climb on the pyre and burn herself to death. Shugan Kanwar's sati is attested by many members of this well-to-do and thoroughly modern family.

I visited Deorala a year after Roop Kanwar had burnt to death and found the villagers angry and embittered. The Rajasthan Armed Constabulary had set up a checkpoint on the sandy track leading to the village. No cameras were allowed beyond that checkpoint. The cremation ground had been fenced off and was guarded by the police, to prevent anyone worshipping the sati. The site of the cremation was marked by a trident, the symbol of Sati, covered by a chunari, the long cloth which Rajasthani women wear over their heads. The chunari had been placed over the trident in a religious ceremony twelve days after the death of Roop Kanwar. Once bright red, it had since faded in the sun. Over the trident there stood the remains of what had been a pavilion. The cloth which had been draped round the bamboo structure to decorate it was begrimed by dust and hung in tatters. Traditionally, a sati shrine should be tended daily, but the police saw to it that Roop Kanwar's shrine was neglected – the government had ordered that no 'glorification' of the sati should be allowed.

I found Prehlad Sharma, a Brahmin who had just retired as a government inspector of cooperative societies, sitting outside one of the houses overlooking the open space where Roop Kanwar had burnt alive. He came from a prosperous family with a large house. It was built of concrete but in the traditional style, around a courtyard. The Brahmin sat on a platform outside the doors leading to the courtyard. Next door was one of the many crumbling brick-built havelis or mansions of Deorala. Many of them have fallen into disrepair because of family disputes over their ownership. Other families can no longer afford to maintain them properly, because they have lost a lot of their land in the government land reforms. Although it is set in the Rajasthan desert, Deorala has been a prosperous village for many years because it has plenty of underground water. Until recently, bullocks used to amble slowly round and round the wells, turning Persian wheels. Now there are electric pumps. Tractors have come to Deorala too, but the most common vehicles are still carts pulled by camels, their noses turned up disdainfully as their flat feet pad slowly but surely through the dust and sand. Deorala is a village where change is taking place, but most of its elders want that change to take place similarly slowly but surely.

Prehlad Sharma said, 'All this talk of progress since independence the politicians are always on about – what changes can you expect in forty years? We are a very old nation and we have our own ways. They have changed before and they are changing now, but forty years is a very short time. Rajiv Gandhi is talking about the twenty-first century. What can we say about that? How can we know about Rajiv Gandhi's life? His is a city life but ours is a village life, and that's different.'

Some of the young men of Prehlah's joint family were standing listening, but they let the old Brahmin do all the talking. I asked him whether he felt it was right to prevent worship of the sati. He replied, 'That's the government ruling, and who can go against the government ruling? No one. The trouble is that our representatives in the government never come to ask us what we want, or what our view is.'

'But do you approve of sati?'

'Approve or not approve, what is there to approve? Some people who have a religious mind approve of it. It's a religious matter, and people do want to worship at the sati sthal [site] when they come here. We can see that they are religious people. They behave very well. Cars still come almost every day, although they can't go up to the shrine.'

Tej Pal Saini, the journalist who had been the first to reach Deorala after the sati, had come to the village with me. He had warned me that the villagers were extremely sensitive about the allegations that Roop Kanwar had been forced to commit sati, so I approached the subject in a roundabout way by asking the Brahmin whether he was upset by what had been written in the press. 'Anyone can say what they want. It is their right,' he replied. 'Because of the press, it's our good fortune that we have become famous throughout the world.'

'But the press – or at least some journalists – said that Roop Kanwar was drugged with opium and then dragged to the funeral pyre.'

'Now look here. I ask you – this is a big village, it's an open place – can anyone do zabardasti [cruelty] here and it not be known? I mean, when there are cases of dowry deaths in towns, inside houses, witnesses come forward. Can it happen that no one would have seen Roop Kanwar being taken to her funeral by force and no one says anything about it? You know, in a village, if a man beats his child once, other men will stop him before he can beat him again. To burn someone is a very big thing, and do you really think that no one is going to stop that? The press thinks that we are very crude and cruel people, that we burn women. We are in fact very decent people.'

Prehlad Sharma had not been in the village on the day of the sati, but he sent one of his sons to call a farmer who had. The farmer, Arjun Singh, turned out to be an uncle by marriage of Roop Kanwar. He wore a red and white spotted flat turban, loosely tied in the Rajasthani style, and a vest which indicated that he had been working in the fields. The Brahmin warned me that Arjun Singh might be unwilling to talk, because all members of the family had been 'terrorized' by the press, but he seemed very anxious to defend the family. I asked him about reports that Roop Kanwar had been forced back on to the pyre. He replied, 'It was not really possible to tell what happened at the cremation. There were so many people there; there was such a crowd and so much pushing and noise that no one can tell exactly what happened, but I am in the family of Roop Kanwar and I am certain that I would have known if it had been wrongly done.'

Arjun Singh felt very strongly about the allegations that had been made in the press: 'They have given very wrong news. I have seen photos and seen it on the television where they have written that Roop Kanwar was given opium and then they burnt her. We are not the sort of people who burn women. It could not happen in my family. Some people have defamed us.'

It was about a five-minute walk from the cremation ground to the house where Roop Kanwar and her husband had lived. It too was built of concrete around a courtyard, but the young couple's room was in the front of the house and its door opened on to a verandah facing one of the village lanes. The house was empty. A peacock strutted across the empty verandah where once eager sightseers had jostled to get a view through the barred window of the small room in which Roop Kanwar was reported to have decided to commit sati. There were some faded decorations above the locked door and blue paintings of elephants on the yellow walls of the verandah. One villager said that Roop Kanwar's father-in-law was returning in a day or two, but no one was willing to say which members of the family still lived in the village or how much time they spent there. The whole village knew that murder charges had been brought against the father and other members of the family, and so they didn't want to give any information about them.

The lane I was walking down eventually widened into the village bazaar, which consisted of a few small shops and two or three handcarts from which vegetables were being sold. The bazaar could certainly not be described as bustling – there was no sign of the hectic commercial activity that Roop Kanwar's sati had sparked off last year. The cloth shop, which had a very meagre selection, was owned by Ram Gopal Aggarwal, who had recently been elected as sarpanch or head of the village council. He was a small, youngish man dressed in shirt and trousers, not the comfortable loose-fitting dhoti that the older generation all wore. He told me that he had not been in Deorala at the time of the sati, but he insisted that it had been voluntary.

'There could not have been any force. Our people are educated – they wouldn't have allowed someone to be burnt like that. I am not in favour of sati. It shouldn't have happened, but it couldn't have happened by force.'

One of the allegations made against the villagers is that they supported the sati because it would make Deorala into a shrine, and that would attract a lot of business. The sarpanch was a bania or member of the trading caste himself, but he denied this allegation.

'Who in this village is going to be able to take advantage of that sort of thing? When huge crowds came to worship Roop Kanwar, I had five stalls. All the rest of the stalls selling photographs and other souvenirs came from outside. Take those photographs of Roop Kanwar showing her on the funeral pyre with her husband. That was trick photography, and there is nowhere in this village where you can do that. They came from Jaipur. Actually, this is a very backward village commercially. You can see the bazaar. When the villagers want to buy anything out of the usual they go to Ajitgarh, which is a smaller village but has a much better bazaar.'

I said to the sarpanch, 'But the government maintains that the villagers wanted to build a temple so that devotees would flock into the village regularly. Then that would surely have benefited you all.'

'Yes, the government thinks that we wanted to build a temple. No one is interested. Anyhow, do you think that we can build a temple in a day? The only people who might be interested would come from outside.'

Although the sarpanch was elected on the ticket of Rajiv Gandhi's Congress Party, he clearly did not support the government line that greed had led to Deorala supporting a brutal murder. But then the sarpanch's links with the village are much closer than his links with the party. He also had a personal grudge against the authorities: the police sent to prevent the worship of Roop Kanwar had forcibly occupied the village dharamshala or rest house. 'We must have a place for people to stay,' he complained. 'When we have weddings in the village and other functions, it is essential that there should be somewhere for people from outside to sleep.'

All the villagers I met at Deorala insisted that Roop Kanwar's death had been 'voluntary'.

Dr Sharada Jain, a leading sociologist and champion of women's rights who teaches in the state capital, Jaipur, said to me, 'Roop Kanwar's death could not have been an act of free will. She was murdered.' Dr Jain is a formidably intelligent academic who does not suffer fools gladly. Doubt is not one of her weaknesses. When I pointed out that Rajput leaders had accused the women's protest movement she spearheaded of being Westernized, she snapped back, 'It is totally false to say that we are Westernized women. The Rajputs have taken to Western ways much more than any other community. The sati was not a question of tradition against modernity.'

Sharada Jain claimed that the sati was a conspiracy by three of the most important castes in Rajasthan, who shared a vested interest in it. 'Take the family which committed this murder,' she said. 'They are Rajputs. They pride themselves on their tradition of chivalry and valour. In villages throughout Rajasthan, the Rajputs were once the main landowners. Now there is little opportunity for deeds of chivalry, the government has taken away much of their land, and so the Rajputs are in search of an identity. A sati by a woman of the Rajput caste was a tremendous boost to their morale and their image.'

The Rajputs are the warrior caste from which the great ruling families of Rajasthan came – the maharajas of Jaipur, Jodhpur, Udaipur, Bikaner and Jaisalmer. They still provide a very fertile recruiting ground for the Indian army.

Sharada Jain went on to explain the Brahmins' vested interest in sati. 'As the priests, their approval was necessary before Roop Kanwar's sati could be accepted. Brahmin's prestige still depends on their priestly role. They only come into the limelight when something unusual happens – a birth, a death, a marriage. They would certainly want to dip into something so unusual as a so-called sati.'

The third caste which benefited from the sati, according to Dr Jain, are the banias. 'The banias', she explained, 'are a very rich and successful caste. You could say they are commercially very daring, but they are also basically superstitious. They are religious-minded, but their religion is based on luck. They would want to touch the ground where a sati was committed because they would believe it would bring them luck.'

Sharada Jain believes that these three castes combined to promote Roop Kanwar's death as sati. 'The banias have the economic power, the Rajputs the political power and the Brahmins the power of religious knowledge. Is it right that a woman's identity should be controlled by these vested interests?'

That mention of a woman's identity is the crux of Sharada Jain's argument. She insists that, whatever actually happened in Deorala, it was the unjust social and pseudo-religious pressures on women in Rajasthan which led to the death of Roop Kanwar. For that reason, she argues that journalists and academics who have tried to find out whether the sati was voluntary or not have got it all dangerously wrong. She wrote in the Bombay-based *Economic and Political Weekly*:

> The climax of the horror story in fact lies not in Deorala, or even in other parts of Rajasthan. It lies in the élitist 'distanced' quarters. It is from the urban educated élite that the oft repeated question came: 'Did Roop Kanwar commit sati of her own will or was she forced?' If, even at this level, the utter irrelevance of the question is not clear and if, even here, the condemnation or approval of the event depends on an answer to this question, then the focus of action has to be deliberated on with great care.

In one sense Sharada Jain is clearly right: it is not possible to justify anyone standing by and watching a woman burn herself, no matter how inspired by religious fervour she might be, no matter how 'voluntary' the act may be. But there is another aspect to this question. The villagers of Deorala could be described as misguided or superstitious if they stood by and witnessed what appeared to be a voluntary sati by a woman overcome by grief immediately after her husband's death and by religious fervour. On the other hand, if the villagers stood by and watched a young woman being dragged to the funeral pyre of her husband and then forcibly held down while she burnt, they can then only be described as condoning a public execution without any legal or religious sanction. There seems to me to be an important distinction between the two. The villagers of Deorala certainly feel there is, and they object to being seen as 'people who burn women'.

The Rajasthan government already had adequate powers and experience to deal with a case of sati: there have been twenty-eight such incidents in Sikar and its two neighbouring districts since 1947. A senior official in Jaipur told me there was a standard practice. 'Book the offenders under the Indian Penal Code, prevent puja or worship of the sati, and prevent the collection of donations.'

It was two days after the sati that the representatives of three women's organizations, including Sharada Jain, called on Mr Harideo Joshi, the chief minister of Rajasthan. They demanded that stern action be taken against those who abetted the sati, which they told the chief minister was a crime. He replied, 'It is a matter of religion. I will do the needful.' When they asked what that would be, the chief minister rang his bell and called for the next supplicant. Investigations were formally launched the next day, but the case was registered as one of abetment to suicide. This certainly did not satisfy the women's organizations: it was their contention that sati had to be murder, that Roop Kanwar could not possibly have chosen of her own free will to die on her husband's pyre. But what really angered them was that no attempt was being made to prevent the public celebration of the twelfth day after the sati: the date of the chunari ceremony, when the father and brothers of a woman who has been burnt with her husband place a coloured headcloth on a trident marking the spot where the cremation took place, which is considered a shrine of the goddess Sati.

The government was well aware of the mounting fervour in the village and the commercialization of the sati. Five days before the chunari ceremony was due to take place, the *Times of India* reporter wrote:

> And now the 'devotees' come in teeming hordes, squatting atop jeeps and buses and spilling out of camel carts. They come from as far as Delhi and Jaipur to this remote village, to propitiate the goddess of Sati . . . Meanwhile, the village economy has got a shot in the arm . . . with an average of 10,000 pilgrims streaming in every day. Jeeps, buses and tractors ply twenty-four hours between Deorala and Ajitgarh, a village four kilometres away. The villagers, recognizing the opportunity to make a quick buck, have set up makeshift shops selling everything from coconuts, sugar canes and sweetmeats to photographs of the couple. A not-so-cleverly engineered photographic card displays Roop Kanwar holding the superimposed face of her husband, smiling resplendent, on the pyre. These crude reproductions are selling like

hotcakes . . . The fervour will reach its climax at the 'chunari mahotsav' [festival] . . . the villagers expect more than one lakh [100,000] devotees on that day.

Still the government did nothing. The women organized a protest march, but it attracted only some 400 people, many of them well-known activists. That was no political threat to the government, and so it continued to regard the celebrations as a matter of religion. It was not until the day before the chunari ceremony, when the women's organizations got an injunction from the High Court ordering the Rajasthan government to prevent the ceremony taking place, that action was taken. Orders were sent to the local administration to control the situation, and senior officials of the police and the civil administration were dispatched to Deorala to enforce those orders. But a senior police officer told me they had been faced with an impossible situation. 'We kept on getting messages from the government: only allow 400 to worship, then only allow forty, then only allow the immediate relatives. But what could we do? Thousands and thousands of people had already arrived and buses were pouring in from Delhi, from other states and from Rajasthan itself. There would have been a riot.'

In the end a deal was struck with the organizers of the ceremony. They agreed to bring it forward by a few hours, so that the authorities on the spot could claim they had been taken by surprise and could not prevent it. But it is quite clear that at no stage did the Rajasthan government actually attempt to prevent the worship of sati, as it should have done according to its own procedures. If it had done, it would not have told the officials on the spot to try to limit the number of worshippers: it would have ordered them to surround the sati sthal and prevent anyone putting that red chunari over the trident.

Why did an experienced politician like the chief minister of Rajasthan not forestall the chunari ceremony? Like most chief ministers belonging to the prime minister's Congress Party, Hari Deo Joshi was little more than a cipher, taking orders from party headquarters in Delhi, which in effect meant the prime minister's secretariat. Those orders didn't arrive until too late. Joshi was already facing a serious threat from disgruntled Congressmen in Rajasthan who appeared to enjoy the support of Rajiv Gandhi, and he was not going to risk offending a politically powerful community like the Rajputs on his own initiative.

The chunari celebrations were widely reported in the press and sparked off a series of predictable responses. The urban liberal intellectuals and journalists jumped into the fray on the one side; on the other side, Rajput leaders leapt to the defence of their community and its traditions.

Journalists – as fundamentalist in their blind faith in modernity as the young Rajputs were in their beliefs – fanned the flames. Promila Kalhan, a syndicated columnist, attempted to make the case that sati was caused by the life that Rajput widows were condemned by tradition to live. She quoted the most senior civil servant in the Rajasthan government as saying, 'Men in their [Rajput] families consider it their prerogative to sexually abuse widows.' The official later denied ever saying this. No one I talked to confirmed that this was part of Rajput custom. The veteran communist columnist Nikhil Chakravarty described the death of Roop Kanwar as 'the murder of a young woman in the name of the outlawed superstitious practice of sati'. He went on to say, 'Reports available now indicate that the hapless victim was repeatedly pushed into the raging funeral pyre by the thugs masquerading as the standard bearers of Rajput chivalry.' He did not mention the reports which indicated that Roop Kanwar had committed sati voluntarily.

Praful Bidwai, writing in the *Times of India*, called sati 'one of the more opprobrious rituals and inhuman customs of Indian society'. He then went on to accuse the Rajputs of attempting to use sati as a powerful symbol to promote their identity in Rajasthan. Very few journalists made any attempt to understand the point of view of the villagers of Deorala. One who did was Prabash Joshi, the editor of the Hindi daily *Jansatta*, which is widely distributed throughout northern India. In an editorial, he suggested that Roop Kanwar did commit sati of her own free will:

Roop Kanwar did not become a sati because anyone threatened her, and neither was there any exceptional unhappiness clouding her own life which left her no option but to burn herself with her husband. Yet she purposely followed the tradition of sati which is found in the Rajput families of Rajasthan. Even among Rajasthan's Rajputs sati is no ordinary event. Out of hundreds of thousands of widows perhaps one would resolve on sati. It is quite natural that her self-sacrifice should become the centre of reverence and worship. This therefore cannot be called a question of women's civil rights or sexual discrimination. It is a matter of a society's religious and social beliefs.

To protect the moral values of society from time to time various types of rules and restrictions are made. These may become corrupted, and they can also be changed. But change can only come by re-moulding the accepted ideas and beliefs of the common people. New beliefs cannot be forced on them.

People who accept that this life is the beginning and the end, and see the greatest happiness in their own individual pleasure, will never understand the practice of sati. They are removed from the society which does not accept that death is the absolute end of the individual, but believes it to be the means of moving forward from one life to the next . . .

The practice of sati should now be totally re-examined. But this is not the right of people who neither know nor understand the faith and beliefs of the masses of India. If such people make a decision it will be torn to shreds in the same way as the decision of the [Rajasthan] High Court and the police at Deorala [at the time of the chunari ceremony].

The next day, about twenty-five members of the Janwadi Mahila Samiti or Popular Women's Committee filed into Prabash Joshi's office, surrounded his desk and started shouting slogans demanding that he apologize for the editorial. Joshi refused, insisting that he had not supported sati but had pointed out that laws should 'emerge from the womb of our traditions'. After two hours the women gave up and settled for Joshi publishing their statement criticizing the editorial.

Some Delhi academics did question the response of the liberal élite. Ashis Nandy, a sociologist and psychiatrist, wrote in the *Indian Express*:

It is the practices of the poor, the powerless, and the unsophisticated – the ways of the strange creatures who populate the countryside of India and whom we the modern Indians have unfortunately to call Indians – which always look self destructive or superstitious and which invite censure . . . However satanic it may look to us, the urban, westernized Indians, sati reaffirms, even in a bizzarre [sic], violent and perverted fashion, respect for self-sacrifice in a culture in which increasingly there is no scope or legitimacy for self-sacrifice, in which even the idea of self-sacrifice sounds hypocritical.

Nandy in no way approves of sati. He believes that Roop Kanwar was given, 'no help to move out of her depression and no chance to retrace her steps'. He also admits that, although there might not have been 'direct coercion', there was 'an atmosphere charged in favour of sati and the rite did become a spectacle for Deorala.' At the same time, he insists that the incident must be viewed as part of the price India is paying for its pursuit of a Westernized, capitalist way of life:

The traditional Rajasthani lifestyle is today facing major onslaughts on it – through the emergence of market morality as the only moral principle in social relations, through the emergence of modern political economy as the only organising principle of material life and the state as the only arbiter in inter-community relations, and through the large-scale destruction of traditional life-support systems which once provided the psycho-ecological basis of the Rajasthani culture.

Nandy ended his article with an indirect attack on the women's protest movement: 'Sloganeering cannot take away the fact that in a deeper sense the responsibility for the ritual suicide of Roop Kanwar will have to be borne by people like you and me.'

Much more typical of the academic response was an article by Kumkum Sangari attacking Nandy. In the February 1988 issue of *Seminar*, she wrote:

The notion of voluntary immolation in any of the cases that have taken place in Rajasthan, including Deorala, is not only absurd but contradicted by the evidence at hand . . . Nandy's pathetic belief in Roop's decision-making powers shows his distance from Deorala to be more comforting and self-serving than that of the modernists he deplores . . . Deorala is for him an apposite moment to criticise the modernists, and to make a sophisticated defense [sic] of Hindu orthodoxy and orthodox sociology.

Rajput leaders saw the attack on the Deorala sati and the allegations about the way they treated widows as an insult to their community and a threat to its traditions. They formed a 'Committee for the Protection of Religion', and under its banner 100,000 Rajputs assembled in Jaipur to hear speeches calling on them to defend Hinduism against the Westernized élite and 'independent' women. Many of the young men in the crowd brandished swords so blunt and rusty that they could cause death only by tetanus – appropriate symbols of Rajput chivalry, now locked away in the cupboard of history. Speakers at the rally described sati as 'a supreme example of a woman's duty to worship her husband' – the very thing the 'independent women' who had organized the protest movement against the Deorala incident and the government's handling of it disapproved of. They too organized a rally, which was attended by 3,000 people. Their symbols were posters proclaiming that sati was an issue of women's dignity and identity and demanding that religion and caste should not be used to oppress women.

A senior official of the Rajasthan government felt that those protests had burnished the Rajputs' rusty swords. He said, 'The outcry against the Deorala sati put the Rajput community in the dock and that gave the fundamentalists among them a platform, which is surely not what the women protesters wanted.'

There were important Rajput leaders who did not condone sati. Bhairon Singh Shekhavat, the leader of the opposition in the Rajasthan state assembly and a member of the Bharatiya Janata Party, which is a Hindu party, told the assembly that he did not believe that sati was a 'religious act'. He blamed the Deorala sati on 'anti-social elements', and pointed out that the Rajputs were not the only caste in which incidents of sati had occurred. But he went on to criticize the protest movement, saying, 'When, on account of such behaviour by anti-social elements, the entire Rajput community has been made to stand in the dock; and when, after making it stand in the dock, abuse is showered on it – then, forgive me, I am a Rajput and I too feel anguished.'

When I went to see Bhairon Singh Shekhavat a year after the incident, he was still smarting under the insults he felt his community had suffered. He showed me letters he had written to the editor of the *Hindustan Times* about the columnist who had suggested that Rajput men sexually abused widows, and the report that Roop Kanwar had been having an affair with a boy from a Harijan caste. The proprietor of the paper, K. K. Birla, had written back an apologetic letter – K. K. Birla is an industrialist with major interests in Rajasthan. Bhairon Singh Shekhavat, a tall, grey-haired man with a commanding personality, is in his mid-sixties, so Mr Birla may well have to reckon with his presence on the Rajasthan political scene for several years to come.

The Rajput opposition leader was particularly incensed by an allegation reported to have been made by Rajiv Gandhi's minister for women and children's development, Margaret Alwa. He said, 'Margaret Alwa has made a statement that when Rajputs come to console widows they pull the hair out of the widows' heads. Can anyone really believe that any community would have such a barbaric custom? What people don't understand is that we have a deep respect for our women, and that the relationship between a man and his wife is considered something very sacred. Because we don't treat our women in a modern way, does that mean that we treat them badly? My own father died when I was sixteen, but I always had the deepest respect for my mother. Would I have seen her badly treated?'

The Deorala sati was a grave embarrassment to Rajiv Gandhi. He was due to attend the Commonwealth Prime Ministers' Conference in Canada the next month, and to go on from there to visit the United States. Roop Kanwar's sati had by this time attracted considerable attention in the international press, and the young prime minister who had promised to bring India into the twenty-first century did not much relish the idea of going abroad as the leader of a country where the burning of widows was celebrated as a joyous occasion. The government had to be seen to be acting, but in India that all too often means legislative, not executive, action. Under the existing law, those who in any way took part in an incident of sati could be charged with abetment to murder or suicide, but, instead of taking measures to see that this more general law was enforced, Rajiv Gandhi ordered the Rajasthan chief minister to pass a new law specifically against sati.

The same politician who had originally described sati as a 'matter of religion' now took the highly questionable step of proroguing the state assembly for one day so that he could issue an ordinance without any delay. But the liberals were not satisfied. They pointed out – with justification – that, if a law against sati was necessary, it ought to be effective throughout India, not just in Rajasthan. So the central government extended the winter session of parliament to rush through its own bill. Ignoring the sensitivity of the issue, the government gave itself no time to consult experts or interest groups. An act made it a crime to commit sati or to abet anyone to commit sati, and banned the 'glorification of sati'.

Even lawyers working with women's groups condemned the act. For one thing, it did not distinguish between voluntary and involuntary sati, so even a woman forced to be cremated with her husband would be guilty of a crime if she were rescued in time. Also, the act classified the organizers of a sati as abettors, for which the maximum sentence was to be just one year's imprisonment, whereas under the law which already existed they could be prosecuted for murder. Since not even the most extreme Rajputs contended that a woman should ever be forced to commit sati, the act was a retrograde step from everyone's point of view.

A year later, the fragility of the provisions of the new act prohibiting the glorification of sati were shown up. In the town of Jhunjhunu, about an hour's drive from Deorala, there is a shrine dedicated to Narayani Devi, a woman who is said to have committed sati centuries ago – exactly when, nobody knows. She was reputed to have been a member of the Aggarwal caste of banias or traders. Her shrine is now known as the Rani Sati, or Queen Sati, temple and has become a very important centre of the rich Rajasthani bania community known as Marwaris. During the last century, the Marwaris moved into the new cities of British India and many of them laid the foundations of great fortunes. Some of today's biggest names in Indian industry are Marwaris. After independence, Marwari money started to pour into Jhunjhunu. The small shrine of Narayani Devi was converted into a vast white marble temple, surmounted by a curved tower in the north-Indian style. Smaller towers were raised over shrines of twelve other satis. A rest house with some 200 rooms was added, as an outer court of the complex. Every year there is a large fair in honour of Rani Sati.

The year after Deorala, some of the women activists decided to test the new act by challenging the holding of this fair, saying that it amounted to glorifying sati. The Marwari temple trustees argued that sati was just an epithet describing a woman who was pious and faithful to her husband. They maintained that the trust was entirely opposed to the burning of widows and said that the goddess worshipped was in fact Shakti, the Hindu goddess of power. Lawyers moved in and eventually the Supreme Court issued a temporary order banning the fair but allowing the regular daily worship in the temple to continue. Some 40,000 people turned up to worship the goddess on the day when the fair should have been held. Had the law been broken or not? Nobody seemed to know.

Once again, both sides had right on their side. Since independence, the Marwaris have built a large number of shrines to satis they have rediscovered in the area surrounding Jhunjhunu. This is also the area in which most of the satis have taken place since independence. There could well be a connection. But the Marwaris can justifiably claim that Jhunjhunu is simply a very important temple of their community, where they come to celebrate all the important events in their family lives.

The new law has had some effect on worship at Jhunjhunu. When I visited the temple, the image of Sati or Shakti – whoever she was – was a simple silver trident standing in an ornate miniature pavilion also made of silver. A picture I bought outside the temple showed that the trident used to have two eyes between its forks and a red and gold embroidered cloth and a necklace underneath it, giving the impression of a human face and shoulders. I had also read that there used to be a macabre model of Narayani Devi's sati: she sat surrounded by red crêpe paper with her husband's head on her lap. The impression of flames licking around her was heightened by a mechanical device which bobbed her up and down and by electric fans which rustled the paper. When I asked the temple's security officer whether I could see this model, he denied all knowledge of it.

The victories of the women who had challenged the Jhunjhunu fair had been won at the cost of the revival of the memory of the Deorala sati, just one year after the event, and the likelihood of legal cases lasting for years which will be continual reminders of sati. These reminders could well increase interest in the worship at sati shrines in villages all over Rajasthan – the law will never be able to prevent worship at all of them. The Marwaris of the Jhunjhunu trust have offered to make it absolutely clear that they are worshipping Shakti, not Sati, in all the temples they control, but the liberals have rejected this as a 'dishonest compromise'. The liberals have certainly not stamped out the worship of Sati. In the temple at Jhunjhunu I watched a well-to-do Marwari couple with their two children walk down the line of smaller shrines celebrating the lesser satis. They stopped to pray at every shrine, and the father gave his daughter a 100 rupee note to put in the collection box outside each one.

Dr Sharada Jain told me that when she and her colleagues started their protest movement they were determined that Roop Kanwar's sati should be seen not as a religious or caste issue but as a criminal act linked to the problem of women's identity in India. 'We didn't want to attack Rajputs,' she told me, 'because we were afraid it would just provoke another clash of the castes.' But the debate did turn the sati into a battle between the feminists 'modernity' and the Rajput fundamentalists' religious and caste traditions. There is no doubt which side the village of Deorala backed, and the reaction is likely to have been exactly the same in hundreds of other Rajasthani villages. The fundamentalists were, as the Rajasthan government official said, given a platform. At the same time, the law was brought into disrepute by legislation which was impossible to implement, and another myth about the barbarity and backwardness of India was spread throughout the world.

Dr Jain gave me a very frank assessment of the protests which she had played a prominent role in organizing. She said, 'In the end we just wanted the whole commotion to stop. There was so much tension. The controversy became a very happy hunting-ground for journalists and film-makers. They were amused and excited. I didn't see a face which was not smiling. Nobody was interested in solving the problem: they were just here to do their own thing. Caste leaders and fundamentalists came into the limelight and made good use of it. Politicians said, "If we can have another sati we can bring down the government."' But Dr Jain did not believe that the protests had all been in vain. She said, 'What was not counter-productive was that the vested interests were clearly identified.'

The cause of all that amusement and excitement was the government's failure to enforce the law. The protest movement in Jaipur was launched only when it became clear that the Rajasthan government was not going to prevent worship at the shrine of Roop Kanwar. If the chief minister had ordered the police and the administration to stick to the rule book, those responsible for the sati would have been charged with abetment to murder, or at least abetment to suicide, and the villagers would have been prevented from putting up any sort of shrine to commemorate Roop Kanwar. An example would have been set which would deter others from encouraging sati, and Roop Kanwar's death would have been seen for what it was – a crime, but a rare one. Three years earlier Dr Jain had told a student that sati was a 'non-issue'. But a non-issue would not have pleased those feminists who jumped at the opportunity the tragedy in Deorala gave to promote their views on women's rights. They turned that crime into an issue without thinking about the damage their campaign could do to the very women whose lives they were trying to improve and without giving thought to the prejudices against India it could create in other countries. The villagers of Deorala said the feminists used the sati to publicize themselves. That is a harsh judgement, but then the villagers felt they had been harshly treated.

— 8 —

TYPHOON IN AHMEDABAD

On 3 April 1990 the body of a Muslim, Yasin Arab, was found near his home in the congested area of Ahmedabad known as the Old City. He had been stabbed to death. Within an hour of that murder, four Hindus were stabbed in separate incidents. Police were baffled by two aspects of these murders. The young Muslim appeared to have been killed elsewhere, because there were no blood stains near his body. That seemed to indicate that the body had deliberately been brought back to anger Muslims who live cheek by jowl with Hindus in the narrow crowded alleys of the Old City. It was also very strange that revenge should have been taken so quickly, with the four Hindus being stabbed so soon after the Muslim's body had been discovered. Both these unusual aspects led the police to suspect that this was a planned attempt to start riots.

A curfew was imposed in the immediate vicinity, known as Kalupur, but the police were reluctant to extend the curfew any wider for fear of causing panic and giving the rest of India the impression that serious communal rioting had started in Ahmedabad yet again. Over the next three days the trouble built up, with police opening fire to disperse groups throwing stones at each other. Stabbings were reported from several different areas. On the fourth day of the riots, 6 April, twenty-three people were killed and seventy injured. Thirty-one shops were looted and burnt. The seriousness of the situation could no longer be disguised so the curfew was extended to all the other areas of the city with a past record of communal violence.

Then on 7 April there was what looked like another deliberate attempt to enrage Hindus. A rumour swept through the city that the mahant or priest of the temple of Lord Jagannath had been killed. This was highly unlikely, because the mahant rarely went out of the temple and, when he did, he was surrounded by a large number of guards and devotees, but even people ringing up newspaper offices were told that it appeared that the mahant had been killed. When the police investigated the report, however, they found that the man who had been killed was a comparatively unknown sadhu who seemed to have been involved in some row over hashish, because he was killed near a shop which was licensed to sell the drug to addicts. All India Radio then broadcast special bulletins denying that the mahant had been killed. The next day the army staged what are known as flag marches through the areas under curfew, as a demonstration of the government's determination to end the rioting. That seemed to work: there were stray incidents of stabbing for a few more days, but by 14 April the violence had stopped.

Inevitably the press interpreted the riots as further evidence of the threat of fundamentalism. The *Hindu*, a sober, national English-language daily which, in spite of its name, is not sectarian wrote, 'The behaviour of the fundamentalists needs to be condemned. It's time the new government took a deep look into the way the communities have been drifting apart.' That assertion ignores the evidence that there had been a deliberate attempt to incite Hindu–Muslim riots. It suggests that religious fundamentalism is making the divide between Hindus and Muslims deeper and deeper. I found exactly the opposite in Ahmedabad. I found that the poor among the Muslims, who are the real sufferers when communal riots start, blame politics, not religion, for the violence. But then most editorial writers don't speak to poor Muslims and so are easily carried away by the fashionable fear of fundamentalism.

Ahmedabad is the main city of Gujarat, Mahatma Gandhi's home state. He founded his first ashram on the banks of the now dried-up Sabarmati river which divides the city, and he formed a textile union for the mill-workers in the city. Because of its cotton mills, Ahmedabad used to be known as the Manchester of India –

rather unfairly, because it remained a particularly Indian city throughout the raj. It might have thought it was better than Manchester, but never that it was Manchester. In *Ahmedabad – a Study in Indian Urban History*, Kenneth Gillion, an American historian, wrote of the city, 'there was little British investment; there were never many Englishmen in the city; there was no higher education to speak of; the English language was understood by few; and there was no English press.' Ahmedabad today is still resisting at least some of the influences of modern Western culture. It is, for example, the only large city in India without a five-star hotel. It is the only large city where prohibition is in force. It is the only large city which does not have an English-language newspaper of its own. It is a city which has seen several declines, but it has always recovered because its traders and its entrepreneurs have had the energy and initiative to find new opportunities. Gujaratis are fond of pointing out that they were doing business in Africa before the British arrived there. The Gujarati traders who went to Britain after they were forced out of Africa have proved their ability to turn disaster into opportunity.

Ahmedabad always had a reputation as a peaceful hardworking city. In spite of its large Muslim population it was not much affected by the turmoil of partition. Communal violence came to the city only when the politics of Gujarat became unstable, and that surely cannot be just a coincidence. The first and the worst riots took place in 1969, when some say as many as 2,700 people were killed in six days – the official figure of 1,200 is bad enough. There were few stabbings then – people were hacked to death with axes, speared or burnt alive. Because the police took no action, whole areas of the city were in the control of the mobs for two and a half days. When the police did move on to the streets, it took them another three days to restore some semblance of order. At that time the hostility in the Congress Party between Indira Gandhi and Morarji Desai, an austere disciple of the Mahatma, had come into the open and the party was splitting. Gujarat, being Morarji's home state, was his political base. The chief minister of Gujarat in 1969 was a Morarji man, and some believe the riots were deliberately engineered by supporters of Indira Gandhi to discredit her opponent.

The riots in 1985 which lasted into 1986 started just after Mahdavsinh Solanki, a loyal supporter of Indira Gandhi's family, had won the election to the Gujarat state assembly by wooing the backward-caste vote for the first time. He himself belonged to one of the backward castes. In spite of their numerical superiority, they had always been ignored by the influential upper castes who dominated the Congress. Solanki reckoned that by clubbing together the backward vote the Congress would be unbeatable. Of course he was not unmindful of the fact that, as a backward, he would be unbeatable as leader of the party too. But the upper-caste Congressmen were not going to take this lying down. It was they who started an agitation against Solanki's decision to increase the quotas of government jobs and places in universities reserved for the backward castes – an agitation which soon degenerated into Hindu–Muslim violence.

Now, in April 1990, I had come to Ahmedabad to report on the aftermath of yet more riots, which had broken out just after a major political event – the rout of the Congress Party in the state-assembly election. The new government was a coalition of the Janata Dal, which had recently come to power in the centre, and the Bharatiya Janata Party or BJP, which was a Hindu party. The success of the BJP in the recent general election and now in state-assembly elections was ascribed by many to 'a wave of Hindu fundamentalism sweeping the country'.

This opinion appeared to be justified by the BJP's support for a campaign to build a temple in the northern-Indian town of Ayodhya on what was said to be the site of the birth of the Hindu god Lord Ram. Unfortunately there was already a mosque there, and Muslim leaders had threatened that India would feel 'the wrath of their community' if it were destroyed. During the months leading up to the 1989 general election, ceremonies and processions were organized throughout most of India at which the faithful were encouraged to buy a brick for the temple and have it blessed. The President of the BJP took part in one of these ceremonies in New Delhi. The campaign for the temple undoubtedly gave the general election a communal colouring, and these provocative celebrations sparked off clashes between Hindus and Muslims in which the Muslims generally came off worst. In the town of Bhagalpur in Bihar, the violence was described as the worst since the partition of India.

In Gujarat there were, according to the official records, seventy-five 'communal incidents' connected with the campaign to build the temple, seven people were killed, and 133 were injured. Yet when I got to Ahmedabad I found that it was still not a Belfast or a Beirut, a city divided against itself. Sound common sense had again foiled the politicians who wanted to play politics with religion.

The first people I went to see were a group of Muslim women. As I have said, the Muslims generally come off worse in religious riots and I wanted to find out whether they believed their community was in danger of being engulfed by a wave of communal hatred. I found them sitting on the roof of an ugly grey building near the Sabarmati, which was the headquarters of a remarkable organization known as SEWA, or the Self Employed Women's Association. The women were stamping coarse cotton cloth with wooden blocks – hand printing. They were members of a cooperative founded by SEWA to protect them from middlemen and help them upgrade their skills.

In Ahmedabad, riots are always known as 'toofan' or 'hurricanes'. One of the younger printing women, Hasina, said to me, 'It's not so much the toofan itself we suffer from as the curfew. We don't have the sort of homes or shops that mobs will loot, and if we stay inside we normally won't be harmed during the riots. But we suffer very badly from the curfews. We are relying on daily work, and so if we can't go out to work where do we get the money? If a man goes out to his work he may get killed, and his family won't even know where he is.'

'Did any of your relatives get killed this time?' I asked.

'Someone was killed just outside our house. We saw the blood. One of my friends said a young man had been killed. He was a good man. His father had died and he was looking after the whole family. He was fasting.'

The riots had come in the middle of Ramzan, the month of fasting. The young man had died of stab wounds. Stabbing is a very common occurrence during communal violence in Ahmedabad, and this time doctors noticed a remarkable similarity in all the wounds of stabbing victims, indicating that the attackers had been trained. This has led some to believe that the stabbings were organized by one of the leaders of the Ahmedabad underworld who had both Hindu and Muslim gangs under him, but no one would name that leader.

For Indian Muslims, the cure for riots is often worse than the disease, because the medicine is administered by the police force, whose members are almost entirely Hindu.

An elderly woman called Jetun Appa pushed a pair of smart but uncomfortable bifocal glasses back on the bridge of her nose and said, 'The police are as bad as the gangs. They come and break down the doors of our homes saying they are searching for bad characters. This time they broke the windows of the scooter-rickshaws our men drive. They also broke the screens of the television sets of anyone who had them.'

'Did the police loot your houses or steal any of your property?' I asked.

'What property?' she shot back. 'We don't have any.' The others broke into laughter, but the elderly lady was not amused. 'This time the police arrested my brother for being out during curfew. He was arrested for two days. We could only get him out by giving the documents for our home as a security. If we complain, the police beat us. Now we can laugh about it – then we were crying.'

Hasina said, 'This time nothing happened. Last time, in my mother's house, my brother was arrested for trying to take out his scooter-rickshaw. He was held for five days and we only got him out with the help of the ladies who run SEWA. The police bashed his head against a wall, and beat his knees so that he couldn't walk for two days when he was released. We had to massage him for two days.'

The elderly and irascible Jetun Appa said, 'We women have to go out to buy what we can during the curfew breaks, because it's not safe for the men to go out. If we are late back, the police make us sit on the ground in the open sun. They make us stare into the sun. They also make us say we are sorry – toba, toba!' She pulled her ears – the Islamic sign of repentance – and went on, 'If they catch a man, they make him walk home carrying his bicycle above his head.'

Apparently, during these riots a group of women had insisted that the police arrest them along with their men. The police lacked the courage to cope with them and ran for it, leaving the men behind.

I assumed that it was the Muslims who were the targets of the police, but Jetun Appa put me right on this. To my surprise, she said, 'They treat the poor Hindus just as badly. It's always the poor who are killed in riots, and it's always the poor who suffer the police zulum [atrocities]. If a Muslim is killed, they go for the innocent Hindus. If a Hindu is killed, they go for the innocent Muslims.'

When curfews are imposed, the local administration as a routine practice announces that arrangements have been made for the distribution of essential supplies, but I can never remember reporting a curfew where essential supplies were effectively distributed. So I asked the women about this.

'We received nothing,' said Jetun Appa – who seemed to have appointed herself as the spokesperson-in-chief. 'We couldn't even get limes to make sherbet. We have to end the fast each day with lime sherbet and dates. We couldn't get them, although according to Islam we should take them to end the fast each day.'

'We couldn't even get bananas,' said a younger woman called Hanifa, who was the comedienne of the party. Everyone roared with laughter, because it's the privilege of the toothless to break their fast with that fruit.

Jetun Appa took up the tale again. 'We had to break the fast with plain salt. That too is permitted in the Koran if it is all you have. We had no money to buy the children new clothes for Id [the festival] and they couldn't understand so they all cried, and we couldn't tell them we had no money. Even though it was Ramzan, the men were not allowed to go to the mosques for prayers. They used to sometimes gather in each other's houses, but that was all. Sometimes the men could get to the smaller mosques down the galis [alleys], but there were no prayers in the big mosques.'

I then moved on to the subject which interested me most. 'In the newspapers, you read that these riots are communal – between Hindus and Muslims. But they must start somehow. Who starts them – the Hindus or the Muslims?'

She replied, 'It's nothing to do with Hindus or Muslims. It's all politicians. When the Congress comes to power, the Bhajpa [Bharatiya Janata Party, or BJP] does it. When the Bhajpa comes to power, the Congress does it. It's just to give the new government a bad name.'

'So this time the Congress did it, because they had just been routed in the election to the Gujarat state assembly?'

'Yes, yes! That's what the public says,' they all replied. 'We are not going to vote for anyone any more, and if we had our way we wouldn't let anyone sit on the throne.'

'But the politicians don't do the rioting, surely?'

Hasina said, 'The big people, they give money to the small people, the goondas [thugs], and they start the rioting. It's very easy to start riots by killing people and spreading rumours. The big people do it to give a bad name to the government in the chair; so that, as we have said, is why the public blames the Congress this time.'

Hanifa, the comedienne, interjected angrily for once, 'How can it be Hindus and Muslims? We sit together all the time and we work together. There are lots of Hindus in this cooperative. We live in the same areas. Even in the curfew we go from one to another's house. Then when the riots stop, always suddenly, everything is as it used to be.'

'Yes,' the women agreed, 'How do they stop if we are such enemies of each other? It's the same Hindus and Muslims who are meant to hate each other who are again living together now.'

I was fascinated by the openness of these Muslim women, who just a few years ago would never have talked with such familiarity to a man outside their immediate family circle – especially not to a foreigner. I wanted to ask them about family planning, because I had never discussed this with Muslim women before, but I thought that would be presuming too much on their open-heartedness and generosity of spirit. Then I had an idea. One of the charges levied against Muslims by those Hindus who want to stir up communal hatred is that their clergy deliberately encourage them to have large families to increase the Muslim population – a similar accusation is made against Roman Catholics in Northern Ireland. I thought that I would put this allegation to the printers and see where it led.

They all thought about my question for a moment and then Hasina's sister said, 'Most women do still have larger families. Our mother had ten children, but then she was brought up to be very traditional and to accept that the Koran says family planning is bad. Now some of us have changed. I had twins six years ago, and haven't had any children since.'

Not surprisingly, the young Hanifa was the most direct in her approach to this matter which I had thought would be so delicate. She said, 'We all know about family planning, and if we want to we adopt it. If an elderly person asks us why we are not having more children, we tell them, "We don't know. Perhaps it's the will of Allah." But we don't favour the operation. We make our own arrangements – like taking pills. All the men are actually happy, because, once you have a son, who wants a big family in these days of such expenditure? But our men don't want to ask us about it.'

'Don't the mullahs preach against family planning?' I asked.

'Oh yes,' Hasina's sister replied, 'but they don't even allow their women out of the house very much. If they do go out, they have to wear burqas. We don't pay attention to them. That's not because we are not good Muslims,' she continued hurriedly, so that I didn't get the wrong impression – 'we are. We all say our prayers together when we are at work. We keep the fast in Ramzan. We show respect to our men. We wear gold nosepins and bangles to show that we are married, and we take them off if our husband dies.'

'Everyone wears gold except me,' said Hanifa with a laugh which showed no trace of shame or jealousy. 'My ornaments are artificial.' Then, running her bangles up and down her arm, she laughed again and said, 'But they look like gold, don't they?'

SEWA has organized women workers in many other crafts and trades too. One of these crafts is the sewing of khols, or patchwork sheets, made from the unwanted rags of the Ahmedabad mills. Khols are another example of India's refusal to allow anything to go to waste, but they are more than that – a top-quality khol is a work of art. Khol-sewers work at home, and so I thought that a visit to a woman in that line of business would give me a chance to get a better impression of the hardships of curfew that the hand printers had described. They referred me to Fatima Bibi, who lived near Prem Darwaza, or the gate of love.

On the way to Fatima Bibi's, my driver said to me, 'Prem Darwaza is one of twelve gates of the old city of Ahmedabad. In the old times they were all closed at eight o'clock in the evening and no one could come in and no one go out. That's why there was some order and peace instead of all this fighting.' Everywhere I go in India, I find that poorer people hate the lawlessness of today. The squat, sandstone Prem Darwaza was still covered with the detritus of the recent state-assembly elections – posters peeling off the walls and slogans painted in black. The gate itself was now the centre of what was meant to be a roundabout, but my driver – in spite of his views on lawlessness – shot straight through it.

We stopped on the other side of a scooter-rickshaw repair shop to ask for the SEWA khol shop. The mechanics hadn't heard of that, but they pointed to a road which they said was the street of the khol-sellers. I decided it would be quicker to leave the car and walk. I passed a pile of garbage – the overflow from skips provided by the municipality. Two cows were ruminating on rubbish, and a big black bull with a magnificent pair of curved horns was sitting contentedly on top of a pile of garbage. A crow was perched on his floppy hump. I don't know whether it's my imagination or whether Ahmedabad really does have even more stray cows than other Indian cities. Perhaps it's another reflection of the Indianness of the place. An old man with sweat dripping off his grey moustache and a woman who could have been his daughter were bent over the crossbar of a handcart, straining to pull their load of cloth bales. An orange municipal bus – far too wide for the narrow street – hooted angrily at the handcart-pullers, but they refused to give ground.

I soon came to the first shop selling brightly coloured khols and asked for the cooperative's office. The owner pointed down the road without a break in the conversation he was holding. I went on until I came to the first shop where women were in charge, which I rightly assumed belonged to the cooperative. No business was being transacted – there were just two women sorting out enormous sacks of rags. One of them agreed to come with me to Fatima Bibi.

Fatima Bibi lived less than a hundred yards away, in a building constructed of old, wafer-thin, biscuit-like bricks. There was little sign of the mortar which had once held them together, and the walls bulged ominously. We went into an extension built on to the original building, and walked along a muddy passage which the builders had still not provided with a floor. We made our way to an open doorway at the end, which led to steep wooden stairs like a ship's companionway. My guide climbed up, poked her head through a trapdoor and shouted, 'Is anyone at home?' Back came the angry reply, 'We are asleep. Don't come till four o'clock.' Rebuffed but not discouraged, my guide suggested that I go to a tea shop and return later.

When we eventually gained admission, I saw a stout woman with frizzled grey hair sitting cross-legged on the floor picking stones out of rice for the evening meal. She looked well over fifty, but claimed to be just forty. Fatima Bibi, like the hand-printers, was not fazed by the sudden arrival of a strange foreigner: she was apparently used to inquisitive visitors from SEWA.

Once again I decided to start by asking her about her connection with the cooperative and the work she did.

She said, 'I joined SEWA out of greed for twenty-five paise. The veparis [traders] gave us one rupee seventy-five paise per khol, and SEWA promised two. Now I only work for SEWA. They also gave me a sewing-machine.' She pointed to a treadle machine in one corner of the room. 'We sew fifty khols a week between us and so make 100 rupees. We need the money because my husband has been laid off by the mill where he used to work. That was seven years ago. He didn't get any compensation because he was not in pukka service. I will take these khols to the godown [warehouse] this evening and get the money. Then we can eat. I have to carry them on my head to the godown. I don't like doing that – it makes you like a coolie – but what can I do?'

'Doesn't the government also offer help to khol workers like you?' I asked.

'The government!' she said scornfully. 'All they do is shoot us. They just shoot us dead.'

'Why do you say that?'

'These riots we suffer from – the government's hand is behind them. I tell you, it's all the government's hand.'

I looked round at the small room where she and the other six members of her family had just been incarcerated for nearly a week during the curfew. The floor was made of mud in which were set a few flat stones on which Fatima Bibi was sitting. The only pieces of furniture were one iron bed, two tin trunks and a wooden chest. The clothes of the male members of the family were hung over a string stretched across one corner. A row of teacups hung neatly from hooks in the edge of a wooden shelf. Water was stored in clay pots. Part of the room was shut off by corrugated-iron sheets and a padlocked hardboard door. There was one tube-light suspended precariously from the roof. Fatima Bibi saw me looking up at the sunlight shining through the gaps in the smoke-blackened wooden struts of the roof. She said, 'Yes, this roof leaks everywhere during the monsoon. There is only one corner where you can sit and keep dry. I am going to ask SEWA for a loan to repair this house, but I don't know whether they will give it to me.'

'You have just had more riots,' I said. 'How did you survive?'

'With great difficulty. My son couldn't get out to work. He works ironing ready-made garments. He couldn't go to work because he had to pass through a Hindu area. It was even worse because of the fast. My family observed it. I must say I didn't – I won't tell a lie.'

'Who started the riots this time?'

'We didn't have too many riots here this time. The local corporator Rasulbhai came and told us not to have riots. But in 1985 it was terrifying. The Hindu people came and did it. They even burnt our men's scooter-rickshaws. We have Hindus living in the galis behind us, but there is no trouble usually. It's loafers, looters, louts, drinkers who come and do it all,' she said angrily.

'But you said the government's hand was behind it.'

'How else do you explain that everything changes so suddenly?' She pointed out of the open window. 'You can see for yourself there are Hindus and Muslims together without any quarrelling, then suddenly all this hatred and fighting starts. The government says it is trying to stop it, but it doesn't. It just sends the police, who give us even more trouble. The only person ever to help us was Latifbhai, and that was in 1985.'

'Who is he?'

'The police say he is a big bootlegger, but I don't care about that. All I care is that he was the only person who helped us. All the government help went to the big people. Even SEWA didn't do much for us then. Latif's men went from door to door and took down the names of the helpless Muslims. Then they arranged for us to be given fifty rupees in cash, wheat, rice, oil and dal.'

'Did Latif help this time?'

'No, he couldn't. The police have driven him away. They say he is a bad man – that there are cases of all sorts against him. But that means nothing, because the police always make up cases against Muslims, don't they? Personally I don't care how Latif made his money. Why shouldn't he be a thief if all these big leaders are thieves too? At least Latif spent some of his money on poor Muslims.'

By now it was clear that Fatima Bibi was becoming a little irritated by my inquisitiveness, so I decided to leave. As we got up to go, she muttered to herself, '*Sakun nahin hai. Taklif hai*' – 'There is no peace, only trouble.' I wasn't sure whether she was referring to me or to the riots.

Latif was one of those Robin Hoods of the underworld that are so common in India. He had started life as a small-time runner or delivery boy for a bootlegger. Prohibition in Ahmedabad has inevitably spawned an illegal market in liquor. Some of the cheaper varieties are distilled in pots buried in the bed of the dried up Sabarmati river – the sand gets so hot that there is no need for a fire to bring the liquid to the boil. Other cheap varieties are distilled by a once nomadic tribe known as the Charas. They came home to rest in a suburb of Ahmedabad known as Sardar Nagar, where their activities became so notorious that the government set up a special police station. That police station is now a very popular posting, and a thanedar or station house-officer could well have to pay up to 500,000 rupees to get transferred there, in the certain knowledge that he will recover that sum and much more from the haftas or weekly payments the distillers and bootleggers pay for protection.

Various vessels are used to transport the cheap liquor, including balloons and cycle-tyre inner tubes. The liquor is sold at open-air addas. 'Adda' is a word which can mean anything from an airport to a bus or pony-trap stand; in this case it means an illegal bar. The addas also sell samosas and other snacks to help the digestion damp down the fire the crude liquor ignites.

Latif controlled the upmarket business of Indian-made foreign liquor – that's the bureaucratic classification for Indian whisky, gin, rum, vodka and beer. Anyone short of a drink had only to ring Latif's local man and the bottle would be delivered to the door. During the curfew of 1985, Latif used ambulances to ferry booze about the city.

The bootleggers buy protection from the police and provide protection to the politicians. It is their gangs who are used to instigate communal violence. Latif was, of course, always able to tell Muslims that he was not instigating but retaliating. He became so popular with the poorer Muslims that they elected him to be a corporator for five different wards in the Old City. He became so powerful that he could hold even the Indian army at bay.

In 1985, when even the army failed to stem the violence, Rajiv Gandhi sent Julio Ribeiro to Ahmedabad. He had been an outstanding commissioner of police in Bombay, whose gang leaders would have regarded Latif as a novice. Ribeiro asked for a list of all the leading bootleggers and then ordered their arrest. Soon afterwards he called a meeting to discuss progress. Each time a bootlegger's name was mentioned, an officer would say, 'We can't touch him – he's such and such or so and so politician's man.' So Ribeiro went and sat in police stations – much to the embarrassment of the local thanedars – and refused to move until the bootleggers living in the neighbourhood were brought before him. Ribeiro himself told me that the trouble died down within a matter of a week or so.

Latif was caught in the Ribeiro net, and that was the beginning of the end for him. It was not, of course, the beginning of the end of bootlegging – that was resumed when Ribeiro moved on to Delhi and then to Punjab. No one quite knows where Latif is nowadays. The courts have banished him from Ahmedabad. According to his lawyer, Mohamed Husen Barejia, he is not allowed within 100 kilometres of the city, but thousands of poor Muslims still cannot believe that the police have got the better of their hero – they still insist that he is in hiding somewhere in the Old City.

Barejia himself had been arrested for fifty days during the 1985 riots, even though he was a leading member of the Congress Party which was in power. He had even been a member of the state assembly for five years. The lawyer lived in the same congested area as Fatima Bibi, and from the outside his residence didn't look much smarter than hers, but when I walked through the doorway I found myself inside a substantial modernized house with an office just below ground level, separated from the hall by a glass partition. The lawyer's daughter sat me down in front of a large desk, and I waited for the statutory five minutes – a man involved in politics always insists on keeping visitors waiting, to demonstrate his importance.

When the lawyer finally made his entrance, he was wearing an immaculate white kurta with pajamas. His thinning white hair was brushed straight back off his forehead. He sat down at his desk and stared at me coldly over the top of his gold-rimmed half-moon spectacles. I thought, 'This is going to be a difficult conversation to handle.' But it wasn't. I didn't even have to ask about his client Latif's background – as soon as I mentioned his name, the lawyer said, 'Latif is definitely a man of the underworld,' and went on to explain, 'He has been charged under the National Security Act, the Prevention of Anti Social

Activities Act, bootlegging, etc., etc. – whenever any liquor is found on anyone, it can be blamed on him. But he is also a symbol of the Muslims' sensitivity. They feel he is being persecuted because he is a Muslim. Bootleggers like him have lakhs of rupees to give to people and earn public goodwill. That was why he became so popular. But I must tell you he is fighting all his cases, and he has been released on many of them already.'

'Was it because you were Latif's lawyer that you were arrested too?' I asked.

'Oh no. That was quite a different story. I was arrested during the '85 riots along with three other Congress Muslim leaders. No Hindus were arrested. It was done to show the majority community – the Hindus – that the government and the administration were with them. That sort of thinking – that groupism – is the root cause of the Congress Party's downfall.'

One of the lawyer's clerks came through the open door in the glass screen which separated the office from the hall. He stood nervously beside Barejia. I could see a client waiting outside. Barejia turned to the clerk and said with obvious irritation, 'What do you want? Can't you see I'm having an important meeting?'

The clerk replied, 'Yes, Sahib. But that man who came to see you about the murder case – he's outside and he says he has a "date" now.'

'Well, tell him I got him put on bail last time and I'll get him out again this time. Take his court summons for the date and tell him to come to my office tomorrow.' Then, dismissing his clerk with an imperious wave, Barejia returned to the subject of his party – the Congress.

'Let me tell you another story about what happened during those riots, which is even more shocking,' he said. 'It was Id – the day the Ramzan fast ends – like Christmas to you. There was curfew and we had been told to warn Muslims that they couldn't come out to the mosques to say their prayers. All right – we accepted that. Then we learnt that the police were going to allow a Hindu religious procession to come right through our area. I phoned the chief minister. He told me that he had not given permission for the procession, but then went on to ask me to make sure the procession passed through peacefully. I said, "That's not fair. Ask the police, ask the army to do that, but don't ask me." '

It is possible that the decision to allow the Hindu procession to continue was not political. Film shot by the security forces showed the procession accompanying the chariot of Lord Jagganath moving forward appropriately enough like an unstoppable juggernaut, with temple elephants contemptuously sweeping army jeeps aside. If the army or the police had tried to stop it, there would have been great bloodshed. But at the same time, the army must have realized there would be violence if the procession went through Barejia's predominantly Muslim area, and violence there was. At least seven Muslims lost their lives. Barejia organized a demonstration by 20,000 women to protest against the shooting of the Muslims.

As Barejia was so clearly dissatisfied with the Congress Party's attitude towards the Muslims, I asked him why he was still a Congressman. He replied, 'The Congress may be bad, but the main opposition in Gujarat is the BJP and they are far worse. They believe Muslims are a burden on India and should be driven out. Actually, you know, there need be no communalism in India if it wasn't for the power-brokers. The power-brokers turn Hindus and Muslims against each other, so that they will become vote-banks. If you arouse communal feelings, you can call on Hindus to vote as Hindus.'

Much of the trouble in Gujarat this time might have been averted if there had not been so much power-broking going on. On 13 March, more than three weeks before the stabbing started in Ahmedabad, Muslims in the Gujarati town of Patan sent identical telegrams to the prime minister, the chief minister of Gujarat, the inspector general of police, the district collector and the deputy collector. The telegrams read, 'Stabbing of Muslims continuing. No control. Property burnt. Muslims' life in danger. Request immediate interference. Matter most urgent.' That should have warned the politicians that there was a danger of tension and violence spreading to Ahmedabad, but their minds were on other things – the elections to the Rajya Sabha or upper house of parliament in Delhi.

Elections to the upper house of parliament are held every two years, with one third of the house resigning each time. That means that a member is guaranteed a seat for at least six years, whatever the political fortunes of his party during that period. The upper house is known as the Rajya Sabha or Council of States, and it has powers to delay legislation passed in the lower house. These powers are intended to guarantee the federal nature of the Indian constitution. Each state has a certain number of seats in the Rajya Sabha, and the members of the state assembly form the electoral college for those seats. A common phenomenon in an election is what is known as cross-voting, or a member of the state assembly not voting for his party's candidate. Cross-voting can lead to splits in parties and political crises, especially when a government has a narrow majority.

The position in Gujarat this time was particularly crucial. In the recent assembly elections, the Janata Dal had won only three more seats than its coalition partner the Bharatiya Janata Party. Any evidence of erosion of support for the Janata Dal in the Rajya Sabha elections could lead to the Bharatiya Janata Party claiming the chief-ministership. The Congress Party, of course, was very anxious to do all it could to discredit the Janata Dal and take revenge for its defeat in the recent elections. Set-backs to the Janata Dal in the Rajya Sabha elections could also have affected the stability of its minority government in Delhi. Although the Congress Party now lacked the required number of members of the assembly to win even one of the Rajya Sabha seats on its own, it believed it could defeat one of the coalition's candidates with the support of independents.

In March 1990, the verandahs and waiting-rooms of the leaders' houses were crowded with politicians, brokers, operators, middle-men and all their retainers too. Everyone who was anyone had to be seen to be in on an act as important as this. There was not a coloured shirt to be seen: everyone wore white, homespun cotton kurtas – the uniform of a politician – and some sported Gandhi caps, which have gone out of fashion even among politicians in most other parts of India. Unfortunately I was not in Ahmedabad for this political drama, but I was given a full report by one of the main actors – Raoof Valiullah, a retiring member of the Rajya Sabha who the previous government had appointed chairman of the Gujarat Minorities Board.

Raoof Valiullah had been given the important job of keeping the Congress legislators happy. He was busy all day – buying samosas from one shop, special bread or roti from another, sweets from the best sweet-makers, chicken biryani for those who ate meat, and the finest vegetable preparations for those who did not. He himself was forced to eat so many rich meals that by the end of the election his stomach couldn't tolerate anything more aggressive than a glass of lassi or watery curd.

The night before the election, all the Congressmen were confined in one house to keep them away from the seductive offers of the opposing power-brokers. Raoof provided ten videos to keep them happy. The sole woman member of the state assembly presented a bit of a problem. Obviously she couldn't stay with the men, so Raoof had to find another house for her. She then showed no inclination to go to sleep and insisted that Raoof stay up to keep her company. When she did eventually go to bed, Raoof had to stand guard outside the door. But all Raoof's efforts were in vain. His opponents got at one of the legislators he was protecting, who accepted a hefty bribe, and the Congress candidate was defeated by one vote.

Raoof is in his early middle age. He's a small, intense man who would like his political work to be a serious contribution to the improvement of society and of the Muslim community in particular. He believes that, as chairman of the Gujarat Minorities Board, he has done much more for Muslim women than SEWA. He points out that the SEWA cooperatives are very small, and he can reel off figures to demonstrate that the number of women he has helped is much greater. Raoof is also very critical of the leaders of SEWA, who he believes have been seduced by international acclaim and spend far too much time at seminars and other jamborees. He has demonstrated his personal commitment to secularism by marrying a Hindu – the only member I have ever met of the Indian Postal Service, one of the less well-known of the élite government cadres.

I went to see Raoof in the family home, situated in what is known as a 'pole' in the heart of the Old City. Much of old Ahmedabad is still divided into poles – small residential areas shut off from the main bazaars by gateways. There are two small mosques in Raoof's pole. Raoof and his five brothers all live in the house with his mother. Each brother's family has a separate room, but they all share a common kitchen. I sat on a wide wooden swing covered with cushions and suspended from the ceiling. Swinging gently creates a gentle breeze, and this is how Ahmedabadis used to keep cool before the invention of the electric fan. The room we sat in was built around a small open courtyard under which was a huge water-tank. There was an adjoining room to which the women generally retired when male visitors called. Raoof's sisters brought us tea and kachoris – savouries made of crisp, fried, unleavened bread stuffed with dal.

I had first met Raoof while making a film on Gujarat eight years before. Since then we had often discussed politics. He would talk with great earnestness about his various disappointments and fears. 'All my schemes and plans to benefit Muslims amount to nothing, because I can't provide protection for their lives and property,' he said. 'This is the most important thing. The problem is, the social fabric is tearing and politicians are losing their grip on society.'

'But whose fault is that?' I asked. 'Surely it's yours, the politicians'?'

'Yes,' he replied. 'We have fallen victims to these sort of people. Politicians use men like Latif and then end up having to seek their support. That's why we are losing our grip. It's like a Frankenstein which has got out of control. We have created them and now we can't control them. During the riots in the eighties, the chief minister even negotiated with that criminal Latif you have been told about. Under those circumstances, what can the police do about bootlegging and other crimes? I once took the commissioner of police to see the illegal liquor on sale on every corner in my area. I said to him, "This is the public distribution system for illicit liquor. It's a lot more efficient than the government's distribution system for rations." But I knew that the commissioner would not do anything about it because of the links between the bootleggers and the politicians, and I was right.'

One of Raoof's sisters reminded him that he had to get his ticket to go to Bombay that night. She said that he would have to ring up the divisional manager because the booking-office had refused to give him a reservation on the quota for ex-MPs. Raoof phoned the divisional manager, who was quite used to dealing with such apparently trivial matters – he 'did the needful and obliged', as they say in Indian bureaucratese. I then brought Raoof back to the subject of the bootleggers.

'Do you believe that it's the bootleggers who are responsible for the riots?' I asked.

'They can be used to start them, certainly. It's very easy to start a riot – all you have to do is set fire to someone's hut and start rumours flying about the place. But communal strife comes because a communal riot is the only thing which can bring down a government. The riots of 1985 and 1986 all started from the anger of high-caste politicians who did not like Solanki, the chief minister, favouring the backward castes.'

'You seem to be agreeing with the poor Muslims I have talked to. They say the politicians start the riots and the poor suffer.'

'That's not entirely true,' Raoof replied. 'My family certainly suffered during the '85 and '86 riots. We took a beating from the public and the police. My family had to deal with a lot of abusive phone calls, and the police were very partial.'

I remembered that the printing ladies said the police treated the poor Hindus as badly as the Muslims, and I told this to Raoof. He was surprised. 'Well, that's the first time I've heard Muslims say that. I have always found the police biased, but what really surprised me was to find the army were the same. They also acted in violation of the law in a very communal fashion. When the army is put in charge of law and order, each section is given a local policeman to guide it. That may be part of the trouble, because the policeman will tell the army when to fire and he will be biased.'

Raoof had good reason to be angry with the army. During fourteen days of uninterrupted curfew in 1985, soldiers patrolling the main streets were often stoned from the rooftops. One patrol climbed on to the roof of a house in Kalupur to arrest some stone-throwers. The stone-throwers ran for it, jumping from roof to roof. The soldiers gave chase, but their boots slipped when they jumped on to a sloping tin roof, and some lost their rifles. Luckily they slid on to the flat roof of a terrace, but they were trapped. Realizing that they were sitting targets for stones, bottles or even bullets, they ran to a staircase but the door was locked. They beat on the door and shouted, 'Let us in, we are soldiers.' There was no response, so they hammered at the door with their rifle butts until they broke it down, and charged into the house shouting, 'Where have you hidden those salas throwing stones?' When the members of the family protested that they knew nothing about any stoning, the soldiers started to break up their furniture and smashed the fridge. One soldier picked up a 28-day-old baby and said, 'We'll kill her if you don't tell us.' They searched the house but only found one toy gun. Eventually they gave up the search, arrested the male members of the family and moved to a house on the other side of the narrow alley whose door was open. There they repeated the same tactics, pushing around an elderly woman and arresting more men.

Unfortunately for the soldiers, the first house belonged to Raoof's grandfather and the second house was his mother's. Raoof was in Bombay at the time, flagging off a ship of pilgrims to Mecca, but when he heard of the attack on his family he contacted senior members of the Congress Party. A brigadier was sent to apologize to Raoof's mother, and the government television carried an announcement that the 'raid' on his house had been a mistake.

There were further humiliations for the army during those two weeks of curfew, as Raoof explained to me.

'The army had orders to shoot at sight, and they did, so no one even thought of going out. I tell you, the whole area was stinking. Most of the people are daily-wage-earners living in one room, and they have to go out to do their motions. They couldn't because of the curfew. Eventually people started getting sick from hunger. Then about 500 women came out in a procession near Kalupur tower and gheraoed [surrounded] a platoon. One woman slapped a major and said, "I have hit you. Now show how brave you are. Kill all of us." The press heard of this and went to the place. By the evening, 5,000 women were on the streets. The army was then withdrawn from the area.'

I also asked Raoof about the arrest of the Congress lawyer Mohamed Husen Barejia.

'I am still not entirely sure what the motive was,' replied Raoof. 'I rang the chief minister and he said he had to take some Muslim leaders into custody as a balancing act, but I couldn't understand what he meant because no Hindu leaders were arrested. I wrote to Rajiv Gandhi about this and was summoned to Delhi to meet one of his close aides. When I met him, he accused me of harbouring "communal elements". I really lost my temper and let him have it. Eventually the Congressmen were released and the local people gave them a rousing reception. There will never be lasting peace here so long as the authorities come down on the side of the Hindus.'

'You have talked about the political reasons for communal violence. What about the economic causes?' I asked.

'The economy of Ahmedabad is almost worse than its politics,' Raoof said. 'Ahmedabad is a dying city, because of the crisis in the textile mills. Thirty-five thousand families have lost their earning members, and most of them are Muslims or Harijans because they are the traditional weavers. They are also, of course, the poorest too. Large numbers of the Muslims aren't even from Ahmedabad – they came here to work in the mills from Uttar Pradesh, in the north, and now they have no roots there or here. Obviously, economic despair makes people turn anywhere to earn some money, so these unemployed mill-workers and their sons make very good recruits for the bootleggers and anti-socials.'

I drove from the bazaar outside Raoof's pole to one of the mill areas of the city. The tall chimneys and red-brick buildings reminded me of Lancashire as I used to know it. Blake could never have described arid Gujarat as a green and pleasant land, but he could well have described Ahmedabad's mills as dark and satanic. I asked a group of men sitting outside a tea stall which mills were closed. They replied sullenly, 'All of them.' So I drove on until I came to the premises of the Commercial Ahmedabad Mills Company, just by the railway line.

Behind the mill's high walls you can still sometimes hear the rush of steam from leaky valves as a metre-gauge engine pulls a slow passenger train out of Ahmedabad Junction, north towards Delhi or west towards the Saurashtra peninsula and the Arabian Sea. But there is no more steam inside the mill – there's no power of any sort. The Gujarat State Electricity Board has disconnected its line to the mill and now stands in the queue of creditors waiting for the mill's liquidators to complete their dismal task.

When I arrived at the mill gate, I found a small and forlorn group sitting outside the office where once 2,200 people had clocked on and off. One of the men had an ancient rifle across his knees: he was in charge of the guards protecting the mill for the liquidators. A bald man with a large gap in his front teeth said he had retired from the mill as a clerk some years ago but somehow couldn't keep away, even though the mill was now closed. He wasn't sure what had gone wrong but thought it was something to do with the malik, or owner, who lived in Bombay and didn't take much interest. At one stage the workers might have hoped that the Gujarat government would help them: it had a scheme for reviving what are described in bureaucratic jargon as 'sick mills'. But civil servants had proved incompetent company doctors. They had already paid more than £100 million to keep 6,000 textile workers in jobs and there was no sign of the mills recovering. I supposed the only hope for the workers of the Commercial Ahmedabad Mills Company was recruitment by Latif or another of his ilk. But then I thought that perhaps I was being too pessimistic. After all, with Ahmedabad's record for recovering from slumps, there must, I felt, be grounds for hope that its fortunes would revive.

I knew of one mill where the revival had already started, but getting there proved difficult as Sanjay Lalbhai, the managing director, was surprisingly publicity-shy for a modern Indian businessman. Eventually he agreed to see me in his plush, modern office in the mill. He explained that the Lalbhais were a large family, owning assets which probably made them one of the top twenty Indian industrial groups. They had never bothered to club all their assets together, because the only value of doing that was publicity and they had always believed that publicity created jealousies as some members of the family would have to be 'up front'. Sanjay himself was the third generation in Arvind Mills, and admitted that he had 'inherited' the managing directorship, but he didn't think his son would necessarily inherit a top job. Whether he had earned or inherited his job, at thirty-five Sanjay was one of the most progressive Indian managers I had met for some time.

There are similarities between the fate of Ahmedabad and that of the Lancashire textile industry. In both cases, family managements ploughed on in the same old way – ignoring new market trends and new technology. They had had it so good for so long that they came to believe they had a divine right to prosper. But in Ahmedabad it was local competition from power looms, not cheap foreign labour, that had undermined the prosperity of the old mill-owning families. Power looms are individual units and can be set up in anyone's back yard, or indeed front room. They have no unionized labour, or safety regulations, and so can easily undercut the traditional mills.

Sanjay admitted that his family had 'taken success for granted' and had 'stopped scanning the horizon'. But a few years ago they had decided to accept that the power looms had conquered most of the domestic market and to find new niches for their mills. The two they had found were denim and the most expensive cottons at the top of the market. Both, of course, meant exports. In three years, Arvind Mills' sales of denim had risen from £4 million to £32 million and they had plans to increase them fivefold in the next two years. Sanjay Lalbhai believed that he would become the biggest denim manufacturer in the world and that Ahmedabad could yet again recover from disaster and become a major international textile centre, if only the government would get off the industry's back. Almost 70 per cent of Sanjay's time was spent dealing with the bureaucracy.

I asked the young industrialist what his plans would mean for the Muslim and Harijan weavers. 'Well,' he said, 'it will mean that a lot of them will save their jobs. Of course we will have to rationalize our labour force, and we have already started doing so. Every worker who leaves gets 100,000 rupees which, invested in a savings bank, gives him 60 per cent out of his salary. The rest he can easily earn. Some people walk straight out of here into jobs with power looms. But you mustn't get this wrong – we will always be labour-intensive compared to Europe, and that will be a disadvantage we will have to overcome in other ways. It's a sad fact of modern technology: you have to automate. You have to get the human beings out, because they make mistakes.'

'You have to get the human beings out' – not a very encouraging message for most of Ahmedabad, especially as the more efficient industry becomes the more of a threat it poses to the self-employed like the hand printers and the khol-sewers. The economists argue that the service industries will grow with the expansion in wealth created by the modernized mills. But then, suppose the service industries like retailing are modernized too: a Marks & Spencer of India would put millions of vegetable- and fruit-sellers out of business, not to mention the small shopkeepers who still dominate Indian retailing.

There are those who believe that industrialists like Sanjay Lalbhai can never bring prosperity to India, who reject the worship of growth rate preached by the World Bank. They don't believe that wealth will 'trickle down' to the poor: they want the growth to start with the hand printers and khol-sewers, not with the mass-producers. They are not socialists, but neither are they capitalists. One of them is Ela Bhatt, who founded SEWA and the cooperatives that the khol-sewers and printers belong to.

Ela Bhatt founded SEWA in 1972. Its annual report for 1988 gave examples of the difficulties faced by the self-employed women it was helping. There was the case of a vegetable-seller in Ahmedabad who borrowed fifty rupees at the beginning of each day to buy her merchandise and had to return fifty-five to the moneylender every night. Her family's land had been made barren by industrial effluent. Then there was a kerosene-vendor who was going to be put out of business by a new order banning sales on the street. A woman who made pots and pans was facing increasing difficulties because of the high price of metal scrap. A basketmaker could no longer afford the price of bamboo, which had been inflated by the demand from paper-mills. The SEWA report classified three main groups of women as self-employed: vendors, manufacturers of home-made products and casual labourers (including agricultural workers). The report pointed out that only 6 per cent of Indian women had jobs in offices, factories, firms or shops which came within the purview of the labour laws of India.

SEWA's answer to the problems of the remaining 94 per cent of Indian women has been to register itself as a trade union and to form cooperatives. The union fights for laws that recognize the rights of self-employed women and for improvements in the pay and conditions of casual labourers. The hand printers are a good example of a cooperative. Hand printers had been reduced to producing very cheap-quality products at the bottom end of the market. They were controlled by traders who provided the cloth and dye and paid them a pittance for their piecework. Those who have joined SEWA now run the cooperative themselves, buying all their own dyes and materials. They have upgraded their skills and employed a manager of their choice. The last problem they have to surmount is marketing.

SEWA has also formed its own bank, since it found that its members were unable to cope with the bureaucratic procedures necessary to get a loan from the nationalized banks. They had also been put off by stories of bank managers demanding bribes before they sanctioned loans. The SEWA bank also gave women the chance to handle their own money, instead of giving it to their husbands. Eleven illiterate women sat up all night learning to sign their names so that they could put their signatures on the documents for registering the bank. In spite of that unorthodox beginning, the bank's deposits have grown to 11 million rupees in fourteen years – all deposited by the smallest of small savers. The minimum deposit is just five rupees, or eighteen pence.

When I got back from Ahmedabad, I went to see Ela Bhatt in her office in the Planning Commission in Delhi. She was surrounded by all the bureaucratic pomp of a senior official of the government of India – personal assistants to protect her from the public, peons to carry her files, bearers to bring her cups of tea. It all seemed a long way from that cramped, chaotic building on the banks of the Sabarmati with the friendly bank on the ground floor, Ela's colleagues who ran the cooperatives and unions sitting at desks crammed into every available inch of space, and the friendly hand-printing women on the roof. But the Planning Commission had not changed Ela Bhatt. She was still wearing a simple cotton sari, with her hair parted in the middle and drawn back severely over her ears. Her round face, which never quite manages to look severe, broke into a smile as I entered the room. 'It's a little different to when you first met me at SEWA, isn't it?' she said.

'It certainly is,' I replied. 'I hope that you're not becoming one of those social workers who get trapped by their own success and end up like politicians or bureaucrats, miles removed from the people they started working with.'

Ela Bhatt didn't quite know whether to take me seriously or not. 'Surely', she said, 'you don't think my roots are as shallow as that. I see my work at the Planning Commission as just an extension of my SEWA work. I have been talking about tendu-leaf workers all morning and about public distribution of food all afternoon – exports against malnutrition.'

Both these subjects were highly political. Tendu leaves are used for making biris – the poor man's cigarette – and the chief minister of one state had introduced a cooperative to keep out the middlemen. These, however, were a very powerful political lobby and were fighting back hard. As for food exports, the new cabinet had been split because of the multinational Pepsi-Cola. The previous government had allowed the company to come into India on condition that it also processed food for export. But, unfortunately for the multinational, the new cabinet included the socialist George Fernandes who twelve years ago had driven Coca-Cola out of India. His argument, and Ela's, was that, so long as India was unable to provide enough food to give all its own people a healthy diet, it should be worrying about internal markets not exports.

I knew how important these things were to Ela Bhatt, although the whole world seemed to be turning against her and against planning. I knew that 'the market', which was now meant to be the economic miracle-maker, would favour freedom for Pepsi-Cola and the tendu-leaf traders. But Ela insisted that there was an Indian answer to India's problems.

'There is an alternative,' she said, 'and Mahatma Gandhi showed us what it is. I am attracted to Gandhi because he thought of human beings in totality, not only in economic or political terms. He also put women in the vanguard of social change. He said that in the struggle for social change, when the weapons were truth and non-violence, women would be the leaders.'

'But can Gandhiism really stand up against the modern world? Hasn't it already been defeated?' I asked.

Ela said firmly, 'I don't accept that Gandhi has failed. I don't believe in success or failure as such. We have full faith in Gandhiji's teaching, and it has worked. Look at the strength of my members. They have achieved even more than I expected. We have made a breakthrough in the concept of a labour union, questioned the definition of a worker and tried to link policy with what is really happening at the grass roots.'

'I agree that you have done an enormous amount for your members, but SEWA is just a drop in the ocean.'

'You have to make a start, and that start will influence society. It's already beginning to happen. Why would I be asked to join the Planning Commission, which is drawing up the five-year plan for the whole of India, if my work wasn't important? What's more, we are creating a new type of social worker. Feminists here have been urban and, because their education has been Western-based, they have looked to the West for answers. Now the new generation are different. They go and live with poor women and try to be more conscious of their needs.'

I have always been uneasy about Oxfam, Christian Aid and other Western relief organizations because, in their efforts to raise money, they do give the impression that only we in the West are doing anything about poverty and backwardness: that Indians, for example, are not doing anything to help themselves. Yet everywhere I go in India I find dedicated Indians – often very young – sacrificing comfortable careers to live and work among the poor.

Ela Bhatt wasn't worried about this aspect of the international relief agencies' work. 'I don't really mind what they do in your countries. If you want to believe that we are not doing anything to help ourselves, that's your business. One shouldn't always be worrying what other people think of you. But there is a feeling of mistrust about the foreign agencies here. They have their own priorities, which are not ours.'

Ela Bhatt smiled at me and then went on. 'If you are so worried about the impression of India abroad, why do you press-wallahs give such a wrong picture of us? Whenever I go abroad, people only ask me about sati and dowry deaths, as if our men were all murderers. Even when I went to China and Korea they asked me about that. Sati is a very minor thing if you take the actual number of cases, and when a girl who is about to do sati is rescued that's never reported. The issue of dowry deaths is also overblown. There are dowry deaths as a result of materialism, but not as many as you say. It's a modern, middle-class phenomenon which has really been over-publicized by the newspapers. The journalists are urban, middle-class people and so are the women's organizations, and so it's easy to blow this up.'

There was nothing I could say to that, so I hurriedly turned to the subject of communal riots in her home city of Ahmedabad. I asked Ela whether she thought that the press exaggerated them too.

'In a way, yes. Whenever there are communal riots we hear all about them, but we never hear about the peacefulness which is there most of the time. When there are no riots, Ahmedabad is such a safe place. Women can go out at night and not be afraid. We don't have any of what you call "mugging" either. Unfortunately we are only remembered because we have a reputation for communal riots.'

'Well, why do you have these riots if Ahmedabad is so peaceful?' I asked.

Ela thought for a moment and then said, 'I agree with those who say that riots are used to change the politics of the state.'

Nevertheless, the politicians and the press continue to blame the riots on religious fundamentalism. This may be convenient for the politicians and fashionable for the press, but according to the victims – who ought to know best – it's just not true. The victims of the riots don't even know the meaning of the word 'fundamentalist', but they do know that it is not religion that divides them. Chandaben Pappubhai, a Hindu who sells old clothes for a living and is a member of SEWA, addressed a public meeting after the dreadful riots of 1985 and 1986. She said, 'In the midst of the violence, we met our Muslim sisters and brothers in Sarkhej. We vowed to prevent any violence, especially by outside goondas. We sat together, talked together, ate together. We know that while big sahibs sit in offices, drawing big salaries, it is we the poor, the self-employed of all communities who suffer. These sahibs are the people in this city who want to divide us, to keep us down, but we will fight back – together.'

— 9 —

THE RETURN OF THE ARTIST

Schoolboys used to jeer at Jangarh Singh Shyam as he carried loads of wood to the bazaar to sell. He had been with them at the government school until he was thirteen, but then his father died and he had been forced to earn his own living. The boys despised Jangarh because he was condemned to a life of collecting wood, working on other men's land, labouring on roadworks or even begging. They were going on to university, and that meant they were in with a chance of getting a government job – the ultimate in achievement for children who go to state schools. The government does not pay generously, but it does confer status on all its employees and it gives most of them plenty of opportunities to use their office to augment their income.

When I met Jangarh fifteen years later, he was the successful member of his family. His nephew, Shiv Prasad Singh, had been to university and had not stopped at his BA but had gone on to achieve MA honours in history and political science. He had then succeeded in getting a government job in the railway police. Eight years later he is still a constable, with a salary of just 944 rupees per month. He believes he has been passed over for promotion because his relatives do not have the clout to do sifarish – to lobby on his behalf. Discipline is old-fashioned and humiliating – the punishment for a constable who returns a few hours late from leave is to run round and round the parade-ground holding a rifle above his head. One constable who did not salute an officer was sentenced to salute continuously for ten hours. Degreeless Jangarh, however, is now a nationally respected artist, with a job in a cultural centre. Some of his pictures sell for more than his railway-police nephew earns in a year. That is some achievement for a young man from a remote village in the tribal area of central India.

Jangarh Singh is a Pradhan, a member of one of the clans of the Gond tribe. The tribes of India – now known as 'adivasis', or 'original inhabitants' – lived in the remote jungles and remained outside the mainstream of Indian life until the British came. They were not considered part of the Hindu fold. The British, with their hatred of bureaucratic untidiness, decided that the tribals should be administered like anyone else. As a result of the opening up of the tribal areas which resulted from this decision, the tribes lost much of their land and were exploited by more sophisticated traders and farmers. There were a series of tribal revolts, put down with the utmost severity, but in the end the British gave up and segregated the tribals so that they could live their own lives and preserve their own culture. Cultured they certainly were, with their gods, their languages, their poetry, music and dance and their customs suited to life in the forests.

The government of independent India decided that the British policy was an anachronism, however, and the tribals' segregation was ended. Because they were considered 'backward', they were given crutches to help them limp into the twentieth century. Seats in parliament and state assemblies were specially reserved for tribals, and quotas of university places and government jobs were allocated to them. Special tribal welfare departments were set up in the central and state governments.

In the first flush of enthusiasm which came with independence, it was thought that grateful tribals would speedily integrate with the rest of society: their special privileges were guaranteed only for ten years. However, it soon became obvious that integration was a much more complicated task than first imagined, and the tribals still have their special privileges. In spite of these, independent India's policies have not proved an unmixed blessing to the tribals. A senior official in the tribal welfare department of the government of Jangarh's state, Madhya Pradesh, said to me, 'The tribals' forests have been slashed, their lands have been taken away for industrial development and they have been penalized for defaulting on loans they did not have the skill to make proper use of.' The tribals of central India have now started a political movement demanding their own state, to be called Jharkhand, where they can, within the limited autonomy India grants to its states, frame and implement policies which will make themselves the beneficiaries of the development of their homelands, rather than the industrialists, bureaucrats, politicians and traders. This movement is inevitably being strongly resisted by the government in Delhi and by the governments of the states who would lose territory to Jharkhand, including Madhya Pradesh.

Independent India has not put all the emphasis on integrating the tribals: there have also been attempts to preserve some of their culture. It was one of these attempts which rescued Jangarh from a life of hard labour and more than compensated for his lack of a degree.

I first met Jangarh Singh at a handicraft fair in Delhi. I saw this small, sturdy, dark-skinned young man, with a lively, open face, selling pictures of his tribal gods. I was attracted by the bright colours, the swirling lines and the strong presence of the gods and I bought some pictures. Talking to Jangarh, I learnt that he had been 'discovered' by Jagdish Swaminathan, an internationally renowned artist on the staff of Bharat Bhavan, a government-run cultural centre in the Madhya Pradesh capital of Bhopal. When I decided to write about Jangarh, I went first to Bharat Bhavan, where I found Swami, as he's known. He looked out of place in a government office, with his black hair streaked with grey falling over his shoulders, his untrimmed beard, his white kurta and dhoti. He was smoking a biri – the common man's smoke despised by all self-respecting government officials – and shuffling papers uneasily around his desk. He cheered up immediately when I suggested going to a hotel for a drink.

Swami describes himself as a 'cultural bastard'. His parents were south-Indian Brahmins, but he was born and brought up at the other end of India, in Simla, which was then the summer capital of the British raj. He has a deep knowledge of Hindi, Urdu and English literature, and says his last ambition is to walk the Hardy country in his dhoti – no matter how cold that might prove. He comes from that generation who had a genuine love–hate relationship with Britain: he opposed the raj but admired some aspects of British rule.

'I believe the British introduced a sense of justice in India. I'll give you an amusing example. When I was young, there was a crowd of us walking in the road in Delhi. A British Tommy bumped into us on a bicycle. We shouted, "Why can't you look where you're going?" He replied, "Why are you walking in the road, not on the pavement?" I then pointed to his cycle and said, "You should have your lights on." He replied, "You are quite right, Sir," and cycled off. Now isn't that justice?' laughed Swami.

One reason for Swami's interest in the tribals was the British habit of supporting the underdog. Another was his own deep-rooted suspicion of progress. 'I was a communist,' he told us. 'I was also a socialist. But now the very notion of progress is obnoxious to me. How can I say I am better than my father or my mother? The three demons of the modern age are Darwin, Marx and Freud. Just look at these tribals. Just because we can destroy their civilization, and are doing so, does it mean that we are better than them?'

'How have the progressives taken your work with the tribal artists?' I asked.

'Just as you would expect, of course. The leftists say we are trying to glorify backwardness. As for the intellectuals, well, they held a seminar at the Centre for Advanced Studies in Simla. What a presumptuous title, isn't it?' grunted Swami. 'What did they come up with? The speakers there said that, as all tribal art was based on superstition, to attach any abiding importance to it is to perpetuate superstition. I call that highly ignorant and arrogant. The stupid fools don't know what effect Picasso's discovery of tribal art had on Europe. Where would we be now, artists like me, without that? Our intellectuals don't even have pride in their own country. You know, we were the first people to collect the work of the tribals as art, not as folkcraft. When we sent an exhibition to Japan, I was criticized for not explaining where the tribals came from and who they were. I said we are running an art exhibition, not an exercise in ethnography or anthropology.'

'You have had this opposition from the intellectuals, but what about the tribals? Have you been able to do anything for them?'

'I think so. Most of the time they didn't take their work seriously until we met them. They weren't proud of it. There was an old tribal woman, for instance. We brought her to Bhopal and she started trying to do representational work. She couldn't do it, and we told her she shouldn't. We said, "Do your own work." But she insisted that was no good. You see, her values had been distorted by the city. That was what we had to fight against.'

'But what success have you actually had?'

'Well, I think that we have instilled some self-confidence into four to five hundred artists, and because of that others are gaining their self-confidence. There was a time when you could buy their works for five rupees; now you have to pay 500 at least. Of course not everyone likes that. Do you know, we have even been accused of spoiling tribal artists by getting them money for their work. Why should we so-called "modern" artists get paid, then?'

'What about the "modern" artists? How have they reacted?'

Swami chuckled. 'When Jangarh had his exhibition in Delhi, most of them kept away. They felt threatened, I reckon.'

Bharat Bhavan was the first place in India to have a permanent exhibition of tribal art. To make his collection, Swami sent teams of art students into the tribal areas to search for artists and their work. They were given written orders, which Swami says his communist past helped him to draw up. The orders were curt and concise, like 'Obey the team leader' and 'Do not under any circumstances offend the villagers.' Jangarh Singh Shyam was one of the artists the teams discovered. Jangarh now works in the printmaking department at Bharat Bhavan, and his wife and two children live with him in Bhopal, but he agreed to go back to his village with us. We had hoped that Swami would be able to come too, but he was called away to a meeting in Delhi. However, he lent us his car, his driver and a 'modern' artist from Bharat Bhavan to be our guide.

We started out from Bhopal at six thirty in the morning on the Jabalpur road, passing unprepossessing square blocks of flats which house the vast army of bureaucrats and their hangers-on needed to man the headquarters of the government of Madhya Pradesh. Although it was still several hours before the bureaucrats would end their preparations for going to work, a few dark-green and red buses of the state transport corporation were already on the road, adding clouds of poisonous fumes to the morning mist. Gilly and I sat on the back seat. Jangarh, Iyer the artist and of course Swami's driver, Prakash, were in the front.

We were soon out in the country, passing through villages of small houses with sloping tiled roofs, many covered with yellow flowering gourds. The landscape was open, with blue hills in the distance and hardly a tree to be seen.

After an hour or so, I tentatively asked about breakfast. In Punjab and the more prosperous areas of northern India the roads are lined with excellent open-air cafés known as dhabas. That did not seem to be the case on the Bhopal–Jabalpur road. The driver, Prakash, grunted in a way remarkably reminiscent of his boss, Swami. That meant that he would decide when and where to stop. When we passed through a small town where the cafés around the bus station were doing a brisk business, I again feebly raised the question of breakfast. Prakash said brusquely, 'Dhabas near bus stations are never any good.' A few miles out of the town he pulled up at a small open-air café in the middle of nowhere. This was the place where he had decided we should eat.

At this stage I was getting a little worried about my relationship with Prakash. I find drivers among the most difficult Indians to get on with. Either you let them take charge, and then you really are taken for a ride, or you try to establish your authority, and that can mean a surly and uncooperative companion for the rest of the journey. Prakash looked as though he could be a difficult customer. He was a small, wiry man with spiky hair and a two-day growth of beard which never seemed to get any longer. His face was thin, with a hooked nose, and he wore a gold earring in one ear. He came from Morena, which is in the heart of the dacoit or bandit country in the north of Madhya Pradesh, and he could easily have passed for a dacoit himself. As we had four days to spend with him, I decided to leave myself a bit more time to assess the situation.

Breakfast showed that we had also still to establish our relationship with the other passengers in the front seat. Gilly and I sat on one charpai, many of its strings replaced with what looked like plastic washing-line, while Jangarh and Iyer the artist sat down three charpais away and Prakash made the first of what were to be many inspections of the car. A young boy who was still less than half awake plonked down our breakfasts of omelettes, parathas and cups of very sweet tea on a none-too-clean board placed across the charpai. There seems to be an age limit above which you can't work as a waiter in a dhaba anywhere in India, and that limit is about ten. This dhaba was set under an acacia tree whose yellow flowers fell on our omelettes.

Prakash banged down the bonnet of the car and then walked into the fields behind the dhaba. Toilets are not a service dhabas normally provide. He then came back for a quick cup of tea. Before we had finished our breakfast he returned to the driving-seat, making it quite clear that he wanted to be on the move again. We hurriedly washed our hands under a pump, paid our bill and took our seats in the car. It still didn't seem to be the time to disagree with Prakash.

Swami's vehicle was a Hindustan Ambassador – still the standard issue for everyone in the government of India who merits a car, from the prime minister downwards. It is a bull-nosed four-door saloon making no concessions to modern aerodynamics – the late-forties model of the British Morris Oxford. It came to India in the fifties and has dominated the roads ever since. Officially the Ambassador has been through several changes during its long life, but each new 'mark' has meant merely a face-lift for the front grille or a new dashboard. The engine behind the grille has remained the same, and the chassis and springs carrying it have not altered. The car has two outstanding qualities: there seems to be no limit to the number of people it can carry, or to the length of its life. Mind you, the Ambassador is a demanding car – it needs plenty of attention to keep it on the road, which is why every Ambassador driver has to be his own mechanic. But despite its stern principles of economic self-reliance, or pulling itself up by its own bootstraps, even India has not been able to withstand the

Japanese invasion. The Maruti is now the fashionable car in the bigger cities. Named after the son of the Hindu wind-god, it is in fact a small Suzuki. Hindustan Motors, the manufacturers of the Ambassador, has replied by putting an Isuzu engine into the body of an outdated Vauxhall and calling it a 'Contessa'. But Hindustan Motors has not stopped producing the Ambassador, as it is still in demand. Although the Contessa is more comfortable and has an engine which can power an air-conditioner as well as pull a car, I still feel safer setting out on a long journey in an Ambassador. Contessas – and indeed Marutis – require new skills and spare parts when they fall victims to India's treacherous roads, and those skills and parts have not yet spread into the countryside.

About half an hour after breakfast we got the first hint of trouble – a sinister knocking under the back seat. Prakash ignored it. We rattled on through villages where women were pumping water into brass pots, smoke was rising from mud ovens and bells in the small roadside temples were clanging as those for whom the day was to be of special importance sought the blessings of Hanuman, Shiva or whoever the temple deity was. The luckier children were on their way to school; the unluckier ones were carrying vegetables and other produce on their heads to the local market. There were no clouds to shield us from the sun, but it was clearly not going to be an unbearably hot day. The knocking continued, and Prakash decided that something would have to be done. He stopped, went round to the back of the Ambassador and jumped up and down on the bumper. We set off again, the knocking apparently cured. Encouraged by this, Prakash put his foot down.

We were on a national highway, which should have meant one of the better roads of India, but this one would not have passed as a minor road in the more prosperous parts of the country. It was barely wide enough for one vehicle, as we found when we got stuck behind a lorry. The usual request 'Horn please' was painted on the back of the lorry, but Prakash's horn had no effect – the driver ploughed on as though he owned the road. Eventually a bus coming the other way made the truck-driver stop. The two heavily overladen vehicles moved gingerly on to the cart tracks on either side of the road and eased their way past each other. Prakash saw his chance, shot forward and overtook the truck before it could take command of the tarmac again.

The highway had almost as many potholes as the cart tracks, but we sped on – bumping up and down and bucking from side to side like a stagecoach in a Scarlet Pimpernel film – until suddenly there was a loud bang. We had hit a particularly vicious pothole. With the Ambassador still moving at a considerable speed, Prakash stuck his head out of the window and saw a tell-tale trail of oil. That struck him as something which could be serious, and so he stopped. A brief inspection of the underbelly showed that the oil-chamber had been holed. Prakash immediately decided that this needed a visit to the nearest village or town. Muttering something about getting oil, he jumped on a passing bus, leaving his passengers sitting under a tree by the side of the road.

It is of the nature of an Indian breakdown that you know it will be repaired but you don't know how many hours it will take. This delay – however long it was to be – forced us to break the barrier between the front and back seats of the car and establish a relationship with Jangarh and Iyer. The whole point of our journey was to get to know the artist better, and India is an inquisitive country, but even after so many years living here I still have an Englishman's reluctance to strike up a conversation with a comparative stranger – especially with a stranger like Jangarh, who seemed unusually reserved. I imagined that he might well resent our interest in him, but, as usual, my apprehensions were totally unfounded. Jangarh was only waiting for me to open the business between us.

Swami had given me a version of how Jangarh had been discovered, but, remembering that philosopher's own words – 'There is always a story behind a story in India' – I thought I would start by asking Jangarh for his version.

Swami had said his team had come across the artist breaking stones by the roadside, but Jangarh denied that he had ever sunk to that level. 'I did work on the roads. I carried baskets of mud on my head and dug mud to fill other people's baskets, but I never broke stones. We used to work in gangs and be away from the village for months on end.'

'How did you live?'

'I lived alone and used to sleep under trees in the hot weather. When it rained or got cold, we used to put up some sort of shelter. The jobs used to last a few months at a time, and then we went back home.'

'What happened when you couldn't get work like that?'

'Sometimes I collected wood from the jungle and sold it to the schoolmaster, and then of course at some times of the year there was work in the fields.'

'Didn't you have any land of your own?'

'Well, there were ten to twelve acres, but there are fifty to sixty people in my family.'

'Fifty to sixty?' I asked in surprise.

'Yes, but I didn't have to look after them all,' Jangarh replied with a smile. 'When my father died, my immediate family split up. He had two wives and everyone went their own way. It was difficult, because I was only thirteen and I was left to look after my wife and one of my sisters. They were the ones I had to work for. Mind you, the women helped too. They used to work in the village whenever possible, but I didn't want them to come and work on the roads with me.'

Iyer, a former college weightlifting champion with prematurely grey hair neatly tied in a pony-tail, unlike his guru Swami's, turned to Jangarh and asked, 'Well, what exactly did happen when the team of artists came? Where were you at the time?'

'I was working in another village, in the fields, when I was sent for. I found these people from the city in my village. They had seen a painting I had done on the walls of someone's house and had been told I had done it. They seemed to like it. Eventually I met Swami and told him I would like to go to Bhopal, and he agreed. At first I just went for a bit, but then Swami gave me a permanent job and I stayed in the city.'

'Did you think that you would learn more about art by going to Bhopal?' I asked.

'No,' replied Jangarh firmly. 'I don't take advice from any city artists. I also tell other tribals who come to Bhopal not to copy but to do their own work. The point of going to the city is not to change your art but to sell it.'

'Surely your art has changed since you went to the city?'

Jangarh thought for a moment and then said, 'Well, it's cleaner.'

'What does that mean? That the lines are clearer, that it's easier to understand?' I asked.

Iyer, the 'modern' artist, laughed. 'No. He means that there are no longer any splodges on the paper.'

'That's right,' said Jangarh, apparently not in the least offended.

Swami had told me that Jangarh's art had 'blossomed' in Bhopal, that his genius had 'burst forth'. Jangarh seemed unaware of that. Iyer then began to defend his guru. 'Come on, Jangarh. You have learnt new techniques. You've learnt etching for instance.'

'Yes, all right. I have learnt etching, and I do now paint with a thinner line, but my art hasn't changed.'

Iyer came back again: 'But Swami says that you are an original because you are the first person to paint pictures of your tribal gods.'

'Yes, that is true. You see, what happened was that our people use geometric patterns to represent the gods. But then I used to see people when the gods took possession of them and that was how I got the idea of what the gods looked like.'

'Didn't people in your village object to breaking the traditional way of representing the gods?'

'No, they liked it.'

'Did anyone in the village teach you to paint?'

'No. Actually I started by copying my eldest brother, who made animals out of clay. I didn't do it in front of him in case he got angry. I was shy too. Then I took to painting pictures on the walls of people's houses. They seemed to like them, and so I went on.'

'But how did you learn to paint the pictures?'

'How does anyone learn? I just copied other artists in the village, and then I got some ideas of my own.'

'Did you charge money for decorating people's houses?'

'No, I didn't think of doing that in the village. Anyway, then people would not have been so keen on giving me their walls to paint on,' said Jangarh, smiling.

After about two hours a bus pulled up by our tree and Prakash jumped down. 'These dehati [rustic] places!' he said. 'I had to walk four kilometres back from the town before I got any transport.'

I wondered vaguely what good the can of oil he was carrying would do if it was just going to pour out through the hole in the chamber, but I need not have worried. Prakash stuffed a piece of rag into the hole, poured the oil into the engine, jumped into his seat and started revving the engine. Satisfied that there was not too much knocking, he told us to get in quickly and set off again.

The next town – it was really just an overgrown village – was Devri. It was off the main road, underneath a hill covered with patchy forest. The biggest building in the town was the police station, which had 'Patriotism and Service of the People' painted on one wall in big red letters. Prakash, however, would not have dreamt of trying out the police's patriotism and service in this or any other difficulty he found himself in – the only service you will get on the Indian roads is from the people themselves.

Devri didn't even boast an Ambassador mistri, or mechanic, but there was an expert in tractors and Prakash persuaded him that removing the oil-chamber of the car wasn't very different from performing the same operation on a tractor. All went well until they discovered one nut of a different size. The mistri tried all his spanners, but none would fit. He turned to Prakash in triumph and said, 'I told you that we should not play around with this, but you wouldn't listen. Now you have lost another lot of oil.'

Prakash was not so easily defeated. He found a pipe, hammered it into something like the shape of the nut and managed to loosen it. After that it was all plain sailing. Devri did have a welder and so the hole in the chamber was plugged somewhat more substantially than before, and we started on the road to Jabalpur again.

Passing through one village, I noticed a small, squat building tilting precariously. It was advertised as 'The Leaning Temple of Lolri'. Unlike its more famous counterpart in Pisa, the Lolri temple showed no sign of becoming a tourist attraction.

At about five thirty in the evening, we hit a stretch of road which was being rebuilt. Unfortunately the government seemed to have run out of money and the national highway deteriorated into a cart track for about twenty miles. The central government provides the funds for national highways but the state governments build and maintain them. That inevitably means that much of the money allocated for national highways gets siphoned off into projects dearer to the heart of the state government. An abandoned road-roller and occasional piles of stones were the only signs of the Madhya Pradesh government's intention to rebuild this national highway between the state capital and Jabalpur, the seat of the High Court.

When the government of independent India merged the British Central Provinces with a collection of princely states to form Madhya Pradesh, there were several rival claimants for the honour – and, of course, the commercial advantage – of being the state capital. In an attempt to satisfy everyone, Bhopal, somewhere near the centre of the state, was made the capital. Jabalpur in the east was given the High Court, Gwalior in the north was given the Revenue Board, and Indore in the south was given the Public Services Commission, which has the all-important responsibility of supervising government recruitment – altogether not a very convenient arrangement considering the condition of Madhya Pradesh's roads.

Thirteen hours after leaving Bhopal we finally reached Jabalpur, a distance of 200 miles. An official of Bharat Bhavan had confidently assured us that it would only take six hours. There was no question of going on to our rest house at Mandla, the nearest district headquarters to Jangarh's village, so we made our way to Jackson's Hotel. The Jacksons have long-since gone and the hotel is now in the hands of the Chadhas, a family who before partition used to have a lucrative contract for providing the army with supplies, including wines and spirits, in Peshawar, the capital of the North West Frontier Province. Fortunately they have not changed the hotel very much. The entrance that night seemed rather forbidding but the staff inside were more welcoming than the condescending young graduates who operate India's new five-star hotels. The rooms were far more spacious and the prices very much more reasonable too. There were notices on the walls of the rooms requesting 'valued guests leaving early in the morning or in the odd hours of the night to get their bills cleared by 10 p.m. on the previous night to avoid inconvenience'. The notice ended, 'Your cooperation is solicited.' We had decided not to leave at an odd hour, though, so there was no need to cooperate in this matter at least.

The front seat of the car decided to sleep three in one room, but I need not have worried – the barriers were not going up again. When I suggested that we all meet in my room for a drink, Iyer said, 'We have a little shopping to do and then we will join you.'

The shopping turned out to be a half-bottle of Jupiter Royal King Whisky. At the top end of the market, Indian whiskies are highly potable; at the bottom they are near lethal. I'd never heard of Jupiter and so I assumed it was in the latter class. Iyer described it as his cocktail, and proceeded to pour handsome pegs into his, Jangarh's and Prakash's beer.

I wanted to know more about Swami, so I told them how much I had enjoyed my two days with him. Iyer said, 'I'll tell you a story about Swami, about the sort of man he is. When I applied for a job at Bharat Bhavan I had just left university, where I'd been a student leader. We were the rough and tough types, ready for anything. The local shopkeepers gave us plenty of respect and we used to drink with the police, so we were well in with them. The problem was that I had no job and no ready cash. But I wasn't going to take any crap from anyone just to get myself a job, and specially not from some government babu. So I came to that interview in a foul mood.'

'What made you apply for a job at Bharat Bhavan? Were you interested in art?'

'No – that's the whole point. I saw this advertisement for a galleryman on a bag of potatoes made out of newspaper and I thought that, being a government job, it would have been fixed in advance. Nevertheless I applied, like I applied for a whole lot of other jobs. I had absolutely no interest in it at all. My mood didn't improve when I saw this long-haired, khadi-clad creep sitting behind the interview desk. I thought to myself: some typical arty fraud bumming off the government. Anyhow, I thought, I'll fix him. Swami's first question was, "What do you know about art?" I replied, "What is art?" Swami didn't take me up on that one but went on to ask me to name three Indian artists. I told him that I didn't know one, but that I had liked a statue I had seen in a film called *Mughal-e-Azam*.'

The statue was a particularly tasteless plaster of Paris representation of a heroine in a sentimental historical drama.

Iyer went on, 'That still didn't faze Swami. He continued with the interview – apparently seriously. His next question was the standard "Why do you want the job?" I of course replied, "For the money. But while I am getting the money I'll also look at your art." It's a hell of a guy who can give you a job after an interview like that, and I have proved he was right. From being just another mindless bolshie student I have become an artist. My pictures have been shown in Delhi and are now going to Bombay. That's Swami for you.'

By this time the Jupiter Royal cocktail had made Jangarh talkative too. He turned to Iyer and said, 'Don't mind if I tell you, but I think you are wrong. I think it's your fate and what you do with your own strength which makes you a success or a failure. I've told Swami to his face that I'll stand on my own two feet and whether I eat chicken and eggs or only dal is my fate, not in your hands or the government's.'

'Come on,' said Iyer. 'You know you owe everything to Swami.'

'That may be so, but I can look after myself. When I was at school I was the champion kabaddi and kho-kho [team games] player. I was a very good singer, and a dancer too. I know nobody really cares about the poor, although the poor are polite. Everybody goes and pays attention to the rich, although the rich are rude. As for these government officials who are meant to do good to the poor, well, I'll tell you my experience of them – they are just blood-suckers.'

'What do you mean?' I asked.

'I once applied for a loan for a cow. The loan was for 2,000 rupees. I knew I was entitled to it because the government always makes such a noise about these schemes for helping the poor, although they never do really help. Anyhow, after the bank manager had taken his cut I got only 900 rupees – not even half what I was meant to get. But I was poor and in no position to argue and so I took the money. I still intended to buy some sort of a cow, but then I found out that the government vet took 300 rupees to certify the cow was fit to be insured. So I just kept the cash. What else could I do? The police still send warrants from time to time because I haven't repaid the loan. I have the cash now, but I'll be damned if I ever repay it.'

I broke the top off a beer bottle as I was opening it. Prakash said, 'I can tell you why that has happened – there's too much gas in the bottle. I used to work in a small soft-drinks factory where we made naqli [fake] Coca-Cola at night. We used empty Coca-Cola bottles, and I swear you couldn't tell the difference between ours and the real thing.'

Jangarh unwrapped his red and white checked safa or headcloth and strained the beer through it to make sure no broken glass got into our drinks. At that stage in the evening no one much bothered whether the beer was naqli or not, and we polished off the last couple of bottles with an excellent meal of tandoori chicken and dal.

We had arrived at night and had received only the vaguest impression of Jabalpur. Most people from whom we asked the way to Jackson's Hotel seemed equally vague. The next morning we were able to see this leading city of Madhya Pradesh for ourselves.

In *The Highlands of Central India* (1889), a British officer, Captain J. Forsyth, wrote of nineteenth-century Jabalpur:

> The steam-horse has torn his way through the parks, and levelled the bamboo clumps that were the glory of the place. Hideous embankments, and monstrous hotels, and other truly British buildings stare one in the face at every turn. Crowds of rail-borne 'picturesquers' assail the Marble Rocks and other sights about the place. Everything has run up to the famine prices induced by the rapid 'progress' of the last ten years.

Captain Forsyth would have loathed the internal-combustion engine even more than the steam-horse. In the Jabalpur of today, drivers of scooter-rickshaws, whose two-stroke engines emit particularly noxious fumes, battle both with their less fortunate rivals pedalling cycle-rickshaws and with pedestrians driven off the pavements by the stalls which have commandeered them. Situated at the exact geographical centre of India, the city should be a place of distinction, but it is in fact most undistinguished. It has an army tradition, being the depot of the Indian grenadiers, but it is a most unmilitary shambles. In short, Jabalpur's growth has been unplanned, uncoordinated and chaotic. Its streets are lined by small shops, tea stalls, purveyors of various sorts of cuisine, sweet-makers boiling great pans of milk on Calor-gas rings – every sort of fire and health hazard. Nobody knows how many of its citizens live in one-roomed shacks whose roofs are held down by bricks, old cycle frames, pieces of wood or any other junk the owners can find. We were only too happy to leave Jabalpur behind and get on the open road to Jangarh's village, Patangarh. It was just 112 miles away, but no one was guessing how long it would take the Ambassador to get there.

We were travelling through countryside which had once been jungle but was now rolling green hills with small clumps of trees dotted here and there. Yet everyone we saw seemed to be carrying wood or grass on their heads, indicating how dependent the tribals still are on the fast-dwindling forests and common land. We passed a gang of adivasis repairing the road. They wore just patched shorts and plastic shoes. Sweat glistened on their black skin as they stirred boiling tar and poured it on the road. Labourers are a common enough sight in India and I wouldn't have thought about them had it not been for Jangarh sitting in the front seat, smartly dressed in a pair of cream trousers and a purple shirt. Now, however, I saw those labourers as men who might perhaps be artists or musicians, who had villages, homes, families and traditions they were proud of.

Road signs warned of the approach of the steeper hills which they described as ghat sections. At the bottom of one ghat section I saw a group of women in startlingly bright saris sitting on the rocks at the edge of a river. On the other side of the bridge were a group of men dressed in white. A barber was shaving their heads.

'It's a funeral,' said Jangarh. One of the men came towards the car. I feared that he might be quite rightly annoyed that we had been staring at his women, but he was just curious. He was the eldest brother of a young man who had drowned in the river, a member of a farming caste from a nearby village. He had buried the boy near the river. When I asked why the boy had not been cremated, his brother said, 'Cremated? Nowadays who can get wood?' The boy's widow, who was only fifteen, would not be able to remarry but would be adopted by some family.

By now the women had started walking back to the village, in single file. The young widow, looking stunned but rebellious, was the only one wearing a white sari – it symbolized her widowhood. The end of the sari covered her head too, which, as custom demanded, had been shaved by the side of the river. She wore no bangles – they had been broken as part of the ritual.

Eventually we reached Dindori, where the collector should have reserved rooms for us at the rest house. A cook whose head and belly had swollen in the service of the government told us rudely that he had not heard anything from the collector and that both rooms were reserved for the superintendent of police. The cook, like all minor Indian functionaries, delighted in being obstructive. We went to his boss, the assistant engineer of the public works department. He too had heard nothing from the collector but, surprisingly, was more willing to help. The engineer suggested that we stay in another rest house which, as luck would have it, was nearer Jangarh's village. When we reached that rest house, the cook there told us that the thanedar, the head of the local police station, had reserved it for the superintendent. Prakash was able to persuade the cook that the superintendent couldn't be in two places at the same time and that, anyhow, the engineer, not the thanedar, was the 'concerned officer for controlling reservations in rest houses'.

Now the time had come for the last leg of the journey. We all fell silent, and I was worried about our arrival in the village – the embarrassment of being a total stranger in a close-knit community, the unreality of my position as a spectator who could never be a participant and, of course, the possibility of putting my foot in it.

It was pitch dark when Jangarh told Prakash to stop at a bullock-cart track going off the main road. This was the way into the village of Patangarh. Prakash didn't like the look of the track very much, but determination to see that his Ambassador made it to the very end overcame caution. We lurched across a shallow ditch, started to climb up a steep hillside and were soon in a narrow lane with small, dimly lit huts on both sides. We stopped outside one of these huts, which was Jangarh's home. The car was surrounded by people shielding their eyes from the lights. Cattle in a small stable shuffled uneasily. There was silence except for the whirring of the cicadas. Jangarh got out and touched the feet of his relatives, but nobody spoke.

It was Prakash who broke the ice. He leapt out of the car, opened the bonnet and fixed up an inspection light which he shone with exaggerated professionalism over the engine, pulling at a wire here, adjusting a screw there. The children couldn't resist this and soon everyone was involved in a discussion on what could be wrong with the Ambassador. I had not noticed anything beyond its normal eccentricities. Eventually Prakash, by now crouched beside a back wheel, shouted in triumph, '*Ek shocker baith gaya*' – 'One shocker has sat down.'

Jangarh led us through a low doorway, across a small courtyard into a room which he announced with pride was his. It was about thirty feet long and eight feet wide, with a sloping roof supported by three thick wooden beams. Jangarh explained how he had carried those beams from the forest on his back, and how he and his wife had 'raised the walls with their own hands' with mud mixed with chaff and straw. That was during the harsh early years of Jangarh's marriage. As often happens in Pradhan society, he had fallen in love and married when he and his wife were just thirteen. When, shortly afterwards, his father had died and the family had split up, he had to build his own house. Three of his children had died before they were two months old. He seemed resigned to their loss, saying that he would have been like a brother, not a father, to them if they had lived.

His room was lit by a wick in a small kerosene-filled bottle hanging from the wall. Some words of that senior official of the tribal welfare department in Bhopal came to mind. He had told me about a new scheme to install one lighting point in every Harijan and tribal house. 'That', said the official, 'will mean that every time they switch on the light they will think of Chief Minister Arjun Singh.' That is how politicians look at tribals – as easily purchasable vote fodder. They insult men like Jangarh, who are proud of their homes no matter how humble they may appear.

Gilly and I sat on a low ledge with our backs against a wall. Iyer sat opposite. Jangarh went out into the courtyard, from where we could hear the sound of low voices. The room had two small, unglazed, oval windows with bamboo bars. There was no furniture except for a charpai and some earthenware storage pots. On the wall was an advertisement for Tiger-brand biris, which Jangarh smokes, and a photograph of his son in Bhopal. He returned with a colourless liquor in a rum bottle, and four glasses. 'This', he said, 'is mahua.' Captain Forsyth said of mahua, 'The spirit, when well made and mellowed by age, is by no means of despicable quality, resembling in some degree Irish whiskey.'

Mahua didn't taste like Irish whiskey to me, but maybe that was because my drop had been sold before it was seven years old. In Patangarh they don't believe in maturing the liquor, which they make from the flowers of the mahua tree – once it's been distilled, it's ready to drink. But even unmatured mahua is certainly not despicable. It has a pungent bouquet and a bitter-sweet taste very like many of the other better country-made liquors of India. Jangarh assured us it was a very clean drink.

Jangarh kept going out to meet his relatives and other villagers and then returning to drink with us. He explained how important it was that he should not cause offence to any of the villagers. 'The whole village thinks, "This one poor small boy with no land is so wealthy today," but I fall at their feet and they are all happy. However much I earn, I give half to the village whose earth I come from. I give the children biscuits and the older people a bottle of booze, and they are happy. I am happy too. If I don't meet everyone, and most of the village are my relatives, they say, "Here he is – yesterday a boy and today he thinks he can ignore us." '

'In what you call "city" society,' I said, 'we all do our best not to give anything away, avoiding income tax and all that.'

'Hold on,' replied Jangarh, 'I don't give away so much that I am left naked.'

Towards the end of the evening, two of Jangarh's sisters – Genda and Shamabai – brought in food for us. Their children stood by shyly, but there was nothing shy or retiring about their mothers. They drank mahua, joined in the conversation and sang with Jangarh. The words of one song, which Jangarh himself had composed, ran, 'The earth calls out, "Tell me, Raja, why are you leaving me? You will never find such love in the city as you find in your village." '

The two sisters were the only villagers we met that night. When we left Jangarh to return to the rest house, the village was quiet, the inhabitants apparently asleep. He promised that tomorrow we would meet everyone, bathe in the River Narmada and drink more mahua.

When we returned to Patangarh at about eleven o'clock the next morning, the village still seemed to be asleep. Genda came out of her house grinning and told us that her brother was still not up because he and his friends had been drinking and dancing until five in the morning. Eventually Jangarh emerged, rubbing his eyes. He suggested we should go to meet the sarpanch, the head of the village council, who lived just two houses away. The sarpanch's wife was another of Jangarh's sisters, but considerably older than him.

After we had waited outside his hut for a few minutes, the sarpanch – Sahiba Singh Tekam – appeared in the doorway, dressed in a grimy vest and a crumpled dhoti. He blinked at the sunlight and asked, 'Who are you?' Without waiting for an answer, he came and sat beside us on the charpai which had been set out in our honour. He looked at us and remarked truculently, 'No one should come to the village without calling on the sarpanch. I am the sarpanch, and everyone should call on me first. After all, I have the power to stop people coming here. They have to take my permission or', and here he broke into English, emphasizing each word, 'No Admission, By Order'.

I explained that we had come to see him as soon as we had arrived that morning. That appeared to mollify him, though he was clearly under the influence of last night's liquor.

'It is good of you to come to see us. We are only adivasis and live miles from anywhere.'

'No,' I replied, 'it's not good of us. We are delighted to be here and are very honoured to be welcomed by you.'

That fatuous remark enraged the sarpanch. 'People like you think you are too grand even to shit in the sort of houses we live in. I'm an important man. I should have a chamber to entertain you in. It's a disgrace that I don't have a chamber. Perhaps you don't know that my sister married Dr Verrier Elwin. He was a great man. He lived in this village and never counted anyone as big or small. He treated everybody alike.'

Verrier Elwin was an Anglican priest who worked in India and became close to Mahatma Gandhi. His fellow Englishmen did not, of course, approve of this. Elwin first came to work among the Gonds of Mandla district in 1932, with his lifelong friend and colleague Shamrao Hivale. They opened ashrams in the area, offering shelter to lepers and education and medical assistance to the villagers. Eventually Elwin renounced his orders, telling his bishop that his contact with the Mahatma had made it impossible for him to believe that there was only one way to heaven, and he remained among the tribals, studying their life. He became a distinguished anthropologist, and his writings show him to have been a humorous man with a great sympathy for the Gond way of life and character.

Elwin was always sceptical about the benefits of modern, Westernized education and medicine. Soon after coming to Mandla, he noted in his diary, published in *Leaves from the Jungle – Life in a Gond Village*, 'Shamrao gives lecture on malaria at Bondar. Asks, "Who are our greatest enemies?" A voice, "Our wives." General impression in villages, as result of health propaganda, that syphilis is spread by mosquitoes.' He went on, 'Dhobi [washer-man] reports popular view of me, that I am immensely wealthy, and live as I do in order so to engage the favour of the Gods that they will give me more money still. Idea, common in Europe, that the ascetic life creates good impression on the oriental mind clearly very erroneous.'

Elwin's wife, the sarpanch's sister, is still alive, with a house in Shillong in the north-eastern hills of India. She visits Patangarh from time to time.

Sahiba Singh Tekam's election as sarpanch had been a close-run thing. When the votes were counted, it was found that he had drawn with his Congress rival. According to the sarpanch, the battle was decided on the toss of a coin. That was two years ago. He had been elected on the ticket of the right-wing orthodox Hindu Bharatiya Janata Party. He himself was still very much a believer in the tribal gods of his community, but such theological niceties did not bother him. He spoke proudly of his great-grandfather, Dani Tekam, who had been a gunia or tribal priest of the Pradhans. Gunias offer sacrifices and, when possessed by the gods, act as counsellors, soothsayers and doctors. Both Elwin and Shamrao knew Dani Tekam, and Shamrao described him in his book *The Pradhans of the Upper Narbada Valley*:

> When the fit is on him, Dani dances in ecstasy. He beats himself with the iron scourge. He thrusts a pointed iron rod through his cheeks. He sits uninjured on his seat of spikes. The goddess comes upon him and reveals the secrets of the other world and of this, the cause of this disease or that death, where a wandering bullock has strayed and how an errant wife may be restored. The house is poor enough but spotlessly clean and it has a sense of dignity and good reputation.

Shamrao recorded a conversation with the gunia during which he described his relationship with the goddess, whom he called 'the 64 Jogini'.

> Sometimes when she wants to show her presence she appears for a second exactly like a lightning flash and then I know she has some message for me. When I have stopped breathing and my tongue loses control, I know it is possessed by the goddess and whatever she wants to say, she says through my tongue . . . Sometimes she wants to dance and I may suddenly find that even in my bed I hear her music and I am dragged to her place and begin to dance . . . Sometimes the Mother desires physical love and then she comes as a most beautiful girl and

sleeps with you and when you have awakened, she disappears but all the same you have had intercourse with her, successful and complete. You are perspiring and breathing hard and there is a discharge.

The sarpanch made no claim to being a gunia himself, but he was anxious to demonstrate the power which still resided in tribal gods. He went into his house and emerged with a trident wrapped in peacock feathers. Standing over Gilly, he said, 'Now you see I can pierce this through your cheek and nothing will happen.' Gilly flinched, and he said, 'Don't worry – I will do it to myself afterwards and nothing will happen to me.'

Fortunately Jangarh persuaded his brother-in-law not to test the goddess's strength. The disappointed sarpanch sat down on the charpai again and said, 'The trouble is that there are no great gunias any longer. They just don't seem to exist.'

There is still one tribal priest in Patangarh. He lives in a house at the bottom of the hill. In his courtyard stands a long pole surrounded by flags, tridents and spikes. There is also a sanctuary in a dark corner of his room, filled with tridents and peacock feathers, each trident symbolizing a god. Nanku Panda, the priest, had long, straight, black hair brushed neatly back – unlike the unruly mops of the other villagers. He was softly spoken and shy, but willing to talk about his craft. He told us, 'Sometimes a god takes a pig sacrifice for curing someone from sickness. Other gods demand a goat. Chickens are only for very small gods.'

I asked whether he was ever possessed by a deity. He replied, 'When the goddess comes, I pierce myself with tridents and dance, and people play instruments and sing.'

'When does this happen?'

'If anyone pays money it can be done. It doesn't cost much. Just enough for mahua, biris and pan for four or five people.'

One of Jangarh's relatives who had accompanied us suggested that we should pay for the priest to go into a trance, but, remembering Gilly's narrow escape from the sarpanch, I decided against it. In any case, it didn't seem right to purchase the gods of Patangarh, even though I realized that I couldn't possibly understand the rights and wrongs of the Pradhans' religion.

Nanku Panda knew all the rituals by heart – nowhere were they written down. So far his children had not shown any interest in learning them, but the priest said, 'If they don't want to learn from me, the goddess will teach them in their dreams. Actually, every house should have one man who knows these things.'

While we were sitting with the tribal priest, his rival – or someone I assumed must be his rival – had entered the village. He was an orthodox Brahmin priest who visited the village regularly to perform Hindu rituals. He had come to collect some money he had been promised for performing the puja or worship of Ganesh, the elephant-god. When I asked whether there was any conflict between him and the tribal priest, he replied, 'No, he is different to me. There is no tension between us. People here often ask me to come and perform pujas. Then, you see, they like to hear me recite the *Ramayan*. I come to do that every year.'

Was this the stealthy advance of Hinduism – the gradual undermining of the tribals' traditions which I had read and heard so much about? I rather doubted it. Jangarh certainly didn't seem to be worried about the Brahmin.

'He is the village Brahmin. Why shouldn't he come here? He came to see me, and I'm glad that he did. I respect him and touched his feet as I would an elder of the Pradhans.'

In fact, anthropologists say that the Gonds have long been closer to Hinduism than other tribes. I was reminded of some of Swami's words: 'There are no full stops in India, only commas.' It's we Westerners who insist on categorizing everyone and everything, and that is why we so often misunderstand India.

It's not religion but materialism which is undermining the tribals' way of life. The Indian forests have been cut by timber contractors to meet the growing commercial demand for wood, by the government and industrialists to exploit resources like iron ore and coal, and by the more prosperous farmers and plantation-owners to cultivate the land. The villagers of Patangarh, whose life and culture depend entirely on forests, now have to walk six miles to collect wood.

The commissioner appointed by the government to review the

safeguards the constitution provides for tribals and Harijans has in his most recent (twenty-ninth) report described those safeguards as 'more or less meaningless'. The report is a tribute to Indian democracy, in that a civil servant has been allowed to publish a damning indictment of the government's development policy. The tragedy of Indian democracy is that other civil servants will try to make out that the commissioner is exaggerating, and will then put the report on a shelf to gather dust. The commissioner says that one quarter of India's population – the poorest quarter – is still denied the right 'to live with dignity'. He puts much of the blame on the survival of colonial legislation and attitudes, and says of the courts which administer that legislation, 'It is well known that a simple person has no hope of getting justice there.'

The commissioner is particularly critical of the way in which tribals have been robbed of their forests. He blames this on 'growing inequality and the rising tide of consumerism'. The only forests which are really well preserved in India are the wildlife sanctuaries set up and managed with the help and advice of the World Wide Fund for Nature, and much praised internationally. The commissioner points out that wildlife is preserved at the expense of the tribals, who are no longer allowed to live in the forests. He says, 'The tribal people and the wild animals have co-existed reasonably well from times immemorial. Wildlife has not been destroyed by bows and arrows, the real culprit is the outsider.'

Patangarh is in the valley of the River Narmada. The government, in conjunction with the World Bank, is planning to dam the river's waters in a massive development project which will lead to what the commissioner claims will be 'the largest displacement of people in the world'. Seventy per cent of the people whose villages will be destroyed are tribals. The government has promised they will all be resettled, but the commissioner is not convinced. He says, 'It is clear, notwithstanding the promise about land for land, that land is not available for rehabilitation, and rehabilitation of people as communities is not possible.' If the Narmada is dammed, Patangarh will apparently not be affected but thousands of villages lower down the river will be drowned and communities similar to Patangarh will be destroyed for ever.

We had been promised a bathe in the River Narmada but were denied it because the mahua was calling again. It was calling in the shape of the sarpanch, who, clad in an immaculately clean kurta, had arrived with the mukhia, the largest landowner in the village, to start the next round of celebrations of the return of Jangarh. This time we were to be included.

We were taken back into Jangarh's house, where a dholak or drum and a traditional harmonium had been laid out. Jangarh's friends followed us into the room. Jangarh took over the dholak, securing it under one leg. There was no shortage of candidates for the harmonium. The singing started – traditional and modern tribal songs, well known by everyone there except, of course, us. The sarpanch sang loudly and made sure that we were plied with mahua. When the instrumental players changed or there was a lull in the music for any reason, he discussed the problems of the village.

Apparently a young man from Patangarh had recently been murdered by his father-in-law, who lived in another village. The girl, who was eight months pregnant, was still in Patangarh. According to the sarpanch, the couple had fallen in love, but the girl's father was comparatively wealthy and the boy was not. It is customary in such cases that the boy should work for a number of years in the home of the girl's parents. This the boy did for four years, but the father was still not willing to give permission for the wedding. So the couple had eloped and set up house in Patangarh. The girl's father came to the village, took the boy into the forest and killed him.

'What about the police?' I asked.

'Oh, they were bribed, and the boy's father is terrified. He put his mark on a statement saying that the boy had died of illness. We are only adivasis without any money – who will listen to us?'

I offered the sarpanch one of the south-Indian cigars I smoke. He accepted, saying that Dr Verrier Elwin smoked cigars. I was glad to find out later that Elwin said his health improved enormously after he started smoking them, and that they cured him of malaria.

The sarpanch kept insisting that I was a big man and that it was a great honour to the village that I had come to visit them. He was sorry that Jangarh had not brought Swami too, because he wanted to ask him for something. He said, 'I won't tell you what it is, because you will write it down and then Swami will think I have been speaking behind his back.' I gathered, however, that the sarpanch's troubles were to do with a provident-fund payment he had not received. He had worked in a government tribal research unit in the neighbouring state of Bihar but had left when his wife fell ill.

By now the mahua was taking its toll. The mukhia was dozing squatting on his heels, dancing had started and the singing was getting louder. The sarpanch was becoming truculent again. He got up, staggered across to the mukhia and then squatted beside him. Puffing fiercely on his cigar, he stared angrily at me. I didn't know what I had done wrong, and Jangarh was not at hand to ask. The sarpanch then talked earnestly to the mukhia and pointed angrily at me. The mukhia shook his head, clearly not at all agreeing with the sarpanch's complaints. Then suddenly the sarpanch straightened his back and started to make a speech. The music stopped and the sarpanch could be heard saying, 'You have come to our village. We have welcomed you because you are big people from the cities and this is an out of the way place. Anyway, unlike you we welcome everyone.' He then shouted, 'You are canjoos [mean]. I am sorry to say you are canjoos.' A crowd gathered round the sarpanch and an argument started up, but he refused to take back his words.

Jangarh appeared by my side and I asked, 'Should I give some money for the party? Is that what he means?'

'Well yes, I am afraid it is.'

I got out my wallet and gave Jangarh 100 rupees. 'No, not as much as that. Nowhere near that.'

I insisted. I didn't want to be accused of meanness again.

Jangarh went across to the sarpanch and told him that I had given 100 rupees. The sarpanch immediately got to his feet and made another speech. 'These are good and generous people who have come to our village. We are very glad that we have been able to welcome them, and that they have come so far to see us.' He then started to sing a song which, as far as I could understand it, went, 'You have come from far, and you will go away, but there will always be a place for you in our hearts.'

All embarrassment was forgotten and the party continued. A 5-year-old boy with a deformed leg and hand danced energetically, and we all sang '*Mahua ke phul charhao*' – 'Let the flower of the mahua go to our heads.'

Jangarh later wrote a letter to us, apologizing for the sarpanch. We replied that we had not been in the least upset by him. In fact I was glad that the matter had been sorted out and that we had not left a reputation for meanness behind. It had been my fault – I should have discussed the question of making a contribution to the party with Jangarh much earlier. We had presumed on Patangarh's hospitality.

We left Jangarh's house with one of his brothers walking ahead of the Ambassador, waving a torch to guide us down the bullock-cart track. When the brother nearly fell over in a pothole, Prakash said, 'There isn't a single person in this village who is not under the influence of mahua.' Prakash was, in fact, the one exception – although drink-driving laws are not strictly enforced in the depths of Madhya Pradesh, he was not going to risk our lives or his Ambassador. By the time we lurched over the last shallow ditch on to the main road, we had picked up Jangarh's police-constable nephew returning to Jabalpur from leave and another young cousin who just wanted to see Bhopal. On the way back to the rest house we fell asleep, ignoring a sinister smell of burning from underneath the car.

The next morning I lifted my head off my pillow cautiously, but Jangarh had been right – mahua was a clean spirit and I had only the lightest of light hangovers. Outside the rest house, Prakash was preparing the Ambassador for the long drive back. I asked him about the burning we had smelt on our way back from Patangarh. He said it had been caused by some nut which had worked loose. I did not let him know that I suspected he had been driving with the handbrake on. Anyhow, there was no smell of burning that morning.

We hit one more vicious pothole on the way to Jabalpur.

Prakash quickly assessed the damage: '*Ek aur shocker baith gaya*' – 'One more shocker has sat down.' Nevertheless, he was confident that we would reach Jabalpur on two shock-absorbers. We did, but not, unfortunately, until after the police constable's leave warrant had expired. I hope he did not find himself doubling around the parade-ground, rifle above his head.

In *The Pradhans of the Upper Narbada Valley*, Verrier Elwin wrote:

> Amid the weary decline of the great Gond race, he [the Pradhan] still stands out, jovial, original and witty. While the Gond now thinks the sum of human ambition is to be a railway clerk, an Excise Inspector or an E.A.C., the Pradhan still believes that life itself matters more than life's achievements, that a poem is more important than a file, that to know how to make love to your wife is a much more important bit of knowledge than how to read or write.

That tradition is still alive in Patangarh, but how long will it survive what is today called progress?

— 10 —

THE DEFEAT OF A CONGRESSMAN

Dharhara is a small village in northern Bihar. In 1951 northern Bihar was still a remote region, cut off from the rest of the state, between the Ganges and the Himalayan kingdom of Nepal. Patna, the capital of Bihar, could be reached only by crossing the river in an ancient steam ferry. Dharhara itself was three miles away from the nearest road. Yet on 19 June 1951 the whole of Bihar – or at least everyone who counted in the state – had gathered in that remote and unremarkable village.

Fifty richly caparisoned elephants, garlanded with marigolds, red sandalwood paste smeared over their foreheads, plodded solemnly down the bullock-cart track to Dharhara, leading a wedding procession of some 2,000 people. A special train had brought the wedding party to the nearest railway station. The bridegroom, Rudrashawar Prasad Singh, a 19-year-old medical student, was carried in a silver and gold palanquin. He was a magnificent sight with his brocade turban and shervani. A large emerald and pearl brooch pinned to the front of his turban glittered in the bright sunlight, and the ostrich feather crowning his ensemble swayed with the movement of the palanquin-bearers. But the bridegroom was not a happy man. He later remembered the procession as 'a nightmarish experience'. The heavy turban, which had been tied five times before his father was satisfied with its shape, had given him a headache, the long-sleeved, tight-fitting shervani coat was like an oven encasing his body and the swaying palanquin made him feel sick.

The bride was the 14-year-old sister of Digvijay Narain Singh, always known as Digvijay Babu. 'Babu' is a term of respect and affection in Bihar. Digvijay was the young head of a wealthy landowning family who lived in a feudal palace of 100 rooms in Dharhara. The only other buildings of any substance in the village were the school and the small hospital built by the founder of the family fortune two generations earlier. Digvijay was setting out on what was to be one of the most remarkable but least acclaimed political careers of independent India. During that career he never sought or held office, yet at one stage he was the most important politician after the prime minister. He spent a fortune on politics, while most of his party colleagues were making theirs. His constituents loved him for his honesty, his generosity and his concern. Digvijay finally gave up politics on a point of principle – or perhaps 'honour' might be a better word.

Many of those who were to play important roles in Digvijay's political career were among the 3,000 guests in the bridal party. S. K. Sinha, the chief minister of Bihar, was there with almost his entire cabinet. He was Digvijay's political godfather. Shamnandan Mishra, an up-and-coming young parliamentary secretary, strutted among the guests with a liveried attendant in train. Mishra was to be one of the conspirators who brought down the only government Digvijay was directly involved in. L. P. Shahi, another aspiring young politician, cut a less glamorous figure at the wedding: according to the bridegroom, 'He served spinach to the less important guests.' Shahi was to be the man who eventually ended Digvijay's political career.

The bridegroom's party stayed for three days and the bride's for four. Elaborate arrangements were made to entertain them. Bismillah Khan, one of India's best-known musicians, played the shehnai, an oboe-like reed instrument, from the top of the arch over the entrance to the family mansion. The arch had been specially built for the wedding and it had no stairs, so the ustad or maestro had to scramble in an undignified manner up a ladder to get to his perch. The bride's and the bridegroom's parties each brought their own nautch or dancing girls. The bridegroom said, 'Most of the politicians were afraid it would damage their reputations if it was learnt that they had gone to watch the nautch girls, but I know of one minister in the Bihar government who could not resist the temptation.' There was a tradition that, on the third day of the celebrations, the nautch girls danced and sang songs insulting the guests from the other side. Apparently that tradition was faithfully followed.

The mansion at Dharhara had been built by Digvijay's grandfather, Babu Langat Singh. He had started life as a railway worker, losing one of his legs when he was crushed between two goods wagons in a marshalling yard. It was a British railway official, short of funds to pay his debts before he went on home leave, who changed Babu Langat Singh's life. Babu Langat Singh lent him all his savings, and when the official returned he repaid the debt by helping the railway worker to become a contractor. In those days the railways were spreading fast, and Langat Singh made a fortune out of construction works. He spent much of his money on establishing himself as a landed gentleman, buying some of his land from a British indigo planter, George Toomey, who, according to Digvijay, 'was forced to sell it because of his wild habits'. Langat Singh also took an interest in politics and became a friend of some of the leaders of the Congress Party. He himself was illiterate but realizing the disadvantage that he had suffered by not being educated, he founded the first university college in northern Bihar. Langat Singh died from the plague which swept through northern Bihar in 1908 – he had been working among the plague victims. He left behind a reputation for philanthropy which was to stand his grandson in good stead during his political career.

Digvijay's father, Shyamanand Kishore Singh, didn't take much interest in the estate, although he was a kindly landlord. Digvijay remembers his father inviting the villagers to come and sit round the fires lit in the garden of Dharhara mansion on winter mornings and evenings. By that time Mahatma Gandhi had started his movement against the landlords of Bihar, urging farmers not to accept their serfdom as their fate. According to Digvijay, the villagers used to say of his father, 'The system is bad, but he is a good man.' Digvijay remembers his father as quick to anger but also quick to repent. 'He was a highly volatile man. He would beat someone, but then he would say I have done wrong and then give him some land; so people wanted to be beaten by my father.' The violent streak led Shyamanand Kishore Singh to support the terrorists in the independence struggle, rather than Mahatma Gandhi's 'non-violence'. Nevertheless, he died a peaceful death, having lost interest in life when he lost his beloved eldest daughter three weeks after her marriage. Digvijay was then only thirteen.

Digvijay was educated at the school his grandfather founded in Dharhara and then went on to his grandfather's college in Muzaffarpur, the largest town of northern Bihar. From there he moved to Patna to study law, but he got caught up in the independence movement. Digvijay distributed leaflets and talked to small groups, working quietly and unostentatiously as he was to do throughout his political career. He could easily have sought the badge of honour of being arrested, which became almost a *sine qua non* for a political career in independent India, but that was not his style. In spite of his low profile, however, he made a deep impression on S. K. Sinha, then the leader of the Bihar Congress Party, who later launched his political career.

I gained much of my understanding of Indian politics from long evenings spent with Digvijay when he was a member of parliament living in a government house in the centre of Delhi. He was trusted by members on both sides of the house. Because of his honesty and lack of ambition, no one saw Digvijay as a potential rival. That meant he was one of the best-informed sources any journalist could have. Parliament was his life, and he brought an acute intelligence to bear on interpreting Indian politics. Policies count for little in Delhi: personalities are what matter, and so politics are a continual battle between individuals vying for the prime minister's favour or the leadership of a small opposition group. Commitment to an ideology is rare, except among the communists on the left and the Hindu BJP on the right. Digvijay was always in touch with the fluctuating fortunes of all the parties and parliamentarians, and I missed him sorely when he left. He was cheated out of the one thing he coveted – his seat in parliament – by colleagues who owed everything to him.

Digvijay left parliament in 1980. I hardly saw him after that until I made a special journey to Patna nine years later. In Bihar the sun does seem to be setting on India's Westminster-style democracy; the darkness of chaos is almost at hand. Cynicism has eaten into the administration, leaving it without the will to act. A senior official in Bihar said to me, 'This is the first place to prove the truth of Karl Marx – the government has withered away.' The police no longer attempt to hold the ring between farmers and landless labourers fighting for just the paltry minimum wage which should be theirs by right. The government blames the frequent bloody clashes between the two on Naxalites, or left-wing revolutionaries, and the police are told to crush them. The police, of course, crush the activists working for the landless labourers, not the private armies of the farmers. Industrial development is stagnant, and there are areas of the state where agricultural production is lower than it was before independence. Land reforms may have removed the zamindars or landowners, but they have not helped the landless.

Every day I was in Patna, symptoms of the wasting disease which has afflicted the administration of Bihar were reported in the press: passengers travelling in a train between Patna and the town of Gaya attacked and robbed by dacoits or bandits; four people shot in one day in different parts of Patna; the police threatening to strike; a six-month strike in one hospital still deadlocked, and medical students in another hospital boycotting classes because the government would not or could not throw out hoodlums with political connections who were occupying their hostel; irregularities in the examination for employment in the nationalized electricity board; the chief minister making yet another promise to bust the mafia which has controlled the nationalized coal mines for years.

A few months earlier, 500 people had drowned when a ferry capsized on the Ganges. The influential *Times of India*, which is no enemy of the Congress Party that was in power in Bihar as well as in Delhi, wrote, in the pseudo-biblical style it adopts when pontificating:

Once more tragedy has struck Bihar. The ample bosom of the Ganges has opened up to take hundreds of passengers travelling by a privately owned steamer to a watery grave. It is a measure of the depths of inefficiency and even inhumanity to which the State has sunk that after the overloaded steamer capsized it took a long time before even the pretence of a rescue operation was launched by the State Government and the steamer's owners . . . Not only are these antiquated craft unsafe, especially in the monsoon swollen, swift current Ganga, they are rendered more so by the overloading of passengers like cattle by lathi-wielding henchmen of the owners, substantial landlords, who in addition to controlling vast estates have diversified into other profitable ventures. Such is their stranglehold over the state . . .

India has been described as a functioning anarchy. In Patna, that anarchy comes near to chaos. It is a violent and angry city, where I am frightened by my own temper. When I arrived at Patna Junction, I was surrounded by cycle-rickshaw pullers and scooter- and taxi-drivers pushing and pulling me towards their vehicles. I forced my way into a rickshaw and shouted the name of my hotel. The rickshaw puller started to climb on to his saddle, but was pulled off by angry rivals who told me to get out. They banged their saddles, rang their bells and shouted, 'It's not his turn', 'He can't take you', 'You can't get into any rickshaw you want.' I shouted back, 'I'll go in this bloody rickshaw or no bloody rickshaw,' and sat where I was. I knew that I would regret my arrogance and rudeness, but I could not control myself. Unfortunately, all too often shouting does achieve results in India, and sure enough the other rickshawmen fell back when they realized that I was not going to budge. After a few minutes, my rickshawman judged that the storm had blown over and climbed back into the saddle.

He pedalled slowly out of the station forecourt and I found myself bumping down a narrow lane, hemmed in on both sides by tin shacks and stinking drains. We swerved to avoid a head-on collision and lurched into a pothole. The rickshaw puller stood on the pedals, and the muscles in his thin legs tightened as he strained to get out of the pothole. There was a crash and he fell forward – we had been rammed up the backside by another rickshaw. A fight ensued again but I did not take part this time. When that was over, I got down so that we could remove ourselves from the pothole. After several more narrow misses, I asked nervously whether this really was the best way to the Patliputra Hotel. The rickshaw puller looked over his shoulder and said angrily, 'This is the road I am taking you.' I didn't feel like arguing – at least we were spared the murderous motor traffic of the main road.

Later that day I went to Patna's famous museum. An enterprising farmer had stabled his cattle outside it, turning the road into a quagmire. The garden was littered with paper and plastic bags. At the door, an official told me with glee that the museum was closing, although the time was only four o'clock in the afternoon. I lost my temper and shouted inanely, 'You are typical of the lazy and dishonest officials in Bihar. What a way to welcome foreign tourists! Don't you know you have some very valuable exhibits here that people all round the world would like to see?'

The official pointed to a scruffy guard preparing his charpai for the night and said, 'Security.'

'Some security he'll provide,' I shouted back.

'What are you shouting about?' the official replied. 'It's on the board – the museum has been closed at this time for sixty years.'

I realized I was making a fool of myself. As I walked away with what little dignity I could muster, I heard the official saying to his colleagues, 'These foreigners have no right to talk to us. We are only doing our duty.'

It is a phenomenon of India that the feebler the local administration the more officious and self-righteous are its petty bureaucrats. Earlier in the day, the tourist officer in my hotel made me fill up a register giving full details of my passport, visa and registration certificate before he would give me a free map of Patna. When I suggested that this was perhaps a somewhat unnecessary formality, he replied smugly, 'We can't waste government money. That would not be right.'

Kipling described Calcutta as the 'city of dreadful night'; I can think of no better description of Patna. Calcutta has grandeur; Patna has none. That night I walked past the vast modern Hindu temple outside the station. Its garish lights symbolized the vulgar, covetous form of Hinduism which is spreading so fast among the Indian middle class. The clanging bells and the loudspeakers broadcasting what apparently passed for religious music clashed with the prayers broadcast from the mosque a few yards down the road – a cacophony which only the bigots of both faiths could rejoice in. For them it meant more hatred, more violence and more power. The shops surrounding the temple were small and mean. Most of them should not have been there at all, but the administration did not have the will to do anything about these 'illegal encroachments' as they are known in bureaucratese. New public latrines had been built into the wall which runs along the railway yards but they had no doors, so the sight of men urinating added to the squalor of central Patna. Outside my hotel, cycle-rickshawmen argued with each other as they waited for the proprietor of a small kerosene stove and a few saucepans to serve them chapattis and dal. Others were playing cards, and one young boy was asleep in a rickshaw. Further down the dimly lit street I watched a mother trying to quieten her baby and at the same time persuade three other children to get under a blanket spread on the pavement.

When faced with the poverty of India, the temptation is to despair. I have always tried to guard against that: it is futile and does not help the poor. Despair is also frightening when you love the person or the country you despair of. Nevertheless, I did despair that night. I despaired of those children, I despaired of Bihar and I despaired of India. I thought then that there did not seem to be any hope for the system, and that must mean bloodshed. But post-colonial history has shown that bloodshed is no answer to a nation's problems. The strength of India lies in the resilience of the poor. That night I, like so many outsiders, had forgotten that the pavement-dwellers of Patna do manage to make lives for themselves, they have families and friends, they have their hopes and their fears. They are to be admired, not pitied. The poor may be fatalists, but that does not mean they have despaired.

The next day the streets were even more congested than usual, and I had the greatest difficulty in getting to the small house with the cramped garden where Digvijay was living. Policemen were holding up the traffic at every crossroads to allow convoys of buses and trucks into the city centre. The buses and lorries were full of men shouting 'Long live Rajiv Gandhi!' and 'Chief minister Bhagwat Jha Azad is Bihar's leader!' Every bus and lorry had a notice pasted to its windscreen with the name of the Congressman who had collected that particular platoon to swell the army summoned to demonstrate support for the chief minister. It was only a few months earlier that Bhagwat Jha Azad had been nominated by Rajiv Gandhi to rule the turbulent state of Bihar, but he was already facing a revolt within his own party. In another part of the city a former chief minster was addressing a rally of his supporters. He threatened to form his own party if his claim to the throne was not recognized by Rajiv Gandhi. Power was all that the rallies were about: there was absolutely no concern about how that power should be exercised.

When I eventually reached the modest house where Digvijay was living with his younger son, I found him small and frail. He had never been big, but his large head and bulky body had given an impression of size. Sitting hunched up on a chair on the verandah, he seemed to have shrunk. There was no obvious trace of the cerebral stroke he had suffered while being treated for depression after the collapse of his political career, but he had lost weight, his face had sagged and two of his front teeth were missing. He looked like a myopic, toothless old bloodhound. Never a man of sartorial elegance, Digvijay was wearing a flowing dhoti and a vest partly covered by a shawl. The stick he now needed to help him walk lay against the side of his chair. Although only sixty-five, Digvijay had become an old man. He greeted me in a soft voice, saying, 'Well, at least you haven't forgotten me.'

We pottered slowly over to a corner of the cramped garden and Digvijay let himself down gingerly on to a swinging sofa. I sat in a chair opposite him. His wife came out to greet me and then retired discreetly to the house. I had never met Digvijay's wife before; his was a very orthodox marriage, and his wife played no role in his political life. In fact I had never discussed Digvijay's family with him – he had felt that family life and politics did not go together. Now he was reliant on his family and seemed to be living only for them.

'My wife is looking after me. She gets very angry because she thinks that I am not making any attempt to take care of myself. She tells me, "You might at least make sure you don't die for my sake, even if you don't care about yourself." I am very lucky with this son of mine too. He works very hard, going to his first surgery at eight o'clock in the morning. He is the best radiologist in Patna and is in great demand, but he still finds time to treat some cancer patients free. If it hadn't been for him I would have died when I had that stroke.'

I asked Digvijay whether he still took any interest in politics. He replied, 'My family want me to. They think it will take me out of myself, give me a renewed interest in life; but I am very depressed about everything. I think the whole system is collapsing. The way lawlessness is spreading, there is no hope for this system.'

'How can the system be changed?' I asked.

'Only by bloodshed. The way lawlessness is growing it is bloodshed already. Now it's not a question of violation of the law but of a breakdown of law and order. It's the collapse of a system like the end of the Mughal Empire. That was followed by the Pindaris. This violence will lead to chaos for some time, but after that I hope things will improve. In India, periods of integration are always followed by periods of disintegration and then integration takes place again. We are now seeing the end of the integration the British brought about.'

Digvijay's brother-in-law, Dr Rudrashawar Prasad Singh, was sitting with him. The young medical student on whose wedding Digvijay had spent a not-so-small fortune was now acknowledged to be one of India's leading psychiatrists. He was professor of psychiatry at Patna Medical College and had a flourishing practice. A more amusing man to sort out your problems it would be hard to find. He was small, with a rounded belly which told of the gluttony he freely confessed to. The betel-leaf he had been chewing since the early hours of the morning had blackened his teeth. He had a round moon face, with twinkling humorous eyes, and a bald pate. Doctor Sahib was getting a little bored with Digvijay's prognostications and said, 'Come on, Digvijay, Mark has come to hear about your life story. Tell him that, and don't miss out the best bits.'

'What do you mean "the best bits"?' Digvijay asked.

'Tell them about Indira and Feroze,' the doctor laughed.

Digvijay was not amused. He turned towards me and said, 'It is quite true that I was very close to Indira Gandhi and to her husband, Feroze. Indira trusted me throughout her life, and just because she's dead it's not right that I should break that trust and tell tales about her. I can tell you they were not pulling on well. You know that – everyone knows that. In fact they were almost separated, except for social occasions. One problem was that Feroze drank a lot. I once went with him to a doctor to discuss his heart complaint. The doctor said, "Please don't drink whisky." But Feroze wanted to die. He felt frustrated; he felt that he couldn't do what he wanted to do in politics because he was Nehru's son-in-law. That was why he continued to drink, and that was why he died.'

Doctor Sahib roared with laughter and said, 'That's not the half of it. Come on, Digvijay – tell him about the time when Feroze and Indira were locked into your bedroom. You remember, when you hid them there for twenty-eight hours, so that they could sort out their differences. You arranged for food to be brought in to them.'

Digvijay frowned, but said nothing.

'Well it's true, isn't it?' Doctor Sahib insisted.

Digvijay replied, 'Look here. I have already told you I don't think it's right to tell tales about your friends, especially when they share their confidences with you.'

Doctor Sahib gave up, and I took over the conversation.

'Well, let's go back to the beginning, Digvijay. How did you get into big-time politics, mixing with the Nehrus and all that?'

'It was really S. K. Sinha, the chief minister of Bihar – the man who came to that last big wedding in my family mansion. I had several links with him. He knew my family well and the work they had done. He also knew the role I had played in the independence movement. Then again, he was a member of the same caste as I was – although caste was not as rampant in politics then as it is nowadays.'

'You were both bhumihars?'

'Yes. It's a strange caste – I suppose you could say we are half Brahmins.'

'What do you mean by that?'

'We were Brahmins until the Buddhist period, and then we converted to that religion. In the fourth and fifth centuries, Buddhists started converting back to Hinduism. The Brahmins said that we could return to the fold but we couldn't be priests and take money for conducting religious ceremonies, and so we became the only Brahmins who tilled the soil. In Bihar we became landlords.'

Taking part in the independence movement and making valuable contacts with leading Congressmen gave Digvijay a taste for politics. After independence, he gave up all thoughts of becoming a lawyer and threw himself into political work. Those were days of hope when it did seem that a new India would be built – an India which was economically as well as politically independent; a socialist India in which giant strides would be taken towards the eradication of poverty. Digvijay thought that, as a young man, it would be appropriate to start his career as a member of the Bihar state assembly, but the chief minister advised him to go for parliament straight away. The chief minister arranged for him to stand from Sitamarhi near the Nepal border in 1952 – the first election since the constitution of independent India had been drawn up. Digvijay won handsomely.

The chief minister had judged correctly: Digvijay soon established himself in the highest political circles in Delhi. Within three years he managed to get on to a much sought-after parliamentary delegation to the Soviet Union. He told me how this had been achieved. 'I had to go and see Nehru himself, to get his approval. He made a spluttering noise, which was a good sign – if Nehru got annoyed with you then you knew that you had probably succeeded. I found Nehru very approachable. When I went to him about my work, I found I got about 70 per cent of it done.'

'What work?'

'The work – the things that I wanted to be done for my constituency.'

Nehru selected Digvijay to go on two more political delegations. He was clearly an up-and-coming parliamentarian. Doctor Sahib said that when news of these delegations and of Digvijay's friendship with Indira and Feroze reached the family, they thought that he was really going places.

'We were very proud of him: we thought that he would certainly become a junior minister in his first parliament. But even in those days Digvijay didn't seem to be like ordinary politicians. He didn't seem to want to make anything out of his opportunities. He was always a king-maker and never a king.'

'Could you have become a minister?' I asked Digvijay.

'Being a minister never attracted me. I am a carefree man, and I never wanted to bow and scrape to anyone, which you have to do if you are going to get a berth as a minister. It was being a member of parliament which attracted me.'

Our conversation was interrupted by another relative who had heard that Digvijay was telling his life story and had come to contribute his bit to it. He was Braja Prasad Singh, an uncle of Digvijay, who had spent eleven years in jail during the independence movement and had gone on to a long career in parliament, mostly in the upper house. He was at least ten years older than Digvijay, but much more sprightly and cheerful.

I asked Digvijay's uncle, 'Don't you think that he wasted his talents and his opportunities? Surely he could have done much more.'

'You know, I never interfered with Digvijay's politics and he never interfered with mine, but I don't think you are necessarily right. It all depends on a man's temperament. He pursued the right career. He did what suited him. Backbenchers also serve who only stand and wait.' Braja Prasad Singh laughed and went on, 'Digvijay was a good, quiet organizer and an excellent lobbyist. Lobbying behind the scenes is something very great. You see, people trusted him.'

People trusted him. That was the hallmark of Digvijay's political career, but in the end he was to be let down by those he had trusted.

Digvijay didn't allow his friendship with Indira Gandhi to influence his political judgement: he became a firm ally of Morarji Desai, the stern, unbending moralist from Mahatma Gandhi's home state of Gujarat and the one man whom both Nehru and Indira did not want to succeed to the premiership. Digvijay was not very clear about his reasons for supporting Morarji.

'I am not sure why I became a Morarji man. He did impress me. Perhaps it was because of his bluntness; perhaps it was because I too am a blunt man. Then Morarji was a very good administrator, and I personally felt we needed someone who could administer. When he came to the centre from politics in the states, I got to know him and he became very friendly with me.'

'You may be blunt, Digvijay, but you are not stern and Morarji certainly is.'

'Of course he is stern. He used to tell me that he had not slept with his wife or any woman since he was very young. He never eats cooked food, and he's deeply religious. He's totally opposed to drinking. He is a follower of Mahatma Gandhi in a far more real sense than anyone else nowadays.'

'Come on, Digvijay,' I laughed. 'You certainly drink – we have often drunk together. I have never thought of you as religious either.'

'I remember once Morarji said to me, "Digvijay, I hear you drink." Of course I couldn't tell him a lie, so I replied, "Yes I drink." Morarji simply said, "It would be better if you give it up." I never heard from him on that subject again. He drinks his own urine and says that it's good for him. Perhaps he's right.'

Doctor Sahib laughed. 'I don't know that there are any medical grounds for that statement, Digvijay, but the old boy is over ninety and still going strong. I don't think that people like us who drink a different golden fluid are going to live to that age.'

'What about religion?' I asked.

'Well, of course I don't spend hours praying or meditating like Morarji. Every morning after washing I say Mahatma Gandhi's prayer: "O God, O Christ, O Muhammad, if I have committed any sin, forgive me. If you can't forgive me, punish me in any way you like."'

'I don't know what you did, Digvijay,' laughed Doctor Sahib, 'but God certainly seems to be punishing you.'

When Nehru died, in 1964, Morarji threw his hat in the ring and Digvijay lobbied hard on his behalf, but the diminutive Lal Bahadur Shastri won. He died less than two years later in Tashkent, where he had just signed the controversial treaty which formally ended the second war between India and Pakistan. This time Morarji's enemies backed Indira Gandhi, just to keep him out, but Digvijay refused to take advantage of his friendship with the new prime minister and stood by his leader. In 1969, Indira Gandhi, feeling herself stifled by the old guard who still dominated the Congress Party organization, took one of the great gambles of her political career: she caused a split in the parliamentary party. It was a close-run race, but Indira was the winner. I asked Digvijay, 'Did you tell Indira that you were not going to vote for her at that crucial stage in her political career?'

'Yes, of course I did, ' he replied. 'She didn't say anything. She never used to talk. Nehru and Morarji used to talk. But, you know, even then she didn't turn against me. In the general election after the split I was one of the few Morarji men to win. One reason, perhaps, was that Indira never campaigned against me. I was told that some people had suggested that a stronger candidate should be put up against me, to teach me a lesson, but Indira refused.'

'How near did you come to defeat that time?'

'Oh, it was a very close fought thing. I won by only 7,000 votes, mostly the votes of my own caste. I remember my son at the counting station saying that he was going home because he did not want to be there when my defeat was announced. I told him, "I am going to win. It doesn't look good if you go now. Stay with me and wait."'

'It doesn't look good' is a phrase which recurs often in Digvijay's conversation. Throughout his political career he was always concerned about appearances: he felt that right should be seen to be done. Right to him meant honesty and loyalty. He stood for a Victorian concept of loyalty which is not practical in politics anywhere today.

The only time that he was totally opposed to Indira Gandhi was during the state of emergency she declared in 1975. That came about because a judge had found her guilty of electoral corruption. The law demanded that she resign but she went to the Supreme Court, which allowed her to stay in office while the appeal was heard. Sanjay Gandhi, her younger son, urged the prime minister not to take any risks. He collected a group of his mother's senior advisers who helped him to persuade her to declare a state of emergency. This she did on 26 June 1975. Ignoring the constitutional niceties, she arrested the leaders of the opposition – including Morarji Desai – in the early hours of the morning, before she got the approval of her cabinet for the emergency. But then the Constitution was to be torn into shreds during the emergency, so perhaps it mattered little that the process started prematurely. The press was censored; fundamental rights, including habeas corpus, which obliged the state to bring anyone arrested before a court, were curtailed; and the prime minister was elevated to a position where she was virtually above the law. The little problem of the corruption charge was dealt with by the simple expedient of amending the law so that election disputes involving the prime minister could not be taken to court.

Indira Gandhi justified the emergency by claiming that there had been a 'plot' against the state. It is true that her infringement of the electoral law had been little more than a technicality, and that in the months before the court verdict the opposition had taken to the streets – first in Gujarat, Morarji's state, and then in Bihar. Nevertheless, no substantial evidence was produced to justify the claim made in an official document that there was a 'grand design' to overthrow the government.

This certainly 'did not look good' to Digvijay. However, remembering his role in the independence movement, he decided against going for the limelight and forcing Indira Gandhi to arrest him too. He was taken into custody once for demonstrating in Patna, but that was a very mild affair: he was held for only two weeks and he was allowed to go to Doctor Sahib's house for a bath every morning. For most of the nineteen months the emergency was strictly enforced, he worked quietly but effectively at breaking the stranglehold of the censors. By paying bribes to a junior official in the Ministry of Information, he managed to get hold of much of the news which was being censored. In that way he did better than the president of India – a Muslim who did not know of brutal slum clearances in a Muslim quarter of Delhi just two miles from his palace until he was told of them by a member of his own family. The slum clearances and an attempt to deal with India's chronic population problem by compulsory sterilization provided plenty of copy for Digvijay. (Both those programmes were spearheaded by Sanjay Gandhi.)

Digvijay distributed his news to foreign correspondents and to some Indian journalists. I asked him what was the purpose of that when both foreign and Indian correspondents were being censored. He replied, 'The Indians were at least able to feed it into the rumour mill, which did enormous damage to the government, and the foreign correspondents told me that they got some of it out to the world. That worried Indira Gandhi a lot. She was always very conscious of her international standing.'

'Was that the only way you distributed the news?' I asked.

'No. I used to travel a lot too, you know. I would deceive the police by buying a first-class railway ticket at the parliament booking-office to one place and then going by second-class to another. I wasn't used to second-class and I didn't find it very comfortable, but there you are. As the train pulled out of stations, I used to scatter leaflets carrying the news. Actually I don't think I needed all that subterfuge.'

'Why?'

'Well, after the emergency was over I was shown a file on which Indira Gandhi had noted that I was not to be arrested without her written approval. You see, she still had a soft spot for me. In fact, after the emergency she herself said to me, "I know that you know a lot of things about me personally, but you never printed them." '

In January 1977, nineteen months after the declaration of the state of emergency, Indira Gandhi surprised her countrymen and the many international pundits who had pronounced Indian democracy dead by announcing that there would be a general election. Censorship was relaxed, and most of the opposition leaders – including Morarji Desai – were released. Digvijay's hour of triumph had come, but he had also started on the road which would lead to his final defeat. The town of Muzaffarpur in northern Bihar was to be the scene of that defeat; so we decided to postpone discussion of that until we had gone there.

The next day, Digvijay's family came on to the verandah to see him off. His wife said to me, 'I am very sorry that my eldest son and his wife are not living in the house at Muzaffarpur at present. He will not be able to look after you properly.' She never referred to Digvijay by name, or as her husband.

A grey-haired servant who was deaf and dumb packed Digvijay's baggage in the boot of the car. Digvijay's wife had found the servant living on the streets many years ago and had taken him in. He was now fiercely loyal to her. Digvijay's baggage consisted of an old-fashioned bedding roll and a battered black suitcase. He explained, 'I always take that suitcase wherever I go, because it travelled with me throughout the emergency. Those were the best days of my life.'

Digvijay's cousin Mahesh Prasad Sahi was to travel with us – Digvijay still retained enough of his feudal instincts to dislike travelling without at least one sidekick.

As we drove down the narrow alley which led from the house to the main road, Digvijay said, 'My wife was very attentive to you. I don't know how she sat and talked to you – she would normally say, "ooh, angraiz [foreigners]!" and go and hide herself.'

I laughed and said, 'Perhaps she does not have the same respect for you now that you are no longer a neta [leader].'

Digvijay smiled.

We crossed the bridge over the Ganges which had replaced the ferries. The river was still swollen because of the good monsoon. We then bypassed the town of Hajipur on the opposite bank to Patna and drove into banana country. Groves of banana plantains with their light-green fronds and red spiky flowers lined the road on both sides. There were also tall tari palms. We were too late to see the toddy tappers shinning up the palms' thin trunks to collect the earthenware pots suspended from their flowers. Juice drips from the flowers into the pots and ferments to make toddy, the poor man's tipple.

The banana groves thinned out and we came to open country and rice fields. The harvest had started. Men and women squatting on their haunches were cutting the yellow rice with sickles. Others were laying the rice out to dry. In some fields the rice had already dried and was being rolled into unwieldy bundles and carried away on the heads of labourers. Women and children were scouring those fields for straw and grain which had fallen from the bundles – to them, every grain counted. I contrasted this traditional harvest with the combine harvesters I had seen recently in Punjab.

A local cattle fair was in progress in one of the small towns we drove through. The thin and unproductive cows were tethered in groups under trees. Again Punjab, with its sleek and healthy cattle improved by Jersey and Friesian strains, came to mind.

Mahesh kept me amused by telling me stories about Bihar politics and Digvijay's campaigning. He said that Digvijay had been very obstinate. 'We always had a lot of trouble with him because he would only do what he wanted to do – he wouldn't listen to us. I personally think he only won because of his own reputation for honesty and because of the standing of his family. No one else could win campaigning like he did. For instance, we could never get him to address meetings like other candidates do.'

'I personally feel', remarked Digvijay, 'that big meetings are not as useful as getting people together and discussing things with them.'

'Did you always talk to the village headman, the sarpanch?' I asked.

'No. I know that most people believe that if you get the sarpanch on your side you get the whole village to vote for you. I disagree. Just talking to the sarpanch doesn't look good: the people think that you are trying to bribe their leader. There are some good sarpanches, but others are rascals. If you talk to the people themselves, they say, "He has taken the trouble to talk to us. He is a good man." That pays off, and is the right way to go about canvassing.'

Mahesh and Digvijay, who were squashed into the front seat alongside the driver, started an urgent conversation which I could not hear above the roaring and rattling of the car. Digvijay then turned to me and asked, 'Would you like to have a cup of tea?' We were only about an hour out of Patna, but I knew this meant there was some reason for us to stop and so I agreed.

When we pulled up in the next village, the reason became clear. A young man who had been waiting by his motor cycle came up to the car, opened the front door and touched the feet of Digvijay and Mahesh. He was a cousin of Mahesh and had obviously been sent to meet us. Mahesh went off to get the tea, and Digvijay called after him, 'Bring me a packet of cigarettes.' Mahesh turned, frowned and wiggled his finger at Digvijay, who was not allowed to smoke because his doctors had warned it would kill him. Mahesh returned with the tea but no cigarettes. Digvijay pouted like a spoilt child, and so Mahesh relented and went off to buy a packet of Wills. After that, discipline collapsed and Digvijay puffed away happily until we got back to Patna.

By a not-so-strange coincidence, Mahesh's village happened to be just a few miles off the main road, and of course I agreed that we should go there. The village turned out to be a model of rural development, proving that even in Bihar such things are possible. The roads were tarmacked and well maintained. There was a school, a bank and a public telephone which worked. Even the Harijans had concrete houses and electricity.

Mahesh's family home had been built 100 years ago. It was a large house with a well-maintained lawn in front of it – a rare sight in an Indian village. The lawn was surrounded by roses and mogra bushes, a form of jasmine, with sweet-smelling white flowers. Fifty members of the family lived in that house. The men sat on the lawn and talked to us while the women watched a test match on colour television.

The head of the family – or at least its effective leader – was a middle-aged man, Yugal Kishore Sahi, who was a local politician. He was largely responsible for the progress that had been made in the village but was as bitter as Digvijay about the general state of affairs in Bihar. When I told him that I was writing a story about Digvijay, he said, 'You don't get men like him any more. It's goonda raj [hooligan rule] now in Bihar. Do you know that there are criminal charges against thirty-three members of the Bihar assembly? The criminals helped the politicians to get elected then they saw that the politicians couldn't do without them, so the politicians were taken over by the criminals. Democracy has become a farce, and politics a business. You need to spend at least five to ten lakhs to become a member of the state assembly, and so you invest that money and expect to get a return on it. Recently they had the municipal elections in Hajipur. Each person paid a lakh [100,000 rupees] to get elected, although the councillors have no power.'

'So what's the point of being elected?' I asked.

'It's just to say, "I have arrived. I am a big man."'

I then asked what was the secret of the success of his village.

'It's really due to L. P. Shahi, who was born here and who is now a minister in the central government. I actually got him the ticket first, and he has helped us. You have to have the support of a prominent politician, otherwise the officials do nothing – they can delay a scheme for ever.'

L. P. Shahi was the man who many years ago had served spinach to the less distinguished guests at the wedding in Digvijay's family mansion. He was also the man who eventually took away Digvijay's seat in parliament.

As we left the village, I noticed that the villagers were building a new temple for the monkey-god Hanuman. He is one of the most popular gods now, because he is believed to be particularly effective at answering prayers. I supposed the villagers were honouring him because he had answered so many of theirs.

Nearer to Muzaffarpur we passed fields of tobacco. Muzaffarpur is famous for its zarda or chewing-tobacco. Vines of pan leaf, India's other favourite chew, sprawled over bamboo frames. Men standing up to their waists in water were fishing in ponds. We crossed over a canal which was dry. Mahesh said, 'They make a canal but there's no water. They will only open the gates when the floods come.' Then we drove under the national highway which bypassed Muzaffarpur, into the town itself. Digvijay's family house stood behind a ten-foot-high wall. Small shops abutted the wall. One boasted of being a medical hall, but was in fact a cramped chemist's shop. Next to it was an equally cramped surgery. The doctor advertised injections for tetanus, polio and diphtheria – all of which should have been available free from the government if the public-service advertisements on the television were anything to go by. Motor cars and two-wheelers in need of care were also provided for, by a battery shop, a spare-parts dealer and a small workshop.

As we entered Digvijay's compound, a man and a boy asleep on the verandah sprung to life. The man was Mohan, another faithful follower of Digvijay, who lived in this house and looked after it when Digvijay's elder son was away. He had a job in a minor irrigation department of the government of Bihar. The department was so minor that the government had forgotten to pay its staff for six months. That, Mohan said, was nothing unusual for Bihar. He was retaliating by not going to work.

It was to this house that Digvijay returned after the end of the state of emergency to fight his own election and the election of one of the heroes thrown up by it, George Fernandes. George was a charismatic trade-union leader – brash, self-confident and an excellent orator – the very opposite of Digvijay. He was one of the few opposition politicians Indira Gandhi did not release when she announced the election – he had been accused of attempting to blow up railway lines, and so was being held on criminal, not political, charges.

Shortly after the release of the political prisoners, the main opposition parties except for the communists merged. The new Janata Party which they formed was a hotchpotch of former Congressmen like Digvijay and Morarji Desai, members of the right-wing Hindu Jan Sangh, politicians whose politics were based on caste interests, and socialists like George. The socialists were very anxious to get George elected, because they were a small party and had few well-known leaders. Digvijay agreed to stand down from Muzaffarpur and to organize George's campaign from there. He himself moved to another constituency in northern

Bihar. In Muzaffarpur, Digvijay's supporters – including his son – took a cart with a life-size model of George, handcuffed and in jail, from village to village. The campaign was an outstanding success. In March 1977, George *in absentia* won one of the largest majorities in the Janata Party's sweeping victory.

After much unseemly wrangling, Morarji was chosen to head India's first non-Congress government. He wanted his old friend Digvijay to be his senior parliamentary secretary – a position of enormous influence, because all the files would have gone through him. Most Indian politicians would have been overjoyed; Digvijay was dismayed.

'I heard about this on the evening before Morarji was going to announce the appointment. By that time I had already had three or four whiskies. I washed my mouth, smoked a cigarette, took a pan [betel-leaf] and then went to Morarji and told him not to make me a minister. I managed to persuade him by telling him that it would not look good if too many members of what had been his party got plum jobs.'

Digvijay was elected Secretary of the Janata parliamentary party, which gave considerable scope to his talent for lobbying. He used to see Morarji most evenings for ten minutes or so and report on the latest plots against him – the two rival claimants to the premiership started plotting against Morarji from the moment he got the job. In fact Digvijay had more access to the prime minister than his cabinet colleagues, and he was regarded by most members of the Janata Party as the one man who could influence the inflexible Morarji. But no one ever accused Digvijay of using his influence to advance his own cause.

One of Morarji's weaknesses was his son, Kanti. The prime minister prided himself on his honesty, but he knew that Kanti was making money by interfering in decisions on industrial licensing and government contracts. This gave Morarji's opponents a stick to beat him with, but, when Digvijay suggested that Kanti should be restrained, Morarji just said, 'You tell him.' Digvijay explained to me, 'You see, there had been a history of suicide in Morarji's family. His own daughter killed herself, and I believe that Kanti was blackmailing his father by threatening that he would commit suicide too.'

Morarji's government lasted only about two years. He was pulled down by one of his two rivals in the Janata Party. George Fernandes defended Morarji's government vigorously in the debate on the crucial vote of confidence in Parliament, but the next day he voted against the government. Digvijay had rung him at midnight and George had given an assurance that he was still on Morarji's side. Digvijay never forgave George and vowed to fight him wherever he stood from in the next election. That election followed very soon, because the plotters who overthrew Morarji failed miserably. Their government fell after six months, paving the way for the return of their arch-enemy Indira Gandhi in January 1980.

During my stay in Muzaffarpur, I met many of those involved in the battle between Digvijay and George which followed the brief, inglorious rule of Morarji's successor. Many of Digvijay's friends tried to persuade him not to fight George directly but to continue to contest from the constituency that Digvijay was then representing. That constituency was very anxious to have him as a candidate again, but Digvijay had pledged his word and he refused to go back on it. A battle royal ensued.

Digvijay's supporters allege that George spent money like water to bribe the local leaders. I put that allegation to George's agent in that campaign, Vinay Bushan – a lean and intense man with a long face, large spectacles and a grey beard. He was one of the old school of Indian socialists, utterly dedicated to his cause and prepared to suffer for it. He introduced himself to me as a 'jailbird', saying, 'Don't ask how many times I have been to jail because of my politics. Whenever I am locked up, I tell the jail supervisor, "I am senior in service to you. I know more about the jail manual than you do."'

I asked, 'How much money did George spend in that election?'

'George didn't open his purse in front of me, so what can I say about what I don't know? George was never short of money, but all those stories about him bribing people with scooters and bicycles are rubbish.'

Mohan strongly disagreed: 'I don't know how you can say that. You could see with your own eyes that all George's workers were riding scooters. Where did they come from? Not from the workers' pockets.'

'Well, I don't know about that,' Vinay Bushan said. 'As I have told you, George never opened his purse in front of me.'

'He wouldn't have dared to, because you would have walked out on him.'

'I dare say so.'

The other allegation made by Digvijay's camp is that George's men captured a large number of polling-booths and stamped the ballot papers with his symbol. His agent admitted that reluctantly.

'You know that this booth-capturing has become a feature of Bihar elections. Both sides captured booths in that election.'

'What exactly do you mean by "booth-capturing"?'

'Well, musclemen of one of the candidates occupy a booth before the polling-day. Then they will explode bombs and maybe fire guns to let everyone know that they are in charge of the booth and to frighten them away. On polling-day itself there will be more explosions, just to make sure no one comes to vote and to frighten the polling-officers. Then they threaten or bribe the officials to allow them to stamp the ballot-papers with their candidate's name.'

'We could have used bombs too,' said Mohan. 'Four hundred or so people came to us and said, "We have bombs. Wherever you are weak we will put the situation right. We don't want money, just some food, somewhere to sleep and transport." They actually brought the bombs and put them in my room, but Digvijay would not let them out of there.'

'But how many booths did you capture?' I asked George's agent.

'I didn't capture any.'

'No, I know – but you know what I mean. How many did George's men capture?'

'How can I tell you that? It was a long time ago. I can tell you that Digvijay was not defeated by money or muscle-power but because the whole election in Bihar was turned into a forward–backward battle.'

That piece of back-to-front political jargon meant that the election had been turned into a fight between the newly prosperous farming castes, the backwards, and the landowning castes who had dominated Bihar before independence, like the bhumihars.

Vinay Bhushan explained, 'George was not very popular. He had not established any connection with the area. Digvijay was very big. But then people thought that Digvijay was bhumihar and that George was a member of a backward caste.'

Whether through forward–backward, bombs or money, George did narrowly defeat Digvijay, who went into the wilderness. Morarji was out of politics and the Janata Party was riven by internecine warfare. The party had done so badly in the general election that there didn't seem to be much to fight over; nevertheless, the leaders fought. Digvijay kept right out of it. This was the first time for twenty-eight years that he was not an MP. The lobbying, the gossip, the friendships of parliament had been his life. Now, because he had to surrender his MP's house, he didn't even have anywhere to stay in Delhi.

Digvijay spent nearly five years in limbo. By the time that preparations for the 1984 general election started, he was thoroughly disillusioned with the Janata Party. Where else could he go? None of the other opposition parties would suit his politics. He could return to Mrs Gandhi. Several of his former Janata colleagues who did not have his old friendship with the prime minister had already done so, but then he had never practised what he called 'opportunistic politics' before. An approach to Indira Gandhi just before she started selecting candidates for the general election would be blatantly opportunist. Many Indian politicians would not have worried about that, but Digvijay did. His family saw it differently: they saw the head of the family declining because he had no other interest in life than politics. So the family put pressure on Digvijay to overcome his scruples and approach the prime minister. Eventually he gave in and wrote her a letter.

It was a long letter in which he said he had been doing 'some detached thinking on the political situation that obtains or is likely to face the country after the next general election if certain issues are not kept in perspective'. After writing off the opposition as at best being able to provide only 'a government of heterogeneous forces based more on personal ambitions and predilections than on principles and programme', Digvijay went on to say, 'I am quite clear in my mind that our polity cannot bear any more the strains of such political experiments' – a reference to the disaster which had befallen the Janata government. He then expressed concern about the nation: 'The dangerous situation that has developed in the country is enough to make us all lose a bit of our sleep. Nothing less than the unity and integrity of the country is at stake.' That was the cry that Indira Gandhi used to rally the nation behind her, although she was most displeased when any foreign journal or broadcasting organization suggested that India's unity was fragile. Digvijay then told the prime minister, 'The only way to run democracy in this vast country is to revive and strengthen the Congress culture which Gandhi nurtured and which you are striving to preserve against heavy odds.' He forgot the years he had spent opposing Indira because he believed that the true custodian of the Congress culture was Morarji Desai and that Indira Gandhi was promoting a personality cult, not Congress culture. After that lengthy justification, Digvijay eventually got round to writing, 'I am therefore convinced that if I want to serve the paramount national interest the only organization that I can look to or give my loyalty to is the Congress (I) under your leadership.' The '(I)' stood for 'Indira', to distinguish that Congress from the other factions which had broken away or been thrown out; but of course many saw it as signifying, 'I, Indira, am the Congress.' Then came the last and hardest paragraph of all for Digvijay. 'I knew it would be difficult to disabuse many minds of the suspicion about my electoral interest due to the proximity of the general elections. But I can assure you . . . that it is part of my groping towards something higher than the promotion of my personal self.' In his heart of hearts, Digvijay was not really convinced of this.

After writing that letter, Digvijay made an appointment to see the prime minister. According to Digvijay, she just said, 'It will be all right so long as I am alive. If I die, I can't guarantee what will happen.' That was on 12 October 1984. On 31 October 1984 Indira Gandhi was shot dead by two Sikh members of her bodyguard. Her comment to Digvijay was not the only premonition of death: in her last public speech she said, 'I do not worry whether I live or not. As long as there is any breath in me, I will go on serving you. When I die, every single drop of my blood will give strength to India and sustain united India.'

Digvijay applied for the Congress Party ticket in the election which followed Indira Gandhi's death and went to Delhi to press his cause. He appeared to have been successful when a leading member of the Bihar Congress rang him and said that he should leave by the next day's flight to file his nomination for Muzaffarpur. That night the Congress Party published his name as its candidate, but the next morning, just as he was packing, he received another call to say there had been a last-minute change. The party had decided that L. P. Shahi – the man who had served spinach at the wedding and who had been dependent on Digvijay for money in the early days of his political career – had been selected for Muzaffarpur. The residents of that town say that Shahi arranged for hundreds of telephone calls and cables to be sent to the Congress Party headquarters saying that Digvijay had suffered a heart attack and was not fit enough to be the candidate. Digvijay believes that Shahi 'managed it' by lobbying the prime minister's influential cousin, Arun Nehru. He said, 'Shahi told Arun Nehru that I thought I was too senior to do sifarish to [ask for favours from] a comparative newcomer to politics like him.'

Digvijay's family and supporters were enraged. When he returned to Muzaffarpur, hundreds of people gathered outside his house shouting '*L. P. Shahi murdabad!*' – 'Death to L. P. Shahi!' – 'Congress are cheats!' and '*Digvijay Babu zindabad!*' – 'Long live Digvijay Babu!' They tried to lift up his chair and carry him to the returning officer so that he could file his nomination as an independent, but Digvijay refused to cooperate. He realized that it would not look good, and he was not going to lose another battle with his conscience – rather the reverse. He felt that, having committed himself to the Congress, he must now campaign for L. P. Shahi, which he did. Shahi won and, what is more, became a minister in Rajiv Gandhi's government.

During the afternoon I was given assessments of Digvijay by many people who came to call on him after the news got out that he was making one of his now rare visits to Muzaffarpur. There was the man who had been elected to represent Muzaffarpur during the Janata government, and there was the sitting member, a Congressman. There were academics, there were businessmen, and of course there were political workers. All – even the Congress member of the state assembly – agreed that Digvijay had been cheated out of the seat. All also agreed that Digvijay was a 'good man' who had given away a fortune. The former member of the assembly waxed lyrical about him. 'Because of his personal honesty and his helping attitude he has himself become needy, but the people still pine for him to be in parliament. The perfume of his popularity is still being carried by the wind to every house in north Bihar.'

When they had gone, we moved inside – Digvijay, myself, his two faithful followers Mahesh Prasad Sahi and Mohan, and a young bhumihar man who had set himself up in the sweet-making business. Digvijay sat with his feet up on his chair, entirely enveloped in a shawl to keep out the cold and the mosquitoes – Muzaffarpur is known as 'Machcharpur' or 'Mosquitopur'. I too was given a chair. The others sat at Digvijay's feet. A bottle of Indian whisky appeared. There was an electricity cut, but by the light of the candles I could see that the whisky was a brand I had never come across, called Dynasty. Mohan unscrewed the top.

'It's a good brand,' Digvijay said – 'you won't be harmed by it. In Bihar they have to keep on bringing out new brands because the bootleggers buy up the bottles and fill them with spurious whisky.'

This was the time to get Digvijay to talk about his last battle. First I asked Mohan what he had thought about Digvijay's refusal to pick up the gauntlet.

'We all wanted Digvijay to fight against Shahi. He had been cheated. All the other parties opposed to the Congress said they would withdraw if Digvijay stood, but he's an obstinate man. Once he makes up his mind, you can't change it. In the election against George, he wouldn't allow us to use those bombs although

George was capturing booths like anything. Officials offered to help us if we would give them a list of the booths we thought George would capture, but he would not cooperate.'

'I do not think I am as honest as people think I am,' Digvijay said grumpily. 'I also crossed the legal limit for expenditure in that election. That was why I could not file an election petition against George's excess expenditure. My people also captured booths. I reckon that my caste men captured sixty or seventy, while George's captured 104.'

'But you refused to use the bombs,' Mohan said.

'Am I a democrat because of that?' Digvijay asked. 'I didn't use bombs possibly because of timidity or because of my family background. It would not have looked nice. I live here, but George was an outsider. I personally feel that it's not right to blame George. He wanted to win, so did I. He used a technique to win.'

'Do you sometimes regret that you didn't fight as an independent after Shahi took your seat away?' I asked.

'No, that would have been wrong. I had made that one great mistake of rejoining the Congress Party. Let's be honest: whatever I wrote in that letter to Indira Gandhi, the truth of the matter is that I rejoined the Congress because I wanted to get back into parliament and that was the easiest way. There comes a time when your metal is tested, and if you are not of good metal you melt. I melted.'

The next morning Mohan took me to the bazaar which was part of the property that Digvijay had sold to pay for his politics. It was prime property in Suraiyya Ganj, the commercial centre of Muzaffarpur. Wholesale cloth merchants sat cross-legged on white sheets covering the floors. Bolts of their brightly coloured merchandise surrounded them as they pored over handwritten ledgers bound in red cloth. Their assistants unrolled the cloth for the customers. The shops were old-fashioned, a foot or two above the level of the street. The whole of the front was open – there were no plate-glass windows or any other form of security except the metal shutters which clattered down only when the merchant was sure there would be no more business that day. Mohan told me that Digvijay had not invested one paisa of the proceeds from the sale of those shops: they had all been spent on politics and on helping his constituents. We saw the college Digvijay's grandfather had founded, and a school too. They were now run by the government, but the original benefactor was remembered by a bust in front of the college. There would be no such memorial to Digvijay's charity.

Digvijay had reluctantly agreed to visit the family mansion at Dharhara on the way back to Patna. 'I hate going there,' he said. 'It makes me so depressed.' About an hour out of Muzaffarpur we turned off the main highway and took the narrow road to Dharhara. As we bounced in and out of potholes, Digvijay said, 'I never believed in using my influence to have the road to my own village done up. It would not look good.' Mahesh muttered sarcastically, 'It might have been better for you if you had.'

Young boys riding on the back of sleek, black buffaloes were bringing the herds home for the night. The cows wore blankets made from sacking, to keep out the winter cold. We passed a derelict building which Digvijay said had been a hospital donated by his father, and the school where Digvijay had studied. In the dusk, that looked derelict too. Then we drove through the high ceremonial arch built for Doctor Sahib's wedding. It had a sloping Palladian roof supported by the small arches under which Ustad Bismillah Khan, the celebrated shehnai player, had sat. The gardens were unkempt. There was a tall, unpruned ashoka tree in front of the house, and in one corner a sad 1949 Packard Skipper which would never move again.

The main house was a two-storeyed building with a balustrade around the flat roof. There was a verandah at the front. Across a lawn was another building where the women of the family had lived. In one courtyard there was a dead tulsi bush. Every orthodox Hindu house has its tulsi plant: it is considered sacred, and it is the duty of the women of the house to water and care for it. There were no women left at Dharhara mansion to perform that sacred duty. The stone platform on which the wedding ceremony had been performed was in another courtyard. Bushes were growing out of its walls. Dharhara House had 100 rooms, and 300 people used to live there. Now there were only a few former servants. One room was maintained for Digvijay's doctor son, who still spent some time amid the ruins of his family's fortune.

Digvijay sat on a verandah, smoking and staring out into the night. It was a new moon but there were no clouds, so the stars cast their light on the unkempt lawn. The servants showed me round the mansion, their hurricane-lamps flickering over broken furniture and dusty floors. A large, bare wooden bedstead stood in one corner of the room which had belonged to Digvijay's father. The temple in which he had worshipped was still alive, however. It was a small room in one corner of the main building. Outside, a candle flickered; inside, an elderly Brahmin was tending the family deities. He still came twice every day to offer them worship and food.

When we returned to the verandah, rickety chairs and hot sweet tea were produced. I said to Digvijay, 'I can understand how sad you must feel.'

'When I go to bed at night, I get disturbed and think what I did for petty gains – for a ribbon to tie on my breast. I have wasted my fortune and put travails on my sons, and my political achievements are nothing.'

'But the people are very fond of you. They think that you are a truly great man.'

'Public memory', said Digvijay, 'is very short.'

Epilogue: 21 May 1991

Early in the morning of 20 May 1991, I was standing outside an ugly modern government office block in Delhi, waiting for Rajiv Gandhi to cast his vote in the general election which he hoped would bring him back to power. I thought back over the previous eighteen months, which had seen Rajiv Gandhi's first term in office ending in defeat by what can only be described as a motley crew – so motley that within eleven months the government it had cobbled together had collapsed. That collapse had led to this general election. Rajiv Gandhi himself had told me that his biggest mistake had been his failure to communicate with the people. Seeing a prominent member of the coterie which still surrounded Rajiv Gandhi also waiting for him to vote, I was reminded that his isolation had if anything increased after his defeat. But during this election campaign there had been a major change. He had left his coterie at home, had abandoned the strict security which had separated him from the public and had gone out to meet the public personally. The people of India had responded enthusiastically, mobbing him wherever he went. He had been pushed and pinched so much that his body was black and blue with bruises. His fingers were so swollen by the hands he had shaken that he had been forced to take off his wedding ring. He had at last felt the exhilaration of the love and affection of the people of India, and he was a happy man.

When Rajiv arrived to cast his vote, he leapt out of his car and walked straight up to the press, grinning from ear to ear. He greeted many of us by name, and said to me, 'I hear the BBC thinks we are winning this time, Mark.'

I replied, 'I'm not quite sure we've stuck our neck out that far.'

He laughed, 'Well, you think it's better than last time.'

'Oh yes,' I said.

Afterwards I reminded some of my colleagues of the previous time Rajiv Gandhi had voted. Then he had been tense and ill at ease. He had looked a sick and defeated man, which was unusual for him – no matter what strain he was under, normally he managed to put on a brave face. I said, 'I know we're not meant to take sides, but seeing Rajiv like this I can't help hoping he's not too disappointed.'

The next evening, 21 May, Gilly met me as I came back from taking our dog for a walk round the block. 'Forget going to sleep tonight,' she told me – 'Rajiv Gandhi's been killed.'

The flash on the United News of India wire gave no details. 'They might just be wrong,' I said.

'I hope to God they are,' she replied.

But, all too soon, details of the assassination started to come in on United News of India and later on the phone from my colleague in Madras, Sam Rajappa. The man whom only the day before I had seen looking confident that he would be given a chance to restore his reputation and revive the fortunes of the Nehru dynasty had been blown to pieces by an explosion just as he was about to address a meeting in a small town in the southern state of Tamil Nadu. It was a meeting he needn't really have attended, because Tamil Nadu, which would not go to the polls until the last day of the election, was one state which he had sewn up. It was a meeting he nearly didn't attend, because the aeroplane in which he was to fly to Tamil Nadu had developed a fault just before dusk, and night flying was not allowed from the airfield where it had landed. He had actually abandoned his flight to Tamil Nadu and was driving into the town where he had decided to spend the night when a police motorcyclist rode past his cavalcade and flagged him down. The policeman said that the fault had been rectified and if Rajiv hurried back he could still take off.

That night I took part in several BBC radio discussions. Time and again I found myself disagreeing with those experts in London who saw Rajiv's death as the death of Indian democracy. Some of them saw it as the death of India as we know it too. I argued that India had overcome much graver crises in the past; that the administration was still very much intact; that the army remained apolitical; that the separatist movements in Kashmir, Punjab and Assam had no hope of succeeding; and that democracy had struck deep roots. I believed all that to be true, but I have to admit that I wanted it to be true too and so I feared that the wish might have fathered the belief.

The events of the next few days allayed my immediate fears. In almost all places, the anger of Rajiv Gandhi's followers was contained by the police and the army. India mourned, but in peace, and India conducted the funeral rites of its most important politician with dignity and a ceremonial which reminded me of its unresolved dilemma. The soldiers, sailors and airmen marching in the funeral procession; the buglers blowing the last post after the pyre had been lit; the band playing 'Abide with me' when the ashes were scattered at that holy place in Allahabad where the Kumbh Mela was held – these all belonged to the British past. The pandits sprinkling Ganges water on Rajiv's body as it lay on the pyre, the instructions whispered into the ear of his 20-year-old son Rahul as he performed the last rites before lighting the pyre, the mantras which were chanted and that sacred confluence of the Ganges and Jamuna where the ashes were scattered all belonged to India.

Rajiv's political career can be seen as a parable of India's failure to shake off its colonial past and build a nation on the foundations of its own culture. Indira Gandhi never gave her eldest son a chance to be an Indian. He was educated at an Indian public school, but it was more British than the British. He did not even learn Hindi properly. Once, when I was interviewing him, he heard me speak to a cameraman in Hindi and said, 'You speak Hindi very well.' I replied, 'Not really – I wish I spoke it better.' He laughed and said, 'I wish I did too.'

After public school, his mother sent him first to Cambridge and then to Imperial College, London, without following the usual practice of wealthy Indian parents who make their children get

Indian degrees before sending them to foreign universities. That is why Rajiv failed to get a degree from Cambridge or London. When he returned to India with his Italian bride, he became an airline pilot – surely one of the most antiseptic professions there is. He didn't even have to meet the élite Indians who are the only people who can fly by Indian Airlines. He lived a very private life in his mother's house. She didn't encourage him to take part in politics, which would have brought him in touch with India – that was left to his younger brother, Sanjay. It was only after Sanjay killed himself doing aeronautical stunts over the centre of Delhi that Indira Gandhi turned to Rajiv.

His political apprenticeship lasted only three years. Then, on 31 October 1984, his mother was assassinated and he found himself prime minister of India.

The goodwill with which he started his premiership was demonstrated by the record majority he won in the general election two months later. But that was not goodwill he had won for himself. He had gained it because of sympathy for his mother and because he had played on Indians' fear that their country might break up – a fear he had aroused by exploiting hostility towards Sikhs after the assassination of his mother by two of her Sikh bodyguards. Five years later, a humiliating electoral defeat showed that Rajiv Gandhi had dissipated his stock of goodwill.

Its constitution commits India to socialism, secularism and democracy. All three had come under unparalleled pressure by the time Rajiv Gandhi stepped down as prime minister. Socialism had become unfashionable in the West, so it was no surprise that Rajiv had attempted to wriggle out of its grip. He had indeed increased India's growth rate by starting to liberalise the economy, but the industrialists he had encouraged all had their eyes on the easiest market – the expanding middle classes. The poor had no purchasing capacity, so they were of no interest to the industrialists. There was a consumer boom, but this only highlighted the difference between the lives of the middle classes and the lives of the majority of Indians. Rajiv's opponents, who knew their India better, were able to present this as a difference between castes – between the so-called backward castes, who by tradition made their living in the countryside, and the upper castes who had cornered the opportunities in the towns. In northern India, where elections are decided, the divisions between town and country, and between upper and lower castes, were deeper than ever before in the election that Rajiv Gandhi lost. Indira Gandhi had said that India would have its own brand of socialism. Rajiv never officially abandoned the search for that, but it's clear that in his heart of hearts he believed that socialism's failures meant that India had no option but to give up the search for greater equality.

Rajiv Gandhi never quarrelled with the principle of secularism, yet during his premiership the relations between Hindus and Muslims degenerated to their lowest level since the holocaust of partition. He was not a religious man himself, and perhaps that, as much as his Western upbringing, was why he failed to understand the power of religion. He behaved as though religious sentiment was just another factor to be manipulated for political purposes. How else can one explain his naïve handling of religious issues?

The crisis started when Rajiv surrendered to pressure from Muslim fundamentalists and altered the constitution to satisfy their objections to the law on maintenance for divorced women. Then, in a crude attempt to achieve a balance, he allowed Hindus to worship in a disputed mosque in the northern town of Ayodhya. There was a tradition that this mosque stood on the birthplace of the Hindu god, Ram, and there had been a long-running but not very energetic campaign for the mosque to be removed and replaced by a temple. The decision to allow Hindus to worship in the mosque put new life into this campaign, and by the end of Rajiv's premiership it had become a major political issue.

But Rajiv Gandhi had not learnt his lesson. During his election campaign he first allowed a Hindu organisation to lay the foundation stone of a temple at Ayodhya, but then, to demonstrate his concern for Muslim sensibilities (or, putting it more realistically, to avoid losing Muslim votes), he prevented the start of work on the temple. Both Hindus and Muslims were enraged, and the Ayodhya issue became even more divisive. Rajiv could only fall back on appeals to respect the secularism bequeathed to India by his grandfather – a secularism he had breached. He did not realise that underlying the Ayodhya issue was growing belief among Indians that Nehru's secularism was hostile to Hinduism – that it was an alien import from India's former rulers. He did not consider that Hinduism's own tradition of tolerance – a tradition that even the new fundamentalists claim as their own – might be a more natural basis for religious harmony in India.

Democracy was not faring too well either when Rajiv Gandhi was assassinated. He must bear some, but by no means all, of the blame for this too. He didn't understand the Indian way of conducting politics – the need for the personal touch, the need to make yourself available to as many people as possible and the need to gather information from as many different sources as possible. He thought that that was an inefficient and archaic way of doing business, and tried to run his office like a modern captain of industry. I remember a senior member of his party saying to me, 'I don't like to go to Rajiv Gandhi's house because it doesn't feel like an open house, which a Congressman's should always be.' Another told me with despair, 'I have heard that Rajiv is now even trying to get the lists of the people who are going to man every polling station in India on his computer.' Indira Gandhi certainly did not run her party democratically – during her later years she made sure there was no one who could challenge her – but she never cut herself off from her partymen. Even in opposition Rajiv remained an isolated figure, dependent for information and advice on a small coterie who had no political clout of their own.

Rajiv Gandhi left behind a party so sycophantic that within twenty-four hours of his assassination the leadership was offered to his widow, Sonia. She had never played an active role in politics, except for working in her husband's constituency, and had shown distaste for the profession. She had lost a husband she loved deeply and was in a state of shock. Nevertheless the Congress Party tried to burden her with its problems because it did not have the confidence to fight a general election unless it was led by a member of the Nehru dynasty – even if that member was an Italian by birth and a Roman Catholic by baptism. This was the party which had once contained so many powerful and independent-minded people that even men of the stature of Mahatma Gandhi and Pandit Nehru could not guarantee to have their own way. Sonia Gandhi rejected the party's offer politely, but the Congress leaders still pined for her.

It has to be said that the Congress Party's rivals were in no better shape when Rajiv died. The Bharatiya Janata Party was energetically pursuing its goal of a Hindu India, but it was still not a national party. The communists had barely advanced out of their two strongholds of Kerala and West Bengal, and the rest were as usual busy fighting their personal rather than their party battles. But it's the Congress Party in which the Indian electorate has placed its faith time and time again, and so the Congress Party must bear most of the blame for the growing disillusionment of the electorate and the violence of elections. When Rajiv Gandhi was assassinated, more than 200 people had already been killed in electoral violence. In the constituency in which he voted, less than 50 per cent of the electorate turned out to vote.

Rajiv Gandhi did in the end realise that he was out of touch. That's why he took the courageous decision to ignore the warnings of his security advisers and campaign among the people of India. That's why he died. Terrible though his death was, I don't think it means the death of India. If – and it's still a big if – the Nehru dynasty does come to an end, another life will be born. Because this is India, where change takes some time, the birth will be slow and perhaps painful. I believe it could be the birth of a new order which is not held up by the crumbling colonial pillars left behind by the raj but is genuinely Indian: a modern order, but not a slavish imitation of other modern orders. For all its great achievements, the Nehru dynasty has stood like a banyan tree overshadowing the people and the institutions of India, and all Indians know that nothing grows under the banyan tree.

Printed in India by Rekha Printers Pvt. Ltd., New Delhi-110 020